Attorney for the Damned

THE FREE PRESS

New York   London   Toronto   Sydney   Tokyo   Singapore

Attorney for the Damned

A Lawyer's Life with the Criminally Insane

DENIS WOYCHUK

THE FREE PRESS
A Division of Simon & Schuster Inc.
1230 Avenue of the Americas
New York, NY 10020

THE FREE PRESS and colophon are trademarks
of Simon & Schuster Inc.

Text design by Carla Bolte

Manufactured in the United States of America

10 9 8 7 6 5 4 3 2 1

Library of Congress Cataloging-in-Publication Data

Woychuk, Denis.
    Attorney for the damned: a lawyer's life with the criminally
insane/ Denis Woychuk.
        p.   cm.
    ISBN   0-684-87438-5
    1. Woychuk, Denis.   2. Lawyers—New York (N.Y.)—Biography.
3. Insane, criminal and dangerous—New York (N.Y.)   4. Insanity—
Jurisprudence—New York (N.Y.)   5. Legal assistance to the mentally
handicapped—New York (N.Y.)   I. Title.
KF373.W64A3   1996
340',092—dc20   95-41089
                                                                  CIP

To a better world

Contents

Prologue

I am an attorney, and as such I am an advocate for my clients. Most of them are patients at Kirby Forensic Psychiatric Center, a mental hospital for the dangerously mentally ill in New York City. Since 1985, when Kirby first opened, I've been advocating for their rights. I've handled over three hundred cases, winning some and losing others. Some people may be appalled at what I do, but my vision of the law is that the more unpopular a defendant, the more compelling is the lawyer's duty to take the case. And my clients certainly aren't popular; they include child abusers, rapists, cannibals, torturers, and killers. They are scary to everyone, including me.

The general public is frightened of the mentally ill under all circumstances, and, on account of the massive deinstitutionalization of the last twenty years, the public is exposed to greater numbers of mentally ill people than ever before; this contact may even make the general public long for a new policy of reinstitutionalization, especially when some mentally ill individual proves himself dangerous and makes spectacular headlines. However, most public discourse about how to deal with the "dangerously mentally ill" proceeds more from ignorance and fear than from real information. People speak anecdotally, or with reference to the lead stories of the eleven o'clock news, without any firsthand knowledge.

Because of my work, I bring an insider's perspective to the discussion, but I don't have all the answers. I'm not a psychiatrist, or a judge, or a penologist, or a social worker. I can only tell the truth as I know it. And what I know is that this is an imperfect system.

This is a book of true stories, but I have made many changes to identifying characteristics of clients—likewise of doctors, lawyers, judges, and others who are portrayed in these pages. Sometimes characteristics and life circumstances of the protagonists are composites made up of grafts from other clients, or other doctors, lawyers, etc., as I found appropriate. Sometimes those portrayed are composites. Some dialogue was re-created; some is fictional; and my personal reflections are post hoc. The disguises are deep, with a single exception. One of my clients, who came to me some years ago and asked if I would write about his case, has insisted that his true name be used. He is Hugh Kelly, of the chapter called "Psycho Killer—*Qu'est-Ce Que C'est?*"

I selected these stories not to exploit their sensationalism, but because they illustrate different parts of the forensic psychiatric system and illuminate different aspects of my own ethical dilemmas as an attorney in a world where each of my clients is, was, or will be dangerous—to himself, to society, perhaps even to me. And although my viewpoint as a lawyer is of one sworn to fight for his client's wishes regardless of how inappropriate, insane, or even dangerous to society those wishes might be, my intention as a writer is to tell the truth.

What follows, then, are six stories in six chapters about people's lives both in the mental hospital and in court. My own story is, of course, a part of this. The seventh chapter is not a story at all, but rather, some thoughts about how we might improve the present system.

Blue Monday

Paranoids are the only ones who notice things anymore. —Anatole Broyard

Strange things had been happening lately. One hot Sunday in July, someone covered the doorknob to my apartment with animal fat while I was out. Someone also hung a dead chicken from a tree outside my window—not necessarily the same someone, but it looked likely. My dog, salivating to get at that chicken, howled all night, and between 3:00 and 6:00 A.M. my phone rang a dozen times. Each time I answered, the caller whispered, "Mr. Woychuk," then hung up. Although I had given quite a few people my unlisted phone number, none would have called me "Mr. Woychuk," especially at those hours. I didn't want to jump to conclusions, but I was concerned—in the past few weeks I'd seen a strange figure shadowing me in the supermarket, at the movies. I made a guess at who the caller was.

"Dr. Pinto? Dr. Pinto? Mercedes, is that you?"

No answer.

But the calls kept coming.

The next morning, Monday, was gray and humid, with distant thunder. The threat of rain made my dog, Ivan, a big furry wolfhound with one-inch-long teeth, somewhat edgy. When I walked Ivan before work, some guy who'd been sleeping on the street cursed us as we passed him. Rising to his feet and swinging a long stick, he ranted that "dog" (like the devil) was the opposite of "God," and he would "smite [us] mightily." The distant rumblings roared closer, and the sky grew dark as Ivan and I crossed the street, went into the park, and went home. Later the skies opened, as I went to work.

Just off the coast of Manhattan's concrete swelter, where the Harlem River turns due south and merges with the East River, is Wards Island, 122 green acres where the state of New York maintains three buildings that rise like white brick mountains above the rolling lawns. The buildings have names: Meyer, Dunlap, and Kirby. The first two make up Manhattan Psychiatric Center, a low-security civil hospital that houses almost nine hundred patients. The third and most southerly building, Kirby Forensic Psychiatric Center, is a hospital unto itself, with about two hundred patients held in maximum-security conditions. Formerly these patients would have been known as the *criminally insane*, but that term has been supplanted in New York forensic psychiatric circles by the term *dangerously mentally ill*.* The former was felt to be too pejorative, but the latter is hardly less so.

You can get from Manhattan to Wards Island, and hence to both Manhattan Psychiatric and Kirby Forensic, by car or bus—or even by foot. (Although the footbridge was closed when an escapee made headlines as the notorious "subway pusher" of January 1995—and security was tightened, fences erected, and the drawbridge raised— the footbridge was reopened several months later, when the furor died down.)

---

* The psychiatric industry prefers clinical terms that are not yet part of the vernacular, and so, like the terms *lunatic, moron, imbecile*, and *idiot*, the term *criminally insane* has fallen from favor. In due time the same will happen to the current euphemism.

In the warmer months the island's lush vegetation is enjoyed by an abundance of rabbits and even pheasants. In the woods just outside the hospital perimeters, human settlements also rise—temporary structures made of corrugated aluminum, used plywood, plastic sheeting, and other odds and ends—as country people exiled in Spanish Harlem try to recreate an oasis of nature away from the city heat. Even on the hospital grounds a few small forests creep up to the river's edge, with Manhattan looming across the water just a few hundred yards away. But most of the hospital grounds are spacious, rolling greens, which are not only attractive but useful for security purposes.

On Mondays I met with clients. I could do this in the wards or at the eleventh-floor rehab center, where the hospital has shops for assembling pens and frames, classrooms, a video room, a weight room and gymnasium, a pottery studio, some pool tables, a pet center (with fish, iguanas, hamsters, and other small animals), and a library.* Since these facilities were all housed together on a single floor, they were not as substantial as they may sound, and they tended to be overcrowded. The evidence of poor personal hygiene—and there were always one or two patients who managed to avoid soap and water—pervaded the sweaty atmosphere of the rooms, the stink exacerbated by the heat.

The only relief to be had was in the sole air-conditioned room in the hospital—the chapel, also located on the eleventh floor. Its climate made the chapel a favorite spot for nonspiritual pursuits in the summer, and on this particular Monday I was able to schedule my meetings with clients there, starting with the anti-darling of New York's tabloid newspaper industry—celebrated in headlines such as CHOPPED SUEY (Death of Delivery Boy) (*New York Post*) and HELL'S

---

* Until recently the library carried books like *Looking for Mr. Goodbar* and other stories involving psychotic murder, as well as manuals of mercenary soldiering, with step-by-step instructions. By mistake, of course. I discovered this while browsing the shelves. And despite my general support for the unrestricted dissemination of information, I felt compelled to point out to the administrative staff the nature of the literature being made available to patient readers.

KITCHEN PSYCHO SLASHER (*New York Daily News*). His name was Derek Diesel.

I had known Diesel almost from the start of my career, when he was an ordinary civil patient who had been arrested but not charged. Even then he was a smooth, soft-spoken character. I'd negotiated his release with the agreement of Dr. Bellows, his treating psychiatrist, without his ever having to go to court. But he would be back.

On the surface he was smooth. When he was well (and I use this term in a relative sense), he was what we in New York call "schmoozy"—more than friendly, more than jovial. He made a point of taking obvious pleasure when I came to see him. He curried my favor as best he could, deliberately voicing respect for my professional skills in front of others. His frequent open hostility to the treating psychiatrists, whose good graces were far more important than my own to his future, led me to believe he was not just attempting to manipulate the system—that he sincerely respected me. But then, I always told him I'd ask the judge to let him out.

When he was not "well," he was sullen, making it clear he didn't want to discuss his case. I do not work face-to-face with forensic mental patients who make it clear they don't want my attention. For one thing, I have too much else to do, and for another, it is my duty to respect their wishes. There is also a safety issue: If confronted by someone he doesn't want to see, such a patient may react violently.

But Diesel was rarely sullen. We spoke often, and not just about the law. He complained about the hospital's food, for example—not about how bad it was, but that the portions were too small. In the years between 1985 (when he was a civil patient) and the present (when he was considered a serial murderer by most members of the staff, even if this had not yet been proved in court), he had spent literally hundred of hours in the weight room, bulking up. And all those muscles needed food. He was only average in height, but with a broad barrel chest and enormous, strong hands. I told him he wasn't doing himself a favor, that he'd make a better impression in court if he looked meek and harmless, but he said he needed to work out to get rid of the tension.

I had thirty other clients, but because Diesel had "beat the system"—by some counts three times—the district attorney and the hospital scrutinized every detail of his treatment, so his case kept me especially busy. Even things that should have been simple were an obstacle course. For instance, the hospital had refused admission to his private psychiatrist when the latter wished to videotape an interview, claiming that the doctor intended to sell the tape to a television tabloid show. There was no basis for this claim, but it took months of fighting in front of three different judges before the hospital was forced to give the doctor access. I had to spend a lot of time on Diesel's case, many times the norm, and he appreciated that I did. The reasons seemed obvious to me: I was his best and only hope.

So I was caught unaware that particular day, as we walked together around the chapel, when he raised his hands and reached for my throat.

Diesel was talking about a murder with which he had once been charged, one that had taken place in the hospital. "They were in his room when suddenly Goldman just puts Silverberg in this choke hold, you know?" he was saying. "I was walking by, not really watching, but I saw Goldman calmly reach out with a smile on his face and grab Silverberg by the throat like this. . . ."

And he reached out so quickly, and I was so close, that I didn't even have a chance to see his arms come up. The left one was suddenly near the back of my neck, and his right arm was coming around quickly across the front of my throat. Sometimes I fantasize (against my will) about what might be necessary to bring someone down were I to be attacked, and I stay in shape, but at this instant I had let my guard down. Fortunately my body, operating entirely on its own, ducked and slipped left.

The disarming smile never left Diesel's lips. He kept talking.

". . . I don't have to show you now, but you know the kind of hold I'm talking about, and he grabbed him like that. . . ."

And I knew exactly the hold he meant. I learned it as a kid as a way to break someone's neck by falling, pulling him down with me, and smashing my shoulder into the back of his head. (According to my own boyhood folklore, it's a U.S. Marine Corps technique.)

"Listen," I said, "I'm going to stop you here for a moment."

". . . and he started squeezing. . . ."

"Stop smiling for a moment and listen to me!" I had to shout. "Do not show me, do not attempt to show me, any choke holds! Do not. . . ." I was rattled by my own carelessness regarding my personal safety, that I had almost allowed a client—especially Diesel—to put his arms around my throat. I was angry at myself and I was angry at him for trying it, for presuming that he had a right to touch me at all under any circumstances—but he just stood there smiling with that same beatific grin.

"I didn't mean anything by it, Mr. Woychuk," he interrupted. "Don't get so excited. You're the best shot I've got."

And he went on talking as though this little incident was of no import. Like we were just a couple of guys talking with body language. "Anyway, I didn't do it," he said, adding, "There were no bite marks on the corpse," as if somehow that were proof of his innocence.

"Well, you beat that rap. That's not our problem right now."

And that was true; there were no charges pending. Officially, Diesel was being held in this maximum-security hospital because of a "current dangerous mental disorder" related to another murder several years prior.

"I looked over the papers you submitted to the court. What made you think you could be your own lawyer?"

"Well, I didn't have a lawyer who would stand up for me at the time. I got hold of a writ of habeas corpus, and for the most part I copied it. But now I've come to my senses. I know we got a tough case. But to come after me in my aunt's house with a fucking SWAT team, it just isn't. . . ."

"Look, Mr. Diesel," I said, cutting him off. "I just stopped by to touch base, to let you know I've looked over your papers, and that I'll be working on them. Your case isn't really active yet. It'll be at least a couple of months before we get to court. We'll be going into all of it in great detail, great detail, but not now. Later."

"Yeah, I know, Mr. Woychuk. But every day I'm in here, I'm not out there. This is my life we're talking about. I know you're a good lawyer; you did good for me before. Just do the best you can. Keep me posted."

We walked down the hall to the frame assembly shop, a patient rehabilitation station where he was a worker, and we said our good-byes.

Later on I thought about the psychiatrist's remark that this client was a total egomaniac, a complete narcissist who would do anything to make a name for himself—that Diesel thought he was in competition with Charles Manson. Had he considered that snapping his lawyer's neck at a maximum-security mental hospital could lead to potential coast-to-coast headlines? Then again, another client of mine had cut his former lawyer's throat—in fact, that was what got him put in the hospital—and the press had ignored the story completely. But I couldn't count on Diesel knowing about that. Although I didn't agree that Diesel had a desire for infamy, I was glad nevertheless that my instincts had reacted for me. I was glad I had ducked.

Leaving the frame shop, I was approached by a tall black patient who had spotted me from the classroom where he studied computers. He looked athletic but not particularly scary. Most of the patients at the hospital, in fact, don't look scary, and for the most part they don't rant and rave as the media might lead one to expect. Moreover, patients have to "prove" their self-control before they become eligible for the rehab programs. Security therefore is not as tight on the eleventh floor as it is in the patient wards. Between programs it is not unusual for some patients to wander a bit; as long as they don't become "agitated," no one comes running.

But this patient cornered me, talking faster than I could take in. I didn't know who he was, but already I had a problem with his rank breath. Some patients do not have the same concept of personal space that I do, and they lean in disconcertingly. When they smell bad, it's worse. I wanted to gag, but I didn't want to make this guy feel he could not get legal counsel. Patients can be paranoid enough.

"Slow down," I said, taking a big step backward. "Take it easy. Now, pause between each word and tell me what it is you want."

He took a gulp of air. Suddenly, despite a strangely staccato speech pattern, he could speak understandably. He told me he had not yet been assigned a lawyer, and that he wanted me to represent him.

"I don't pick up cases freelance," I said, "but if you tell me your name, I'll see that you are assigned someone soon, perhaps even myself."

"I don't want a woman and I don't want a hippie. I want you. You have to take my case," he said, with a gulp between words. "I know who you are."

"What is your name?"

"Anderson. My name is Lyle Anderson."

His name hit me like a brick. I actually went weak and blacked out for an instant. Then I wanted to smash my fist into his face. I wanted to leap on him and bang his head against the concrete floor.

I always try not to let my personal feelings interfere with my duties as an advocate—but tragedy has a way of changing things. On another Monday, June 8, 1991, I had learned that Alexis Walsh, a woman I knew, was killed by a "deranged ex-convict wielding a carving knife" (New York Post) while walking her cocker spaniels in the early morning hours near Central Park. I did not know her well but she was in my circle, a group of dog walkers that communed almost daily in the park. Tall and beautiful, a former Rockette, she strove for fame all her life—in death, ironically, she made the cover of New York magazine. In all the years I'd specialized in helping violent offenders, never before had I personally known a victim.

The defendant, one Lyle Anderson, was formerly a mental patient at Kingsboro Psychiatric Center. I had expected him to be sent to Kirby eventually after being found not guilty by reason of insanity. But he had arrived, much sooner than I expected, as "not fit to stand trial."

"I can't take your case, Mr. Anderson," I said, stepping away and into the shop where patients put ballpoint pens together.

"Just give me some advice. I can beat this. My criminal attorney is William Kunstler. He stinks. I just want your opinion."

"I can't give you an opinion. It would be unethical. I do not want to listen. I have a conflict of interest."

"What do you mean, you can't give me an opinion?!" He stepped in after me, his voice suddenly a roar. Abruptly a crowd gathered—all patients, and not a therapy aide in sight.

"I can't take your case because I knew the victim!"

I felt sick. Anger flashed in his eyes; his hands curled into fists, and he took a step closer. My arms and back tensed involuntarily, and I bent my knees for greater mobility. Then another voice came in.

"He can't take your case! So just step back, Anderson!" It was Diesel, his big shoulders pushing between us. "You heard him! It would be unethical."

Anderson stepped around Diesel, raising his arm. Immediately he was surrounded.

"Back down, Anderson," growled burly Rafael Ruiz, who had crushed his father's skull against a wall.

"Get back, Jack," echoed Diggs, who had broken the mirror into which his aunt had been gazing and then slashed her pretty face and gouged out one of her eyes with a piece of the broken glass. "He ain't representing you! And anyway, I'm next!"

With that, Diggs stepped between Anderson and myself.

"Me! See me, now, Denis, I'm next!" he cried. "When am I going to get out of here? It's nine years I been locked up! Let's get an office."

Diggs liked to call me Denis, especially if other patients were around—to imply familiarity, I suppose. I always made it a point to call my clients *Mr.* (or *Ms.*, or *Mrs.*, or *Dr.*, when appropriate), for a long while following our introduction. A respectful tone on the part of both lawyer and client produces an atmosphere in court that is conducive to a favorable decision, and good habits should be started early.

"No, Mr. Diggs, you're not next," I said calmly. "Mr. Ruiz is ahead of you."

While Diggs pouted, I said to Ruiz, "Let's talk privately. We can be alone in the chapel."

The whole incident happened so fast that the hospital staff never noticed. Anderson drifted into the hallway, still muttering. For the rest of his stay at Kirby I avoided him. I don't know which lawyer was assigned to him, though eventually I heard he was convicted of murder. But that Monday at rehab had given me pause for thought.

How did I get into this business?

One year out of law school, I had what passed for a promising career in the private sector in Manhattan. I spent each day surrounded by six hundred thousand pages of bad photocopies—including doodles, initials, and numbers without reference—trying to determine how the defendants, a prominent family that included the mayor of a large southern city, had illegally cross-traded their shares in three hundred privately held corporations. My firm's client, a foreign bank, had lent one of the defendants millions of dollars, with selected stock as collateral. The stock in question had somehow become worthless, purportedly as a result of fraudulent trades; that was the heart of our case.

Amidst the endless paper, I was drawn to the human drama: a prominent family (with a wayward son who had blown his inheritance) creating a scheme to bilk a foreign bank of millions through stock manipulations. But I wasn't supposed to be interested in the human element. "If it's not billable, don't do it," my boss told me, and I knew he was thinking of his three kids in college and a new boat. My job was to connect names, or just initials, with numbers that supposedly represented shares of stock or dollar amounts. I was supposed to break whatever code there was. "Just get the facts as they appear on paper," my boss said, but as far as I could tell the reams of documents were just a lot of memo paper littered with doodles. A quarter of a million dollars in litigation fees later, there were still no "facts" proving fraud. But every month the bank paid its bill.

I knew I'd never get beyond the paperwork. Although I worked in the firm's litigation section, I couldn't expect to see the inside of a courtroom for years—especially not in this case, for which the trial would be held in Atlanta, Georgia. Our offices were clean and corporate, with a spiral staircase we used to show off, but once I closed my office door I began to feel I'd died and gone to hell. I was drowning in paper, and working seventy hours a week did little to lighten my heart. "Pay your dues," I said to myself, but payment apparently went on forever. Here at the firm the partners were working as hard as I was—and as long. If I tried to leave before 9:00 P.M., one partner (whose marriage had supposedly soured from his long hours) would snidely ask if I were taking the rest of the day off. "No," I generally replied, "I'm just going out for a bite." "Pick up the phone and order in," he would say. "Don't waste valuable billable time 'dining' when you could be reviewing defendant documents—the firm will gladly pay for the sandwich." Then he'd go back to work, and usually I would as well.

Apparently people got used to seventy-hour weeks eventually, and I imagined that I could, too, if only the work weren't so boring and repetitive. But it had dawned on me by now that most of the practice of law was like that. Well over 90 percent of the legal practice in big corporate towns like New York is business law, and almost none of it ever goes to court. I tried to embrace the corporate culture, but deep down I somehow thought I could eventually become the kind of lawyer I'd grown up believing in—a defender of the weak, a champion of justice who got out before the bench and made his case.

Life was too short to rely on a vague promise that in some future year I might get to court, if only to carry some partner's briefs to the lawyers' table. I began to scan the papers, the *New York Law Journal* especially, to see what employers were looking for. One little ad caught my eye.

MENTAL HEALTH INFORMATION SERVICE
Seeks aggressive self-starter to handle own caseload
for heavy court contact, psychiatric clientele.
Class of '82, '83, '84. Contact NYLJ box Z7T49

I hadn't a clue what the Mental Health Information Service was; it looked like a state government agency. Although I could guess right away the job didn't pay well, the words "own caseload" and "heavy court contact" had real appeal. I wasn't particularly qualified to work with a psychiatric clientele, but I hoped my Class of '84 law degree would be enough to get me at least an interview so I could find out more about the job. Of course I was interested in why people were the way they were, what made them do the things they did, although deviant behavior *per se* didn't fascinate me any more than the next guy. I didn't read books about psychology, deviant or otherwise, stayed away from true crime books, and pretty much avoided psycho-killer movies and television (although Hitchcock's movies,

Psycho and others, I considered to be exceptions and above the general fray). I sent in a résumé.

To my surprise I was called for an interview. It was held not at a psychiatric hospital but in a typical midtown office building on Madison Avenue. "Welcome to the offices of the Mental Health Information Service," said Mr. Barque, a balding black man with a gray goatee, as he offered his hand. "I am the executive director of M.H.I.S., as we generally call it, and this is my deputy, Mr. Bedrosian." The other man nodded at me. They were friendly, more relaxed than the lawyers at the firm. Mr. Barque clasped his arms behind his back and turned to the forty-third-floor window: A golden dome rose like a crown below us to the east, and the Empire State Building was visible to the north. "It's a spectacular view," he said with a sigh. "But you wouldn't be working here. You'd be on location."

"Yes," said Mr. Bedrosian, "on location at a mental hospital, where you'd get an office. And you'd start going to court almost immediately. If we made you an offer, that is. But you should be aware that our clientele is unlike most of the clients you've known. They come from poorer backgrounds, and a high percentage are minorities.

"We are an agency of the Appellate Division, First Judicial Department, of the New York State Supreme Court," he went on, "and our purpose is to be advocates for hospitalized mental patients who want legal representation. Our name is misleading because when this agency was formed we merely advised the court, investigating and then providing information—hence we were called an information service. But our role has changed, and now we are full-fledged advocates for patient rights. The legislature is expected to change our name officially to Mental Hygiene Legal Service to more accurately reflect the fact that we advocate for mental patients.

"We represent mental patients at private hospitals as well as state and city facilities, but the bulk of our clientele is in public hospitals. At state institutions in New York City maybe half of the patients are black. A quarter are Latino. A quarter are white. They've all had hard lives."

"C'mon, Gus," Mr. Barque said. "Let's not mince about. These people are mentally ill. They are not street hoodlums. They are patients. The vast, vast majority have never been involved in criminal activity of any kind. . . ."

"However . . ." Mr Bedrosian interrupted.

"Don't interrupt me, Gus," Mr. Barque said with an affable smile. "However—and I was just getting to this—there is a new hospital that is just opening up, and that is one of the reasons we're looking for another attorney. It's maximum security, for what used to be called the criminally insane. They are patients, too, but they are pretty tough, at least some of them. It's probably not for someone like you. Anyway, the slot over there. . . ."

"Slots," interjected Mr. Bedrosian, but Mr. Barque just kept talking.

". . . will probably be filled by someone with a great deal more experience. The cases are much harder fought, the district attorney's office is involved in almost every case, and we'll need someone seasoned to oppose. But that makes for a slot somewhere else. We've got six offices for attorneys scattered in hospital facilities throughout the First Judicial Department—Manhattan and the Bronx—and a number of satellite offices with part-time coverage. We've got a wide variety of clientele. The important thing to remember is that each one is an individual. The only thing they have in common is that they are all mentally ill. We need someone who is comfortable speaking with all kinds of people and who wants to go to court pretty much every week. We want someone who believes that the state does not have the right to lock up its citizens without very good reason; our job is to put the state to its proof. We want to be sure that our clients are in the least restrictive setting that can reasonably accommodate them. Mental illness alone is not enough to lock someone away, and some people who are mentally ill can nevertheless survive and even flourish outside of an institutional setting. We are freedom fighters. Are you still with me, son?"

I nodded my head in assent.

"I cannot stress enough that there is no one type of person that we represent," Mr. Barque continued, "just as there is no one type of mental illness. Each case is different. Heh, heh, I guess maybe that's a selling point, eh? It can be unpleasant, but the casework is never boring. Our lawyers fight for a very unpopular class of people. We get a lot of blame for our work—the homeless, for example. As though the only alternatives for housing the mentally ill are hospitalization or the street. Well, that's another story. . . ."

His voice had dropped and he had begun to mutter. Then he perked up brightly and looked at me squarely.

"But enough about us. What about you? What makes you want to work for an outfit like ours?" Without letting me answer he moved on to the next question. "Do you have any background in psychology or mental health?"

"No."

"Do you have any work experience with patients, prisoners, or other institutionalized individuals? And what about minorities? I don't see anything like that on your résumé."

"No."

"What makes you think you can handle this extremely multicultural and difficult clientele?"

"I'm from Brooklyn," I said. Both men looked at me with blank stares.

Stupid answer, I thought. I have to do better. I hadn't prepared properly for this kind of interview because I had little idea what I was walking into.

"I grew up in a neighborhood with all kinds of people," I began again. "Most of the lawyers I know grew up in suburbs and had relatively sheltered lives, but where I grew up there were riots at my high school, and drugs were everywhere." Once more I wondered why I was saying such dumb things. "There were good kids and there were tough kids—wild, even crazy kids," I continued. Mr. Barque and Mr. Bedrosian looked at me attentively, even respectfully. I wasn't sure why. "And all sorts of kids, every race, every nationality—Jews, Italians, Irish, Polish, American black, were all around me. Then Puerto Ricans and Dominicans began moving in and whites began leaving and their places were filled by an influx of Haitians. My family stayed and I got along with everybody. I could talk to all of them.

"It gave me a view of the world that I've since discovered is a far cry from my life in Manhattan. Every lawyer at my current firm is white and male. They say they're planning to hire a woman like it's some big deal, but it shouldn't be. They say they'd love to hire a minority, but they're lying." I hoped they wouldn't see this as manipulative and transparent.

"What about court?" Mr. Barque said. "Are you interested in going to court? Are you comfortable standing up for a politically unpopular position?"

"Court is what I want," I stated flatly, evenly, with emphasis on the words *court* and *want*. "I've always envisioned myself a litigator. And as for taking unpopular positions, frankly, I think it's more interesting to fight against the current." They looked at me as though they were expecting more, so I added, "Particularly when your cause is just!"

That seemed to satisfy them. They looked at each other and then at me and then at each other again, nodding and smiling slightly. They seemed like a sweet but goofy couple of guys.

"When could you start?" asked Mr. Barque. "If we made you an offer, that is."

"Oh, three weeks," I blurted out. Then I paused. "If you make me an offer. And if I accept."

"Fair enough," said Mr. Bedrosian with a grin. "You'll hear from us either way." He stood up, motioning me to follow, and moved toward the door.

"But wait," I protested. "I'd like some information about the job."

"What is it you want to know?" he asked, looking at his watch and not inviting me to sit down again. I looked back at Mr. Barque, who was suddenly on the phone. He smiled and waved at me, and then swiveled in his chair and put his feet up on the window ledge. Apparently I had not made a good impression on either of them, but I felt determined to come away with more information. "I'll be very brief. What does the job pay?"

"Oh, I'm sorry," Mr. Bedrosian said. "Of course you have a right to ask about pay, vacation, promotions, etc., and if I had more time I would elaborate in great detail. But as it is, I'll be brief as well. The Office of Court Administration pays our salaries—which will be going up next month, so I can't give you an exact figure—but I can tell you that we pay a starting salary that's roughly half of what the big firms pay. Everybody gets a raise every year, but we don't give bonuses. You won't be making six figures within two or three years if you work for us. But neither will you be working seventy hours a week. You'll have a life. That is, if you want one." He smiled at his own joke. Then he opened the door. "I'm sorry to be so rushed. That's a call from the commissioner that Mr. Barque is taking. I'm needed as well. We'll be in touch." With that, he ushered me out.

I hadn't really intended to give up the money of corporate litigation but the appeal of actual court appearances continued to play in my mind. Since I wasn't expecting an offer in any case, I felt free to consider what I'd do if I got one. Six months, I thought. I could do that psychiatric stuff for six months, get some courtroom experience under my belt, then go back to become a stellar corporate litigator. Of course, I wouldn't go back to the same firm. The bad marriage of the partner I worked for meant he was having a bad day every day. Not wanting to be miserable alone, he chose me to receive his harangues, his barking commands, and other manifestations of his sour, unhappy life. He seemed to confuse the firm with the military. Needless to say, I wasn't happy working for him.

So when I did get a call from Mr. Barque, I gave my notice. Two weeks later, I closed the door to my office, walked down those gray corridors with gray carpeting and the neatly aligned desks of the secretaries and support staff, pressed the down button at the elevator banks, and never looked back.

I'd never been to a psychiatric hospital. I was put on a six-week training rotation at various hospitals in Manhattan and the Bronx, but I spent most of my time at the two big state facilities, Bronx Psychiatric and Manhattan Psychiatric. There were six or eight lawyers at each; what struck me first was that except on court days, none of them wore a suit. I liked that. It made the dirt not quite so bad. I had doubts about whether I would like this job, but then again, I was sure I didn't like my other one.

My first training assignment was at Bronx Psychiatric under Susan

Bianco, a blonde woman not much older than I. Susan had been on the job about three years. She had a terrific sense of humor, which she claimed was necessary for survival. On my first day there she took me up to a women's ward, then disappeared; I was locked in while thirty patients slowly surrounded me.

"Let's get married," one whispered, stepping closer, tugging at her skirt.

"Let's party!" insisted another, with a giggle, as she moved to my left.

"Let's make a baby!" cried a third, fanning out to the right.

I was frightened by the wild look in their eyes, and also somewhat fascinated to find myself surrounded this way. My overwhelming feeling, however, was pity—that these women were somehow so damaged that they had to live here, in a psychiatric hospital. Their bodies quivered and shook; one or two had saliva dripping from their mouths. I stepped back and around, quickly, out of their circle. The pity I felt for these women made me forget the world of Wall Street and high finance bankruptcy. I forgot my doubts.

When Susan came back after thirty minutes, she found me in the chart room reading histories of some of these hypersexual patients. "Do you think you could go to court and ask a judge to let one of these women go?" she asked. "You can always ask," I replied, "and I bet there's at least one of them whose mental condition is such that she is probably ready to leave this hospital. I could find her if I spent some time with these charts." "I bet you could," said Susan, "but we have an appointment somewhere else. Maybe you can come back later." But I was never on that ward again.

I guessed that the purpose of this episode was to help me find out quickly whether I could handle the exigencies that were a part of daily life at the mental hospital. I believed that I could. But suppose I did help one of these women win her release. What kind of life could she have? This was not a question I could answer. I could only help her try to reclaim her life, knowing that she might fail, or that the system might fail, or both.

So even today, I still have doubts. And I'll have them tomorrow as well. Learning to live with doubts, doing my duty and making tough choices, has been central to my professional life since I joined the agency. In a way, it was what I had missed in business.

After my initial training I was stationed at Manhattan Psychiatric Center. Salvatoro Guam, a veteran litigator who had recently returned to the agency after a stint at the Brooklyn district attorney's office, convinced me that the real action was at the newly opened Kirby Forensic Psychiatric Center. In the weeks that followed I studied him, his presentation before the judges, his handling of both the district attorney's and the attorney general's offices in adversarial matters, and I could see he was a man from whom to learn. There were several lawyers vying for the Kirby slot, but he and I struck up an understanding, and he recommended me to be the first attorney assigned there full-time under his supervision. My entry into the forensic psychiatric world had begun.

Back at the chapel, Mr. Ruiz and I reviewed the results of his latest hearing. He'd been one of my first Kirby clients years before, and I'd recently represented him when the hospital had applied to the State Supreme Court for an additional two years of treatment in maximum security. What was interesting about the current hearing was that Kirby had made this application for continued retention even though the treating psychiatrist had determined that Ruiz was no longer dangerously mentally ill.

Rafael Ruiz's story was a sad one. His alcoholic, mentally ill father, a one-time bodyguard, had often beaten him as a boy, grabbing young Rafael by his shoulders and banging his head against the floor or wall until he lost consciousness—supposedly to "knock some sense" into him. Rafael had been hospitalized a number of times with head trauma, but released back to his family after testing because neither his intelligence nor his motor skills seemed impaired. There was no further intervention by child welfare services, and Rafael continued to absorb brutal beatings—and to see his father rape his frightened, submissive mother and his sister—throughout his childhood.

Despite his grim home life, Rafael was resilient and talented enough to get himself into Syracuse University on a football scholarship. Then one day, while he was home for Christmas vacation, lost in thoughts of a summer internship outside the city, he'd nearly missed his stop on the subway—and left his school books behind. When he got home, his father, drunk and in a foul mood, attacked him. "The books, where are the books?" the old man demanded. "Good money for those books. Dumb college boy. Bang some sense into that thick head of yours."

"I don't know what happened," Rafael told me. "He slapped me hard in my bad ear, the one he used to bang against the wall when I was a kid, and the next thing I know I have him in a headlock. Then I must have grabbed his ear with my other hand—I know because he bit me on the thumb—and I went wild. I don't understand how it happened. I don't." Somehow Rafael had ripped one of his father's ears from his head and then, in an eerie echo of his father's actions, slammed the man's head against the wall until the skull imploded on one side. When it was all over, the room was in wreckage, the bloody, one-eared corpse lay sprawled amid the debris, and Rafael was waiting for the police.

Rafael Ruiz's mental state was difficult to categorize. Over the years, he'd been given a variety of diagnoses by different psychiatrists, including "isolated explosive disorder" and "schizophrenia with major depressive features." Because several doctors suspected some underlying organic brain damage, Ruiz was sent for a battery of neurological tests. One medical hypothesis was that he had killed his father because of his brain injury; another was that he had reacted to a history of abuse. In any case, he was acquitted of the murder of his father by reason of mental defect and sent to Mid-Hudson, a maximum-security hospital in upstate New York. Several years later, Ruiz was transferred to Kirby; when the latter petitioned to extend his treatment, I was brought into the case. The file on the case contained horrific, full-cover photos of the crime scene, and I'd looked at them in disbelief.

At the most recent hearing, as at those prior, the important issue for the court to decide was whether Rafael Ruiz would again act violently. Dr. Millerg, his psychiatrist, was convinced that Rafael did not represent a danger to himself or to others, despite the brain damage. Known widely as "the grand old man of rehabilitative psychiatry,"

Dr. Millerg believed that because Kirby was a new hospital under close official scrutiny, its administrators were being overly cautious. He stated that there was no evidence Ruiz would attack anyone who didn't badly abuse him. But the presiding judge, no doubt a father himself, had cringed when he heard the details of the underlying act. Two other psychiatrists, called by the hospital, both testified that it was too early to tell if Ruiz was no longer dangerous. Each pointed out that, as a muscular athlete, Ruiz had the physical potential to do real damage if he were ever violent. They both recommended two more years of hospitalization and the judge was quick to comply. I believed the judge based his decision on what I call the fear factor. Would he be afraid to meet this man on the street some evening alone? Apparently he would.

As Ruiz and I reviewed the latest setback in the chapel, I looked at my client's broad shoulders and reflected that he could be at Kirby for a long, long time. It was hard to be encouraging. He wanted to know why I hadn't gotten him out. We went over the testimony again and again. During his years of hospitalization, he hadn't fought, screamed, or acted out. He'd followed the rules. He'd accepted authority. What more could he have done to "prove" he was no longer dangerous? What kind of lawyer was I? Hadn't his own doctor said he was ready?

Yes, I told him, his own doctor had. But what advice could I give him? It wasn't an easy case. Perhaps I shouldn't second-guess his criminal defense attorney, but either self-defense or some other form of justifiable homicide—similar to the "battered-wife syndrome"—might have been argued successfully. Or a defense based on extreme emotional disturbance might have been used to plea-bargain the charges into something that wouldn't have required a long spell at Kirby. Unfortunately, you can't unbreak a glass, and Ruiz had to live with his "successful" insanity plea.

Two months after our interview, on another blue Monday, someone gave him some cocaine.* It was smuggled into Kirby, probably

---

* Although Kirby is a maximum-security facility, it is not uncommon for street drugs to be smuggled in to patients, usually by visiting family or friends. Because of the high security, however, there is much less access to street drugs than at the less secure hospitals on Wards Island, which have roughly the same profile, in terms of street drug availability, as the rest of Manhattan.

by a relative of another patient, and Ruiz got hold of it. He snorted some, then began to hear voices, and after seven years in a maximum-security hospital without a violent incident, he shoved the sharpened end of a toothbrush into his left ear in an attempt to shut the voices up. He did some real damage to the ear, but the toothbrush shaft broke before it got deep enough into his head to pierce his brain.

Thus the court's judgment was vindicated. Ruiz was a danger to himself, if no one else, and in need of maximum-security hospitalization.

Diggs, whom I met with after Ruiz, was another story. He was a little black guy, 130 pounds or so, and quick as a cat. As always, he was clowning around when we began our interview. He was feeling pretty good about himself that day. He rarely maintained good behavior long enough to be allowed to visit the eleventh floor, and he didn't seem to care if he jeopardized a chance for transfer with a moment of violence. But he'd been in good self-control for the three months just prior to our recent court appearance, and as a result he had been recommended for work, at an hourly wage, in the frame assembly shop.

We'd just been to court, and again we'd lost—not a real surprise, because most of my cases are losers. Ninety percent of the clients I represent have no chance whatever of transfer or release. Mental defects do not disappear overnight, and there is a good reason for the existence of maximum-security psychiatric facilities. But many of my clients, even knowing that they have no chance, like to go to court. Diggs was one of those. Like Ruiz, he had pleaded insanity, and the plea had been accepted by the district attorney's office. Later, when he discovered how much he enjoyed being the focus of attention in court, Diggs regretted not having gone to trial. He really had no interest in leaving Kirby, the best home he'd ever known. But of course, he insisted he wanted to be transferred or released.

That day we discussed why he'd been hospitalized in maximum security for so long—nine years and counting—and what he'd have to do to get out. It was our usual conversation. We'd been having it since I became his lawyer.

"Well, first of all," I said, "you'll need some positive psychiatric testimony to get anywhere. So listen to Dr. Benne, make her your friend, and stop telling her how sexy she is. As your psychiatrist, she thinks it's inappropriate."

"That old thing," said Diggs with a laugh. "I'm trying to make her feel good, that's all."

"And I understand you ate all the fish food in the pet center."

"There was real shrimps in that food, Denis. They was tiny, but they was real! They don't serve us real shrimps. Besides, it was a joke."

"That's part of the problem. Everything's a joke to you. You make fun of the therapists, the team leader, the psychiatrists, everybody."

"You do, too, Denis. I seen you do it in court."

"Dr. Benne says you have no insight, and that until you know why you did the crime, you won't be going anywhere."

"There's nothing wrong with me. But I'll tell you why I did it. I did it because . . . because Aunt Lorraine was fixin' to step out again. Yeah, she was always going out, always pickin' up guys. But you can die from that. You can get beat up, or get a disease. And she's my aunt, she always took care of me. I didn't want her to die. So that's why I did it. I cut up her face and took her eye out. She was puttin' on her lipstick and smelling so fine, and I looked at that mirror and thought how she'd be dead if she didn't quit going out and pickin' up those guys. That's why."

"That's not what Dr. Benne says."

"Aw, what does she know? I was there, right? I ought to know what happened. What does Benne say happened?"

"What does she say happened?" I asked him. I knew they'd been through this many times.

"She says my auntie's boyfriends was raping me. She called them my uncles, whatever. But that's a lie. I never been raped by no men. That's a sin. She says that I think my auntie supposed to protect me, I was living with her and she supposed to. Another lie. Like some thin little woman can stop a big man from raping a ten-year-old boy. How that Dr. Benne get to be a doctor, anyway? It was me protecting Auntie. From getting hurt. And anyway, I wasn't no little boy. I was growed. All growed up, and I said to myself that she was gonna get hurt unless I do something. That's why she's alive today. Thanks to me."

I thought to myself, Diggs could be here for a long time, too.

Whether the cause of brain impairment is genetic or environmental, past violence is still the best predictor of future violence. Like Ruiz, Diggs had performed only a single brutal act. In Diggs's case, though, Dr. Benne had testified that his mental condition wasn't much different from when he'd arrived, that his refusal to discuss what had led up to his crime was a form of denial that fortified his failure to change. And, of course, if Diggs was dangerous upon admission and had failed to change, he must still be dangerous now.

My best legal argument for Diggs, as with Ruiz, had focused on the isolated nature of what he had done. But I didn't have an expert witness to back it up. When we lost the case, I didn't feel as bad as I had with Ruiz. Ruiz really wanted to go; Diggs was having too good a time at Kirby.

"So we go back to court again next year?" he asked with a giggle. "She must like me! How long she want to keep me, anyway?"

Just then a therapy aide knocked on the door of the room where we were talking and said that Diggs needed to get back to his ward, where lunch would be served. Always a fan of lunch, Diggs was up and ready to go before the aide had finished his sentence. While the aide passed a metal detector over Diggs, who stood spread-eagled against the wall, I left and took the elevator to my first-floor office.

I was really tired. Those intermittent phone calls throughout the night had shattered my sleep. And what I saw as my complicity in Diesel's criminal life, since I had negotiated his initial release all those years ago, exhausted me emotionally. I had still not gotten over it, and I had recently been directed by a judge to renew my representation of him. Now my sorrow over Alexis Walsh, the murdered Rockette, forced me again to question the value of what I was doing professionally.

I understood that, each in his own way, Ruiz and Diggs were victims turned victimizers. Almost every violent mental patient had himself been preyed upon when young; like a kind of vampirism, violence infected each generation anew. I also realized that a lawyer's focus must be on his clients and not their victims, and that tactically, the client's status as yesterday's victim was often one of the few possible points for sympathy. And I understood that all patients need legal counsel so that they won't be railroaded by nervous hospitals or pushy district attorneys or because they have the bad luck to be in the wrong place at the wrong time—nevertheless, my efforts had enabled Diesel to gain his initial release. True, I hadn't believed he would go as wrong as he did; not even close. But some unfortunate children had paid the price.

I began to reflect on my own potential as a victim. Most homicides, after all, are committed by someone well-known to the deceased. Sunday's events had unsettled me. I suspected that the greasy doorknob, the hanging chicken, and the late-night phone calls were all the work of an ex-client, not just a series of strange coincidences in a strange city.

But there was no time to brood about it. That Monday afternoon, I went up to the women's ward to visit with a kindergarten teacher who had pushed a nine-year-old boy from a roof to avenge his mother's suggestion that she was a prostitute. Her name was Betsy Faye. The hospital administration seemed to think Ms. Faye was making good progress. Not for the first time, I thought about how race, class, and educational achievement were subtle forces in the legal process. Almost regardless of mental condition, small, educated white women like Ms. Faye had a clear advantage over big young men, black or white, because people aren't frightened by little women. Judges pity them, often finding their potential for further violence to be small.

Later I was back in my office, trying to concentrate on the file of an upcoming case when my private line rang, startling me.

"Hello?"

"Hello, Mr. Woychuk, this is Dr. Pinto," said a voice with some pressure behind it.

Dr. Mercedes Pinto, a thirty-eight-year-old white woman from the island of Jamaica, had given up her medical practice there to relocate to Manhattan and spend time with her parents while they were still alive. A small, pretty woman, she was not intimidating to look at, and when she was relaxed she had a lovely lilting voice. Despite her previous history—she had murdered her mother by lethal injection—a judge observing her in court might not be afraid of meeting her on a dark street. I'd played up Dr. Pinto's frail appearance when I represented her at Kirby, and after she was transferred to Manhattan Psychiatric I continued as her attorney until she was released (with a five-year "order of conditions," a status similar to parole) two years ago. The whole process of shepherding her through the system took about five years, a rapid rarity for someone charged with multiple murder. After being released Dr. Pinto had been accepted to an outpatient living arrangement at the Stratford Arms, a well-run single-room-occupancy hotel that catered primarily to former mental patients and the elderly. Now she lived in my neighborhood, just a few blocks from my house.

"Dr. Pinto. How are you?" I asked into the telephone receiver.

"Bad! Bad! Bad! Mr. Woychuk, that medication was making me ill!" she screamed back. There was static on the line. Her lovely Jamaican lilt was gone, and her voice was flat and shrill.

"Have you been to the clinic? You know your order requires you to go to the clinic once a week."

"I don't like the clinic. I don't like the doctor. I don't have to take medication anymore. My new lawyer said so, and if they want to force me to take it, they have to take me to court. My new lawyer said. . . ."

"So why don't you call your new lawyer instead of me?"

"I didn't call to discuss my lawyer. I want to discuss . . . I heard . . . I heard you again on the radio last night, Mr. Woychuk. Why won't you leave me alone? I can't stand it. All night! I shut it off, I pulled the plug, and still your voice. You must stop it!"

"I wasn't on the radio last night, Dr. Pinto. Maybe you should talk to your doctor, and. . . ."

"I heard you! I heard you! . . . It must have been a recording. Yes, that's it, it was pre-recorded. I checked. I called . . . I, um, I checked it out, and. . . ."

"Did you call me last night at home?"

"I don't know what you're talking. . . . It's none of your business what I do at night! Okay? So stop following me. Stop it! I saw you in the supermarket. And at that movie, too. Leave me alone. Stop it. Return my identity! Give it back!" She was working herself up. "And return those funds to my trust account immediately or something bad could happen, something very bad! Maybe to you."

"When did you last see your psychiatrist, Mercedes?"

"How dare you call me Mercedes! Dr. Pinto! Dr. Pinto! I don't call you Denis, do I?"

"Sometimes."

"Liar! Give everything back! All of it! My identity, my soul, my money! Give it back! Today!"

I didn't know anything about a trust account. I had been paid to represent her by the state.

"Dr. Pinto, where are you? I want to help you."

"Never mind where I am. When I want to meet with you, I'll tell *you* where. And I do. This afternoon. So follow my instructions carefully."

"I'm not available this afternoon. Maybe you should meet with your psychiatrist first."

"You're just like my mother! But I showed her!"

And she had. She had given her mother a lethal injection and later claimed it was mercy killing; voices had told her not only to perform euthanasia but exactly how to do it. When she was apprehended, she pleaded insanity. When the D.A.'s doctor examined her, even he said that she was operating under a psychotic delusion and did not appreciate the nature of her acts, so the district attorney's office agreed to accept her plea.

She was one of those patients who responded extremely well to psychotropic medication, and after only a few months her symptoms had abated. Now she was psychotic again, and no one was doing anything about it.

Was it up to me, then?

The phone call put me in a difficult position. I knew that Dr. Pinto's veiled threats were a cry for help, and I wanted her to get psychiatric attention, but I didn't want to be the one to turn her in.

I'd worked hard for her trust when she became my client—she'd been so paranoid at that first meeting, calling me a KGB, FBI, or CIA agent. Eventually I gained her confidence. Then, over five years of careful legal management, I had guided her through the psychiatric system, from maximum security all the way to community living. She'd grown to depend on me. To betray her now would violate my position as her lawyer, her mouthpiece.

It seems absurd, I know; she had killed her own mother and was possibly threatening me. Ethically, though, I could only report a lawyer-client communication to the authorities if and when an actual threat was made against a particular individual. I wasn't sure we had that here. And I didn't even want to turn her in anonymously. I felt I owed her every benefit of the doubt, and if I could find some way to avoid betraying her, I would.

She no longer had access to the kinds of dangerous drugs she had been able to get when she was a practicing physician. And even if she could somehow get her hands on those drugs she'd still have to get close to me to inject me with anything. If she'd done her killing with a gun, I would have felt less constrained. And it was antithetical to my role to substitute my best judgment for hers, however flawed that might be. I wanted her seen by a psychiatrist for her own sake, if not mine. I realized I had a conflict of interest, so I called Salvatoro Guam, now the director of legal affairs at Mental Hygiene Legal Service (renamed, as Mr. Bedrosian had predicted), for advice.

"The Office of Mental Health already knows she's off her medication," Guam said. "But so far she hasn't done anything. They have no evidence she's been dangerous or threatening, and all they can do is request a hearing on the issue of medication. At least that's our position. They haven't made their move. If you feel threatened, *you* can report her for harassment as an individual," he said, "but how would it look, an attorney calling the police on a client, even a former client? Look, it's up to you. Maybe it'll blow over. Maybe it won't. If you want, call the police."

I didn't.

I put the file I'd been reviewing aside and sat at my desk thinking until it was time to go home.

It turned out that the animal fat on my doorknob was the act of a neighbor, someone I barely knew, who was convinced that I was responsible for her lost job, her missing boyfriend, the fact that she'd never had children, and the general misery of her life. She apologized after she entered therapy, explaining that the apology was part of her recovery.

The voodoo chicken never was explained. I have concluded that it was just another part of life in New York, another group, another ritual in the hours after midnight, and nothing to do with me.

Dr. Pinto's phone calls continued for several weeks, maybe a month, and then she faded from the scene. I heard she was calling her new lawyer with stories of sexual harassment by a bank officer. I have no idea whether the stories were true.

The Jury Trial of Mac the Knife

Once I decide to take a case, I have only one agenda: I want to win.
I will try, by every fair and legal means, to get my client off—
without regard to the consequences. —Alan Dershowitz

A banker, a shipping clerk, a social worker, two secretaries, and an architect—two men and four women—sat in the jury box and watched expectantly as the assistant district attorney, Kim Mulligan, lumbered across the courtroom to stand in front of them. A saleswoman and an aerobics instructor sat behind them, ready to step in as alternates if one of the regular jurors became sick or was otherwise unable to fulfill his or her civic duty. All their faces were open, interested.

Mulligan, Jim Berris (the assistant attorney general), and I had ended up with these eight individuals after spending the better part of a week haggling over a pool of almost one hundred and fifty potential jurors. I liked all eight, although I would ordinarily have fought to keep a banker off a case like this. I wanted minority men in any occupation, and anyone in a liberal profession such as social work or teaching. I wanted people who could sympathize with others, recognize the oppression of mental disease, and understand what it means to struggle for life and dignity. But I didn't want nurses or anyone else who worked in a hospital, because of a potential loyalty to such institutions. And certainly no relatives or friends of policemen, let alone an actual cop. I was looking for rebels willing to defy authority or at least concede that institutions can be wrong. If the banker hadn't been an actor for a while after he finished college, I might have exercised my last peremptory challenge and had him bumped. But after extensive *voir dire* in which he, like the others, was questioned about his family, his career, his friends, his hobbies, and his neighbors, I felt he was a reasonable guy who would listen to the evidence. Perhaps what tipped the balance for me was that he lived in a neighborhood noted for liberalism and creative arts, not stuffiness. I thought he, along with the rest, would be fair to my client.

As Kim Mulligan approached the rail separating the jury from the rest of the courtroom, he looked down, towering over them. In a brilliantly white shirt, dark blue suit, and a somber striped tie, he was the picture of a serious trial attorney. He was a big man, ruddy and blond, and passion was part of his style. It seemed he could turn it on just when it suited him. He would build toward his display of righteous anger carefully, almost too carefully. He calculated how to play to the jury's emotions, but once he got himself going, his passion looked perfectly real. As a lawyer, I respected that.

As he did in every case we'd had together, Mulligan began his opening statement quite gently. "Ladies and gentleman of the jury," he said quietly, "what you will hear today is the true story of a man gone mad—the story of a man who has killed not just once, but at least twice. This much we know. His victims were unfortunate innocents whose only mistake was to be in the wrong place at the wrong time. As a result, this man has spent six of the last ten years of his life as a mental patient." Mulligan's voice now began rising, in both volume and intensity. "As recently as ten months ago, he was found to be suffering from a *dangerous mental disorder* by a judge of the Supreme Court, this very court where you sit as jurors today. That judge ordered this man retained in a maximum-security hospital from which there could be no escape. No escape!

"And why is that so important? Because when this man was a mental patient in a low-security hospital—after killing one man and almost killing another—*he did escape!* And he returned to a life of drug dealing and drug abuse on the streets of Manhattan." Mulligan was practically shouting now. Already he had begun to sweat. "*He ran away!* And for years we looked but couldn't find him.

"And that is why *only* six of his last ten years were spent as a mental patient—*because he ran away*. From treatment. From the people who could help him. And what did he do? Out there on the streets? He took drugs. By his own admission, he *sold* drugs. That's what he told his psychiatrist. In fact, he was busted on at least three occasions for possession with intent to sell, but the police never discovered his real identity—not until he threw acid into the face of another man.

"You will hear testimony about how it was discovered that that man"—with this, Mulligan gesticulated wildly toward my client, who sat there in his wheelchair like a stone—"was discovered to be *the same man*. He'd avoided capture by adopting new identities. He is not stupid. No. No one ever said he was stupid. But he is crazy."

"Objection," I said as I jumped to my feet, knowing that I was playing right into Mulligan's hands. The term *crazy* would now get even more attention than if I had merely chosen to ignore it. But I had to make the objection to preserve the record in case I needed to appeal. I looked at the judge intently, straightening my back. I wore a gray suit, because minority jurors often subliminally associate dark blue with police department authority, and four of the regular jurors were either black or Latino. In an effort to avoid a totally formal look, I wore a powder-blue shirt and one of those lemon-yellow ties that were popular that year.

"This is opening statement," said the Honorable Carol E. Martinbrook-Rodriguez somewhat stiffly, "and I will allow some latitude, but you've gone too far with that last remark, Mr. Mulligan. The jury will ignore Assistant District Attorney Mulligan's last remark about 'crazy,' " she directed from the bench. Now the word would register with even those jurors who weren't paying attention. "Proceed, Mr. Mulligan," she said. The judge looked bored.

"I'd like to rephrase, Your Honor, if I could," said Mulligan. He cleared his throat. "No one ever said the defendant was stupid. . . ."

"Objection!" I leaped to my feet.

"On what grounds?" asked the judge, looking at me over her half-moon glasses.

"There is no defendant in this proceeding, Your Honor. Mr. Mac-Knight is a psychiatric patient. There are no charges pending. This is not a criminal trial. To call him a defendant is inaccurate and misleading. We are not here to try him for a crime but to determine his mental condition. This is a civil matter."

"That it is, counselor," said the judge flatly. She pulled off her glasses and wiped the lenses. "Mr. Mulligan, do not call Mr. Mac-Knight 'the defendant.' Now let us proceed. But please, remember, this is opening statement," she said, half-turning toward me from the bench. "Let's not have so many objections, okay, Counselor?" She seemed less than friendly. Despite her ruling, she was making it clear that my client didn't have her sympathy.

"As I was saying," Mulligan continued, "the mental patient in question is not stupid, but he is dangerously mentally ill, and you will hear testimony from three expert witnesses who have examined him and concluded that he continues to suffer from the same mental disorder as when he killed one neighbor with a knife and badly wounded another ten years ago.

"You will hear expert testimony that *only in his mind*"—here Mulligan started waving his arms—"were his neighbors pumping poison gas into his apartment. Of course, there was no poison gas. He was hallucinating; he was paranoid and hearing voices. When he was arrested, he said that God had told him to grab his knife and go next door to the neighbor's; that God told him to plunge his knife into that young man's chest; that God told him to cut that young man's father so badly he spent six weeks in the hospital while his son lay dying in the next bed.

"The experts will tell you that the patient's mentally disordered mind manufactured his perception of poisoned gas, manufactured the voice of 'God,' manufactured the paranoia. *His own mind.* And because of this dangerous mental disorder, he was acquitted of murder by reason of insanity, found not responsible for a killing that he admittedly committed, and sent to a mental hospital. He became a ward of the state. And when the state attempted to prolong his life by providing him with medical care at one of the many fine hospitals located here in New York City, he found an opportunity to slip away, to escape. And claim another victim.

"He was clever, but he wasn't better —his whole life has been one paranoid fantasy—and he was as mad then as the last time he killed. And when was that? We aren't sure. But we do know that he killed *his twelve-year-old brother* with a knife."

I could see horror sweep across the jurors' faces. I jumped up, ready to object.

"But let's forget about the victims for a moment," Mulligan continued, and I sat down. "What does *he* want? What does the killer want? What does the mental patient want? Let's think about that.

"This mental patient would like to be set free." He spat the words *mental patient* like a slur or a curse. "He wants to go back to the streets of Manhattan and roam from one neighborhood to the next. He wants to live as a free man. He wants you to believe that his mental disease is behind him, that he is no longer mentally ill, and that he can safely live in society.

"Certainly, that is what he wants most, but he has another attractive alternative. If you do not find he is ready for outright release, this killer would like you to find that he at least is ready to 'graduate' to a non-secure psychiatric hospital, the kind of hospital where some patients are free to come and go, the very kind of hospital that he left so abruptly—*that he escaped from*—four years ago.

"He wants you to believe he does not have any mental disorder, but he is willing to settle for your believing he does not have a dangerous mental disorder, but merely a mental illness. He wants you to believe that a few months of demonstrating self-control in a setting where his every move is monitored is enough justification for his transfer to a low-security hospital—and we already know what has happened when he has an opportunity to make a run for it."

I thought Mulligan was off to a pretty good start. After initially acting as though this was a criminal matter, a very common mistake among assistant district attorneys, he had clearly grasped that the issue was MacKnight's current mental condition. But then he surprised me.

"He doesn't want you to know that a knife was found hidden behind his locker only three months ago," Mulligan continued. "They call him Mac the Knife, but he doesn't want you to put two and two together. Even though a judge found him still to be dangerously mentally ill only ten short months ago, he wants you to believe that's all behind him now."

I stood to object. The judge glared at me, though, and I was intimidated into sitting back down. I couldn't think clearly of a basis for objecting other than that I didn't like what Mulligan was saying. I wasn't expecting this reference to the knife. The evidence was far more ambiguous than his statement would lead one to believe. Could I turn this to my advantage?

"However, the evidence is clear," Mulligan said, "and you will conclude, ladies and gentlemen, based on the evidence, that this monster. . . ."

"Objection!" I cried, rising. Once again I knew I was playing into his hands by drawing attention to his remark, but I could not let such a statement stand. I had to get control of this trial and set the tone of the discourse.

"Withdrawn," said Mulligan quietly, looking pleased with himself. "I'll rephrase," he added after a brief pause. Then his voice rose, full of sarcasm and scorn: ". . . that this mental patient suffers from a dangerous mental disorder even as I speak. Based on the testimony of Drs. Vronsky, Wu, and Baker and all the other evidence you will hear and observe, you too will conclude that *this mental patient currently suffers from a dangerous mental disorder.* That is the only conclusion you can reasonably reach. Thank you."

Mulligan stood before the jury for a moment, glaring at them, impressing them with his seriousness. By now beads of perspiration rolled down his face. He looked drained. Then he turned abruptly and strode back to his table, which he shared with Assistant Attorney General Berris. Respectfully, the judge allowed them several minutes to confer, thinking perhaps that in the long run it would save time, and she was right. Because both attorneys were seeking the same result—the continued retention of my client in a maximum-security psychiatric hospital—much of the evidence they wanted to show to the jury was the same. Although Berris technically represented the hospital itself, whereas Mulligan represented the people of New York, in this case they were in complete agreement. In fact, Mulligan had already said everything Berris wanted to say. I wasn't surprised. The fact that there were two of them made it look as though I was outnumbered, and that can work for you as well as against you, particularly before a jury. I intended to turn that to my advantage as time went on.

"Mr. Berris," asked the judge, "do you wish to make an opening statement?"

"No, Your Honor," said Berris crisply, rising to his feet. "I waive opening statement." His clipped style of talking contrasted with his appearance, which was lanky and relaxed. He wore a tan suit with a striped blue shirt and a brown knit tie, loosely knotted—certainly not the attire of a lawyer intending to make a powerful statement.

The judge turned to me. "What about you, Counselor? Are you ready for your opening statement?"

"May I have a moment to confer with my client?" I asked.

The judge nodded.

I leaned over toward MacKnight. "I'm doing this strictly for show," I whispered, "so the jury can see us talking things over. After that D.A.'s opening, we've got to humanize you, make you an individual. And by the way, how are you holding up?"

"Fine," he said in a weak, raspy voice, clutching the arms of his wheelchair as if he'd fall out if he let go. His dark brown complexion was chalky and dry. He looked terrible—which was good, from a tactical point of view. Maybe we could get some sympathy.

Like Berris, I had never before made an opening statement to a jury, because I had never before done a jury trial. But unlike him, I could not afford to waive. He and the district attorney's office were on the same side, united in their interest to keep MacKnight locked away. My client was alone. I rose to my feet.

"Yes, Your Honor, I am."

"Counselor," said the judge, "we got a late start this morning, and I'm sure the jury would like their lunch. Why don't we recess until two o'clock—that's just over an hour—and you'll begin your opening statement when we return."

I dined in Chinatown, just a few blocks from the courthouse with Mulligan and Berris—as I expected I would, although neither Mr. MacKnight nor any other client in a similar position would have understood this as anything but a betrayal. But Mulligan, Berris, and I didn't have any personal animosity toward each other. Like me, Mulligan was now a specialist in mental health law, and I faced him in court hearings quite regularly. You might even say he broke me in: in my very first court case, just over a year before, he had beaten me handily. Of course, that was an unwinnable case, but in my end of this business so many are.

Berris covered a rotation of hospitals that did not include Kirby, and we had only just met. I understood he had done appeals at the attorney general's office before joining the Mental Health Bureau, and he had a good reputation for writing briefs even if he was untried in court. As we sat down, Mulligan and Berris were joking with each other about how they would bury me. Good, I thought; maybe I can pick up a useful tidbit or two to use on my client's behalf.

Mulligan was in a jovial mood. I could see why. His opening statement had painted a convincing picture, and my client's chances looked bleak.

"Just give it up, Woychuk. Your guy is nailed." He asked for a beer with his lunch, but the restaurant didn't have any. The three of us had the traditional Chinese tea. "No jury in the world, not even a Manhattan jury, would cut this guy loose," he continued, "so just give it up. C'mon. Look at the judge's face. She's seen it all and even her skin crawls when she looks over at your guy. You want that dirtbag on the street? You live here, too, so think about it."

But I didn't think about it. Well before I entered mental health law, it was clear to me that my job as an attorney was to do my best for my client—whether I represented Monsanto Chemical, an accident victim, or an alleged drug dealer. And when I worked on behalf of mental patients, acquitted by reason of mental disease or not, the standard did not change.

My role was to represent MacKnight to the best of my ability. That was my ethical responsibility as a lawyer. I was not there to judge him, to patronize him, to consult my personal rather than professional opinion about what was best for him, or to allow my feelings (or even my fear) to color my capability. I was there as a tool, a hired gun—period. I was his mouthpiece, his technical expert, not his superego, his minister, or his conscience. My responsibility was to him alone. As long as I did my job, my adversaries did theirs, and the judge did hers, I felt society would get a fair result. That was all any of us could ask.

"Woychuk. Woychuk! Snap out of it! Our food's here," said Mulligan, and it was. "So before I begin on the highlight of at least my day—lunch—what do you say? Will you roll over on this one? I'll owe you one—and it's a loser anyway."

"Oh, stop it, Kim!" I said, thinking that only a beefy guy who's almost six foot five could get away with a name like Kim. "You want a deal? Okay, let's transfer the guy to a non-secure on stipulation and we won't go for release."

"You're crazy! He should be in jail—not summer camp."

"We're not even trying the same case. You act like it's a criminal trial."

"That's what I do. Criminal trials."

"We are not here to retry the crime. Okay, he killed that guy; we admit it. But that isn't the issue. None of that stuff you promised them should be allowed before the jury."

"Opening statement, Counselor. I'm just telling them what to expect. It's not evidence. It's only my opinion of the evidence. And you're not supposed to object. I'm surprised the judge allowed it."

"I'm keeping it out when the case really starts. I won't let it get into evidence."

"Oh, yeah?" said Mulligan with a laugh. "Good luck! Martinbrook-Rodriguez doesn't keep anything out!"

I didn't know if he was bluffing. I had never appeared before her. All my hearings had, until that time, been held at the hospital, not downtown.

Berris snorted with Mulligan. Mulligan had a reputation for knowing his way around a courtroom, and Berris was content just to ride along and let his ally carry the case. "He's all bluff!" Berris stage-whispered to Mulligan, grinning slyly at me.

Lawyers tease each other when they feel friendly, but my confidence was shaken. I didn't know how much I could control in the course of a jury trial. I hadn't any experience. But even Mulligan had never before done a jury trial like this one. No one had. It was the first such case in the history of Manhattan.

Unlike in criminal trials, there is no immediate right to a jury when the matter before the court is continued hospital retention.* Because liberty is at issue, however, the New York state constitution mandates an opportunity for a jury trial at some point. The state legislature saw fit to afford a jury trial only after a continued retention pursuant to a court order. According to the statute, a jury review should be had within thirty days of such an order, but as a practical matter it often takes about a year before the trial gets started. This *de facto* delay discourages jury reviews because patients don't want to wait a year; a trial before a judge alone can be had in a matter of eight to ten weeks.

But there had been no such trials for secure hospital patients in Manhattan until now simply because there were no secure hospitals. Jury trials for maximum-security forensic patients had taken place upstate in rural Orange County, where the Mid-Hudson Psychiatric Center had served what is now the Kirby patient population. The great wave of deinstitutionalization without adequate discharge

---

* Although a jury may have been involved regarding the finding of "not guilty by reason of insanity" on the criminal level, once such an acquittal has been had, the right to a jury on the issue of continued hospitalization is provided for by statute only pursuant to a proceeding known as a "rehearing and review." However, this term is misleading because the courts have almost consistently found that a rehearing and review with a jury is a trial *de novo* (a trial afresh from the beginning), and what the jury is to consider is the patient's current mental condition and not his mental condition at the time of the prior hearing.

planning and the great surge in homelessness have statistically as-sured growth in the psychotic-killer business, though, and Kirby was opened to deal with the additional population of dangerously mentally ill psychiatric patients.

MacKnight, well aware that a conservative upstate jury wouldn't have much sympathy for a black, inner-city drug addict who was also a killer and a mental patient, felt he'd get a fairer trial in Man-hattan, and entirely on his own he successfully lobbied for a transfer to this jurisdiction. It wasn't until after his transfer to Kirby that we met. He was intelligent, but in ill health. He spoke knowledgeably about strategy and tactics and how important impressions can be, but he was not well versed in the law. Like so many patients, he felt he had a convincing argument that he had been illegally detained for years, and he even seemed to think he was owed serious money by the state for damages. I quickly dissuaded him from pursuing any-thing other than his freedom at this time, and I explained it was nec-essary to pursue his freedom in steps: first transfer, then release. If he were lucky, I told him, it was possible to accomplish this within two years, "but I don't want to get your hopes up. It's really a long shot."

"But I'll be dead in two years," he said grimly, "and I don't want to die in a hospital, especially a mental hospital."

"Well," I said, "this will give you something to live for. And be-cause you're physically not well, I can push your case to a jury more quickly. The court won't look so good if you die a year after you've filed for your thirty-day review and rehearing and the case still hasn't come before a jury."

"They been fucking with me like this before," he said. "Do what you can." So I did. And as the first such case tried before a Manhat-tan jury, MacKnight made history.

When we returned from lunch I stood and faced the eight people in the jury box. I was a little nervous, but I put aside my notes and began.

"Ladies and gentlemen, over the next several days you will hear a great deal of evidence. And, just as the judge has asked of you earlier this morning, I know you will not make up your minds until you have heard it all and considered it all. And that is important. It is important to be fair, to weigh all of the evidence, and not to jump to conclusions because something looks bad before all the evidence is in. It is important to wait until you know all the facts. It is important to listen to the judge and follow her instructions. And it is important to remember that we—my client and I—*we* don't have to prove anything. They," I said, waving toward my adversaries, "have the burden of proof.

"Now you probably won't find what I have to say nearly as exciting as what my esteemed colleague, Assistant District Attorney Mulligan, told you this morning. I won't be telling you stories of crime and violence—because that is not what this case is about. It is not a criminal trial, and you are not here to decide guilt or innocence.

"It has already been found that ten years ago my client, in a psychotic delusion, killed his next-door neighbor. There's no getting around that. But ten years is a long time. In ten years some people get sick. Some people get better. This case is not about the past, it is about the present, and you are being asked to decide my client's *current* mental condition. You will hear from experts on this subject, and some of them will have different opinions. For that reason, you will not be able to believe them all. You will have to choose whom you believe, and whether your belief is total, or only in part. Furthermore, you will probably hear from my client, and you will have to evaluate his testimony.

"Now, as I've mentioned, the burden to show that my client currently suffers from a mental illness or a dangerous mental disorder is entirely on my adversaries. We don't have to put in any evidence at all. We can do nothing, say nothing, deny nothing, just sit, and still, if the attorney general and the district attorney don't establish their case by a preponderance of evidence, then you must find for my client. What that means, preponderance, is that if the evidence is evenly balanced on both sides, fifty-fifty, then you must find for Mr. MacKnight. The judge will tell you that that is the law. It will be your duty to listen.

"We are not contesting that ten years ago Mr. MacKnight was a very sick man. Mentally sick. Psychotic. But that was ten years ago. He is still a sick man, but the nature of that sickness has changed.

While ten years ago he had a mental disorder, a dangerous mental disorder, the evidence will show that today he is mentally much improved but physically infirm. He sits there in a wheelchair, has lost 90 percent of his lung capacity due to inactive tuberculosis, and is slowly dying from AIDS. . . ."

"Objection!" shouted Mr. Berris.

"Overruled," said the judge, "but you are trying my patience, Mr. Woychuk. This is opening statement. Stick to it."

"Yes, Your Honor," I said, turning again to face the jury. My tactic was to play for sympathy, to make MacKnight the victim to whatever degree I could. Berris knew it, Mulligan knew it, and now Judge Martinbrook-Rodriguez knew it. She wanted me to stick to what evidence I would present and not make speeches. Although the issue of his health was central to my argument that he did not represent a physical danger, physical incapacity was not technically at issue. Still, now the jury had it in their minds.

"My duty is to stick to the issue," I went on. "Your duty is to stick to the issue. And what *is* that issue? The sole issue for you to decide is the current mental condition of Mr. MacKnight.

"You probably will hear a great deal more than necessary about what happened ten years ago, but ten years is a long time. More important is what is happening now. Does my client *currently* suffer from a mental illness? Does he currently suffer from a dangerous mental disorder? Different doctors will say different things. Dr. Freerick will tell you that certainly he does not suffer from a dangerous mental disorder and that even his mental illness is in remission. *Remission;* the symptoms are gone. And all the other doctors, even the D.A.'s doctors, agree. Furthermore, Dr. Freerick, a psychiatrist in practice for almost fifty years, can find no evidence of a mental disease or defect that would require secure hospitalization of Mr. MacKnight. You will hear how well-behaved he's been back at the hospital, with no fights or other negative incidents, and you will hear this not just from Dr. Freerick—who is paid not by me or my client but by the court to give his testimony—but also from Drs. Vronsky, Wu, and Baker, who are my adversaries' witnesses and in the employ of the hospital.

"You probably will hear a great deal more than necessary about

what happened four years ago, as though a fight between Mr. Mac-
Knight and another man is by itself a sign of my client's mental disease—but my adversaries aren't interested in the details of that
fight, and they don't want you to be. And why not? Because *Mr.
MacKnight was attacked*. And the man Mr. Mulligan calls 'the victim'
was the attacker.

"My adversaries would have you believe that such an attack
couldn't have happened. Not here. Not in New York City. Not even
on 146th Street. That Mr. MacKnight's mind *manufactured* a life-
threatening situation. That his version of events was somehow a hallucination, a delusion. But you know better than they do, I trust,
that such things *do* happen in New York City, that homes are broken
into, that people do have to fight to protect themselves, sometimes
for their very lives."

Two or three faces on the jury suddenly softened. I saw tight lips
loosen, set jaws relax. People who seemed so rigid during Mulligan's
opening were now hearing both sides of the story. I pressed on.

"So, as you hear the evidence on this incident, ask yourself this:
Why was Mr. MacKnight never charged with a crime? Why did the
victim refuse to press charges against Mr. MacKnight?" Whenever I
said the word *victim* I made quotation marks in the air with my fingers, just in case someone on the jury wasn't hearing my sarcasm.
Would MacKnight as victim of an armed attacker play before this
jury? We would find out.

"If this, quote, victim, unquote, were the injured party, and not
someone who could be charged with breaking and entering, assault
with a deadly weapon and worse, why did the victim disappear?

"You will hear how my client, Mr. MacKnight, was struggling fi-
nancially in the community but still making ends meet, living in his
own apartment, staying out of trouble, not showing any symptoms
of mental illness that would bring him to the attention of the police
. . . for years. For four years! And for those four years he was sufficiently balanced to survive on his own, without social services, without help. When he left the hospital without consent, the hospital
felt he wasn't ready, but by living those years without trouble and
without making trouble, he showed that he was. He wasn't in the

hospital for punishment. He was in the hospital to be treated until he could survive without danger to himself or others. When he was attacked in his own apartment, the result was *he* was the one incarcerated. Thrown back into a maximum-security hospital, more jail-like than jail.

"So listen carefully to the evidence and follow the instructions of the judge. Do not make up your minds until you've heard everything and then use your best judgment to come to a reasoned and fair decision. You will find that you can only conclude that my client, despite his serious physical health problems, is mentally much improved—that his mental condition today makes him an entirely different man than ten years ago—and that he should have the right to die with dignity, outside of a hospital setting. Thank you."

I wanted to concentrate the jurors' minds on MacKnight's in-hospital record—to show improved mental condition. But I was willing to address the acid-throwing incident for two reasons, one of which was that I had no choice. Mulligan had chosen to make it central to his case, and the patient's history is always deemed relevant in a psychiatric proceeding. Even so, I thought I could show that it had no relevance to MacKnight's current mental condition and that the assistant district attorney really had no hard evidence of a current dangerous mental disorder since my client's readmission. If I presented it properly, MacKnight's recent hospital record could look very good.

By now I considered Berris, who was deferring to Mulligan on every issue, to be along only for the ride. This was a tactical error on his part. He could have made an independent opening statement to the jury that would have supported his cause but used an entirely different approach. For example, he might have based his approach to the case on cause and effect, with medication being the former and sanity being the latter. He could have called this theory "synthetic sanity" and had a catchy phrase of his own to bandy about. But because he somehow didn't know better, he let Mulligan carry the ball alone, surrendering the advantage of numerical superiority.

As far as Mulligan and I were concerned, our jockeying for the minds of the jurors had begun, with each of us trying to define the ground upon which we would do battle. But of course this battle had begun long before. Many lawyers believe that you win or lose your case before you even enter the courtroom, when you pick your jury from among the many waiting to be called: pick the right jurors and you win. Consequently, a great deal of strategy is devoted to jury selection.

Ultimately, though, it is the evidence that determines the winner and the loser. Now Mulligan and I—and MacKnight—were at the point where the evidence would be introduced and the true education of the jury would begin. The trial was adjourned, to resume the next day.

The courtroom was a high-ceilinged affair left over from a time when architects understood the importance of overhead space. Thirty-foot ceilings today are no longer the norm, but the grand, sweeping rooms of yesterday continue to do duty at 60 Centre Street, where civil trials are held in the state courthouse. Not everyone saw the grandeur— MacKnight noted only the peeling paint, the creaking doors, the worn floors—but I saw a room still regal in its dark authority, with the judge's wooden bench rising like an altar before all that surrounded it. It was an impressive room without being ornate. The only other public rooms with as much dignity are banks—the old ones, where the authority of money speaks of a time gone by.

Closest to the judge's bench was the witness stand, a much more humble perch, and the jury box was further off to one side. Two dark lawyers' tables were directly in front, the one closest to the jury for myself and my client, the other shared by the prosecutor and the hospital's attorney. Behind these tables was a carved wooden rail meant to restrain spectators. But there would be no spectators here, of course, because this was a closed trial. In order to protect the privacy of the mental patient, the public and the press would not be permitted to attend.*

A court reporter would take down everything that was said, and

---

* Only recently has the Appellate Division, the second highest court of New York, recognized officially that there is some right to know on the part of the public; now, subject to judicial discretion, such proceedings are open.

he sat between us and the judge on a portable seat, punching buttons on the little machine between his knees. As the jury was led into the jury box most of them looked around, as though the setting helped to reinforce the seriousness of the task that lay before them.

Mulligan called Dr. Lucas Vronsky as his first witness. As Dr. Vronsky strode up to the stand and raised his hand to be sworn in, I realized how strong a witness he would be. As supervising psychiatrist for the Kirby facility he often gave testimony, and I didn't want him to recite his long list of accomplishments for the jury to hear. His cultured European accent already gave him enhanced credibility with any jurors who felt a psychiatrist trained in Vienna was better than one trained in Poughkeepsie. Vronsky was articulate, relatively young (in his mid-forties), and good-looking. His full credentials would only bolster the case against MacKnight.

"Dr. Vronsky," Mulligan asked, "what is your occupation?"

"I am supervising psychiatrist at Kirby Forensic Psychiatric Center since 1985."

"And what is your educational background?"

I rose to my feet. "Your Honor, we'll stipulate that Dr. Vronsky is an expert in psychiatry." This was legal jargon saying that I wanted to admit the point and move on. Mulligan agreed, which I thought was a tactical error; he could have insisted in bringing out the doctor's qualifications in detail.

Then Mulligan proceeded to question the doctor about the number of forensic patients he had examined, asking him to describe to the jury what forensics involves.

"Forensic," answered Dr. Vronsky, "means dealing with cases that are brought before the court. This can include anything—such as a civil suit where, for example, someone gets hit by a car and says there is damage. Forensic psychiatrists are also frequently called in on criminal cases to testify as to someone's mental state at the time of the crime. So forensics covers a wide area."

Mulligan and Dr. Vronsky were educating the jury. This would continue for a while before they got down to the specifics of this case; it was important for all parties that the jury understand what type of hospital Kirby was. Because the district attorney's office went first, the task fell to them.

Dr. Vronsky explained that Kirby was a maximum-security hospital that treats three types of patients.

"The first type," he said, pulling at his chin, "are those remanded after committing a crime and being found not fit to proceed with trial—which means these patients have a mental illness and cannot go to trial because of that. We treat them, and once their symptoms are alleviated, we send them back to court to stand trial."

Already the doctor was wrong, and his bias was clear—to me, at least. In fact, many of the patients admitted to Kirby as not fit to proceed had *not* committed crimes; and certainly they were legally innocent in every case *because* they had not been to trial. I didn't intend to make much of this, however, because I didn't think it would play well for the jury. I studied Dr. Vronsky's style and felt relieved he didn't have a beard. With a beard he'd have been perfect.

"The second type," he continued, "are those who have been to trial already, and because they were found not responsible for what they did due to their mental illness, they come to Kirby for treatment until they are no longer dangerously mentally ill, and then we would apply for a transfer to a less secure facility.

"The third group are known as civil patients. Maybe they have never committed a crime, or their charges have been dropped, but they may be too violent to be managed in a civil hospital, and they would also be kept at Kirby."

Now the general background was done; the focus hereafter would be on MacKnight. The doctor had examined him twice in preparation for this trial and diagnosed him as suffering from chronic paranoid schizophrenia, which is characterized by auditory hallucinations and persecutory delusions—in other words, he heard voices and thought people were after him. But what Mulligan was really after was the incident that led to MacKnight's insanity acquittal and other violent acts. He asked Dr. Vronsky to tell the court his understanding of the incident in 1976.

"In July of 1976," said Dr. Vronsky in his melodious yet guttural Viennese voice, "while acutely psychotic, Mr. MacKnight, believing his two next-door neighbors were pumping poison gas into his apartment and responding to auditory command hallucinations, attacked them with a knife, killing one and wounding the other."

Then Mulligan asked about MacKnight's history.

"Mr. MacKnight had a history of prior psychiatric illness," answered Dr. Vronsky, "but the exact details are not available to us. We do know that he was seen by a school psychiatrist at the age of about nine or ten. . . ."

"Objection!" I shouted, and I leaped to my feet. "Your honor, what happened forty years ago has absolutely no bearing on Mr. MacKnight's current mental condition." If I could keep the information I knew was coming from the jury, I would be doing my client a great service. I was sure, however, that the judge would overrule my objection. Because psychiatrists always consider past psychiatric condition as a factor in determining current mental condition, and because they are expert witnesses, anything they have considered is admissible. I hoped I wouldn't lose credibility with the jury if she overruled me, but I had to give it a try.

"Overruled," said the judge. "That goes to weight, not admissibility." She obviously wanted to hear it. "Please continue, Doctor."

"When he was seen by the school psychiatrist at that young age, nine or ten, he was experiencing paranoid ideation, specifically that people in his family wanted to hurt him," Dr. Vronsky continued. "He subsequently killed his twelve-year-old brother with a knife."

I thought I heard a juror gasp. I looked over at the jury box. The banker was wiping one eye with a handkerchief. The others were looking down, or at the doctor. None of them would look at me. This seemed to be a bad sign—but hardly a surprise.

I kept my mouth shut as Dr. Vronsky talked about MacKnight's life on 146th Street and St. Nicholas Avenue just a few days before he stabbed his neighbors. He spoke of how MacKnight was threatening strangers in the street and of how he was taken by the police to Columbia-Presbyterian Hospital, where he was treated for several days, given medication, and then released. Dr. Vronsky noted that after MacKnight left Columbia-Presbyterian, he stopped taking the medicine.

Then, in response to further questioning, he coughed and said: "Mr. MacKnight believed he was hearing God's voice and that he was the son of God, the messiah. This is a relatively common hallucination. He also believed his natural father had been killed by Jews through voodoo. He was grandiose, insisting that he, too, was a psychiatrist. And he swore that the acts that he was charged with had been committed by somebody else.

"After being found not guilty by reason of mental disease or defect, he was sent to Mid-Hudson Psychiatric Center. Later, although he was still dangerous, he was transferred to Bronx Psychiatric because of his physical health problems; Bronx Psychiatric is close to a medical hospital which he needed to visit for TB treatment. During one visit, he escaped. Then he was on the streets for a number of years. After he was apprehended for throwing acid into another man's face, he was again sent to Mid-Hudson. The D.A. never prosecuted him for the acid-throwing incident, but the original finding of NGRI—that's 'not guilty by reason of insanity,' or what they now call 'not guilty by reason of mental disease or defect'—was still legally in effect. A court hearing was held at Mid-Hudson, and Mr. MacKnight was retained in the hospital. Because he had lived in the New York City catchment area—the geographical region designated as a part of the jurisdiction of Kirby Forensic Psychiatric Hospital—and because he agitated for the transfer and the doctors in Mid-Hudson were happy to get rid of him, he was transferred to Kirby in 1985."

Dr. Vronsky was talking well and had lowered his voice, a technique that made the jury lean forward in their seats and pay close attention. Mulligan loved this stuff. "And what did the patient tell you about his life at Mid-Hudson?" Mulligan asked.

"He said he felt that people were laughing at him, that he was in danger from them."

But then the doctor began to discuss MacKnight's condition after being transferred to Kirby. The hallucinations were gone, he said, although less severe delusions continued. This testimony about MacKnight's improvement, although it was not a surprise, seemed to chill Mulligan's enthusiasm. MacKnight just sat at my side impassively, occasionally coughing into a handkerchief. I found myself distracted, thinking about tuberculosis and wondering how often doctors are wrong when they say a disease is no longer infectious.

"Mr. MacKnight was beginning to understand that he had indeed suffered a severe mental illness," Dr. Vronsky testified, "and he took medication voluntarily, but his acceptance of that was still incomplete, and the most dangerous thing about his thinking at that time was his insistence that he was fine now, this couldn't possibly happen again, and that he didn't need the medication anymore."

"What medication was he taking?" asked Mulligan.

"Haldol, 20 milligrams a day."

"Was his improvement caused by taking medication?"

"There is no question."

"If he had not been taking medication would he have improved?

"No, the passage of time might have brought some changes, but there's no way he could have improved so much. At this time he is taking only 5 milligrams a day; he's so much better. He appears to be free—"

"Thank you, Doctor," Mulligan cut him off. "Please just answer my questions."

"Your Honor," I said, rising from my chair, "Mr. Mulligan might not like the answer, but he asked a question and I believe the doctor should be allowed to finish his answer." I didn't think the judge would side with me, but she did, and Dr. Vronsky was directed to continue. Mulligan look shocked and stupefied, as though he had been betrayed by a trusted associate, and he sat down glumly.

"I was saying," said Dr. Vronsky, "that the patient is currently free of hallucinations. His acceptance of what happened and of the risks of any future noncompliance, and, particularly, his acceptance of his need for lifelong treatment is substantially improved. However, he is not free of the grandiose images of himself that he had, which is a kind of minor delusion. For example, he refuses to call me Dr. Vronsky, referring to me instead by my Christian name, Lucas. This is indicative of his belief that we are social equals and that he is not there as a patient and I, a doctor."

"Is this delusion indicative of psychosis?" asked Mulligan, emphasizing the word *psychosis* and looking at the jury in an attempt to reinforce the idea that MacKnight had a serious current mental condition.

"Yes, but. . . ."

"Thank you, Doctor," Mulligan said quickly and hurried on to his next question before I could object. "Now this is an important question coming up: Was a lethal object found in the area of Mr. Mac. . . ."

I jumped to my feet. "Objection! Your Honor, Mr. Mulligan is leading his witness. Mr. Mulligan is cutting off his witness. Mr. Mulligan is. . . ."

"Overruled, Counselor," said the judge.

I knew I'd be overruled, but I'd objected for two reasons. If, to my surprise, she sustained my objection, then Mulligan's attitude of invincibility would have deflated. Sometimes a juror may allow the appearance of success to influence his or her decision unknowingly, and up until a few minutes ago Mulligan seemed brimming with success. But perhaps more significantly, I had some good evidence on this issue. Not only did I want the jurors to pay special attention, I wanted Mulligan to make a big deal out of it. I sat back down, and Mulligan finished his question.

". . . a lethal object in MacKnight's dressing area?"

"Yes," said the doctor quietly. "A knife was found taped behind his dresser."

"You say, 'A knife was found.'" Mulligan was shouting again. "Is that significant?"

"Yes," said Dr. Vronsky. "Particularly because he continues to insist that the knife was not his. He may be in denial, or he may be aware he is prevaricating."

Now it was time for Mulligan to hit us hard. MacKnight leaned over to me from his wheelchair and I bent my ear to hear him. "I'm just doing this so the jury will see us talking," he whispered. "I don't really have that much to say. Not until I testify."

I straightened up, and Mulligan continued. "Doctor, this man escaped from a non-secure facility in 1979 and threw acid. Isn't the very act of throwing acid into another man's face indicative of dangerousness—a dangerous mental disorder?"

Again I leaped to my feet. "Objection! Your Honor, he's leading the witness."

"Sustained."

But the doctor continued, "Certainly, such an act by a man with his history. . . ."

"The objection was sustained, Doctor," the judge interrupted. "Do not answer that question. Mr. Mulligan, please go on."

This was the finale coming up. Mulligan asked Dr. Vronsky to tell the jury his recommendations regarding both transfer to a non-secure hospital and release. And Dr. Vronsky told them what Mulligan wanted them to hear.

"Mr. MacKnight has a history of escape. If he discontinued his treatment for any reason, whether because he escaped or because he started refusing his medications in a hospital, he would relapse to an active and dangerous psychosis. He is afflicted with a dangerous mental disorder, and although his insight and acceptance of need for treatment is substantially improved, the risks of his not continuing with treatment, either by escape or release, are just too great. Furthermore, it would be an enormous stress to him if he were suddenly to find himself outside a hospital setting; that stress alone could cause him to decompensate."

"Thank you, Dr. Vronsky," said Mulligan, heaving a big sigh. He turned to the bench. "I have no further questions of this witness, Your Honor."

"We will take a short recess," announced the judge. "I'm sure the jury can use a stretch." She banged her gavel with a crack. "Ten-minute recess!"

Although the doctor's conclusion—that my client continued to suffer from a dangerous mental disorder that required treatment in a maximum-security facility—was damning, the basis upon which he reached his conclusion seemed open to other interpretations. I knew from my review of the hospital record that observed manifestations of current psychosis were probably nonexistent. That Dr. Vronsky testified MacKnight still suffered delusions—citing as support MacKnight's calling him by his first name, rather than using his title—might even have helped us, given the silliness of this example. In any case, I felt Dr. Vronsky had testified to his honest beliefs, and I respected that. It's really all a lawyer can hope for.

Next it was Berris's turn to question Dr. Vronsky, which he insisted on doing—and he said this next part with a big flourish—as a matter of right on behalf of the attorney general of the State of New York! He was not with the district attorney's office, he said; he represented the hospital, and his concern was the proper treatment of patients with dangerous mental disorders and the safety and welfare of society at large. That was the high point of his appearance. Then he proceeded with an uneventful, if businesslike, examination that repeated Mulligan's in almost every detail. He could have made my job much harder by building on the foundation laid by Mulligan, emphasizing MacKnight's past failures to take medication when he was not in custody and underscoring the synthetic nature of a sanity brought about by drugs alone. But Berris must have felt confident that Mulligan could carry the case without him. He rested without giving the jury anything new.

Then it was my turn.

I opened my cross-examination by focusing on the knife—both because jurors always remember a knife and because the record was much less conclusive than the doctor had indicated. By showing the jury that his conclusions were not founded on scientific principles, I could challenge his credibility without damage to my client.

Dr. Vronsky admitted he had never seen the knife; he couldn't describe it, didn't know it was only two and a half centimeters long—about an inch. But he did know that the hospital had conducted an investigation about this knife.

"What was the procedure in this investigation?" I asked him.

"The investigator was asked to determine how the knife got there, and whose it was, if possible. He spoke to everybody he could to try to do that, and the results were that it was not possible to determine that."

"Doctor, didn't this investigation go to the incident review committee, and didn't they determine that it was not Mr. MacKnight's knife?" I asked.

"I'm not sure if they specifically concluded that it was not," he backpedaled. "I do not know if they felt they were in a position to be any more sure it wasn't than it was. My understanding of the conclusion is that we don't know, and we're not going to be able to find out."

"Did you speak to Dr. Bernstein, Mr. MacKnight's treating psychologist, about the knife?"

"Yes."

"Was it her opinion it was not his knife?"

"Yes."

The jury looked on attentively.

"Did you speak about this knife to a Mr. Copeland, the therapy aide who found it?"

"I did not."

"Didn't he write in the hospital record repeatedly that he felt it was not MacKnight's knife?"

"Yes."

"Do you have any information that would contradict this conclusion?"

"No," said Dr. Vronsky, his head drooping. I knew he was sure it was MacKnight's knife, based solely on his own intuition. But intuition doesn't fly in court.

I had not expected the knife to feature so prominently in Mulligan's direct case because of the ambiguity surrounding it. I suppose Mulligan felt the jury might be impressed by the tangible presence of a deadly weapon, whatever its size, in a trial that otherwise revolved around theoretical opinions about the inner workings of one man's mind.

Because Dr. Vronsky had testified that MacKnight's denial of ownership of the knife was significant, the opinions of Dr. Bernstein and Mr. Copeland that the knife in fact was *not* his provided a basis for the jury to question Dr. Vronsky's overall credibility. It therefore was tactically appropriate, at this juncture, for me to show them that he was participating in this trial as a paid employee of the hospital, not as my client's treating clinician. That took about two questions. The jury looked bored, but I wasn't there to entertain them. I was there to make the point.

The next step was to make MacKnight look good—or at least sympathetic—despite Dr. Vronsky's conclusion. Given MacKnight's history, that would not be easy. But I had witnessed several interviews between my client and Dr. Vronsky during which MacKnight had agreed that medication was something he needed, something he would always need. The doctor quickly admitted as much.

"Doctor," I continued my questioning, "you've just stated that Mr. MacKnight agrees he needs medicine; did he make an analogy that he needs the medicine like a diabetic needs insulin?"

The doctor didn't like this question; we both knew the answer. I could see him sweat. "Yes," he finally replied in a soft voice. "He said that Dr. Bernstein explained to him"—I was glad he didn't say "coached him," although that is actually what she did—"that he would have to take it for the rest of his life. He said he didn't want to get sick again, and that he had come to understand that the medicine prevented recurrence of his illness and that he would always have to take it for that reason."

"Now, you asked him what would happen if he didn't take the medicine, and he said the voices would come back and he would get sick again?"

"Yes."

"And doesn't that show insight into his condition?" I asked.

Insight, the understanding that you have a mental disease, is by everyone's account a big step toward getting that disease under control. If you don't know you have it, you can't seek treatment; however, the logic goes, if you know the warning signs of an oncoming mental problem, you can get help before it is too late.

"Yes," Dr. Vronsky replied.

"Isn't that what you were looking for in an answer?"

"Yes."

Now I shifted my line of questioning to MacKnight's condition in 1976 and had Dr. Vronsky compare his condition then with now.

"Doctor," I asked, "what is your present diagnosis of Mr. MacKnight?" We both knew the answer to this question, too, as we did to almost all the questions. Unlike those on television, real-life courtrooms have very few surprises.

"Chronic paranoid schizophrenia," he answered, but he might just as well have admitted "in remission" immediately rather than have me ask him the inevitable follow-up: "Is he in remission?" Once he answered, "Yes," I asked the doctor to explain that term.

"Remission refers to abatement of acute psychotic symptoms, such as hallucinations or delusional beliefs," he said. "People with schizophrenia in remission still show symptoms of psychiatric after-effect, impaired interpersonal and social functioning, autistic or idiosyncratic thinking, and sometimes—but this would not apply to Mr. MacKnight—such things as inappropriate affect."

"Doctor, does he have any delusions now?"

"Not significantly."

"Does he have any hallucinations now?"

"Not as far as I know."

"Does he have any ideas of reference, Doctor?"

"No, not as far as I know."

"What is an idea of reference?"

"Ideas of reference are beliefs—and they may be held to a delusional extent or not—that other people are talking about you, people whose conversations you can't hear are talking about you, or that other stimuli, such as what you are hearing from the radio, has got special messages meant only for you—beliefs that stimuli refer to you when they do not."

"And Mr. MacKnight doesn't suffer from that?"

"At this time, not as far as I know."

"And Doctor, what is magical thinking?"

"Magical thinking is a less well-defined term. It usually refers to the thinking—and again, it may or may not be of delusional proportions—that certain events have a causal relationship when logically, that is not a warranted conclusion. Such as, to give you a trivial example, if I take my umbrella with me, it won't rain."

"Does he suffer from magical thinking, Doctor?"

"No."

I then proceeded to question the doctor regarding MacKnight's behavior in the hospital—specifically, his complete compliance in taking medication, the total absence of fights with patients or staff, and his demonstrated understanding of what he had to do to prove he was not dangerous. Dr. Bernstein, MacKnight's main therapist, had worked hard with him on this last point, and MacKnight had mastered his lessons. Dr. Vronsky couldn't cite a single slip. Still, in order to serve my client I had to discredit Dr. Vronsky further. I sought to do that by showing that he hardly knew MacKnight.

"Doctor," I asked, "you had two interviews with this patient, correct?"

"Yes."

"Both of them lasted about an hour?"

"About."

"How much time have you spent reading his record?"

"Maybe another hour and a half."

"So altogether you've spent three and a half hours on this case?"

"Approximately."

"Now, Doctor—"

"That doesn't include conversations with staff," Dr. Vronsky interrupted with a scowl.

Here was an added bonus. In his attempt to show the jury he had worked hard on this case, Dr. Vronsky had opened the door to a new line of questions. I asked him whether he had spoken to Mr. Bromley, Ms. Fish, or Mr. Stafkey, all of whom were therapy aides at the hospital. They were not people that a testifying doctor would ordinarily consult because they were not clinicians, but the jury didn't need to know that. They saw more of MacKnight than any clinician could because their job was to watch the patients. I had spoken to all of them; Dr. Vronsky had not.

"Did you speak to Dr. Freerick, the court-appointed witness?"

"No, he's not on our staff."

"You didn't think it was important to speak to the court doctor who recommended transfer?"

"No."

"Have you read his report, Doctor?"

"Yes, I have."

"He thinks Mr. MacKnight's ready for a transfer, isn't that right?"

"Yes, he feels that it is time enough, and I feel that we need to see this improvement sustained for longer in a secure facility."

"Does Dr. Bernstein, Mr. MacKnight's treating psychologist, believe that he could be transferred to a non-secure facility?"

"She said she thought so."

"Doctor, if he had the exact same condition that he has right now for a longer period of time, you would recommend his transfer?"

"If his improvement continues in the direction he's been going, he will eventually get referred for transfer."

"There is no question that Mr. MacKnight's mental health has improved, is there, doctor?"

"No."

"But his physical health has deteriorated, isn't that so?"

"Yes."

"Doctor, how old is he now?"

"Fifty-one."

"Doctor, what is Mr. MacKnight's life expectancy?"

Mulligan jumped to his feet. "Objection!" he shouted.

I expected as much. In fact, I was pleased with Mulligan's vehemence. Several members of the jury seemed to shake themselves awake from their daydreams. "How long the patient is expected to live has no relevance as to his current mental condition!" Mulligan cried. "Counsel's sole purpose is to elicit sympathy from the jury. Furthermore, there's no foundation for the question, and it calls for pure speculation."

"I'll withdraw that question, Your Honor," I said to the judge graciously, not looking in Mulligan's direction. I wanted to appear cooperative, willing to compromise. But I continued my questions regarding MacKnight's health. Aside from sympathy, I wanted the jury to realize that MacKnight *physically* couldn't act on a dangerous impulse even if he had one. I asked about the wheelchair, just in case the jury hadn't noticed. Mulligan was on the edge of his seat. I was onto something.

"He needs that wheelchair, doesn't he, Doctor?

Mulligan jumped to his feet. "Objection! It is irrelevant to his mental condition whether or not he needs a wheelchair."

"Your Honor," I quietly explained, "one issue before this court is dangerousness. It is certainly relevant that Mr. MacKnight is confined to a wheelchair and physically incapacitated."

"Mr. Woychuk," said the judge, stifling a yawn, "do not belabor this point."

"Doctor, isn't it a fact that even if Mr. MacKnight wanted to do violence, he would be unable to due to his poor health?"

"Objection!" Again Mulligan was on his feet, this time with Berris joining him.

"Sustained," said the judge.

But I'd made my point with the jury—and I'd make it again.

"Isn't it a fact that Mr. MacKnight is dying?"

"Objection as to form!" cried Mulligan.

"Sustained," ruled the judge.

That was fine with me. I proceeded to lay a foundation for discussing MacKnight's impending death.

"Isn't it a fact that Mr. MacKnight is HIV-positive?" I asked.

"Yes."

"He has AIDS, doesn't he?"

"Not exactly."

"He will get AIDS, isn't that so?"

"Very likely he will, if he lives."

"He has other health problems, doesn't he?"

"Oh, yes."

"Isn't it a fact that if Mr. MacKnight is not transferred or released as a result of this hearing he will die at Kirby Forensic Psychiatric Center?"

Both Berris and Mulligan were on their feet. "Objection!" they cried.

"Sustained," said the court, but I didn't really need the doctor to answer this question. I just wanted the jury to hear it.

"No further questions of this witness," I told the court, and I sat down.

The next day Drs. Baker and Wu testified. Dr. Baker, a young Yale graduate, was Mr. MacKnight's treating psychiatrist, seeing him in passing every day and spending a half-hour session with him once every two weeks. But Dr. Baker had only been at Kirby a matter of months, and he had never testified before a jury. Although he supplied essentially the same opinions as Dr. Vronsky, he was nervous, and his voice broke on several occasions. Dr. Wu had been a member of the group of Kirby doctors who reviewed the treatment team's recommendation for MacKnight's continued retention. He too had good credentials, but his English was not good and deteriorated as his testimony went on; even the court reporter had trouble understanding him. Neither doctor had anything to say that hadn't already been said by Dr. Vronsky, and neither captured the hearts of the jury. As the afternoon drew to a close, Mulligan, as the representative of the district attorney, and Berris, as the representative of the attorney general, rested their case against my client. Things were moving relatively quickly. It was only Wednesday.

Now it was my turn. I called Dr. James John Freerick as our first witness. He was old—semi-retired—with a bushy white beard that almost always obscured a red bow-tie set askew. His eyebrows were like the wings of a small bird and his clothing was disheveled and poorly matched, but he spoke with authority in a slow midwestern baritone. His report had already been available for review by the judge and by all parties, and his position clearly supported my client's transfer. The question now was who the jury would believe.

"Dr. Freerick," I said, "please tell the court about your educational background."

"I did my undergraduate at Harvard. . . ."

Berris cut him off. "Your Honor," he said, "we will concede the doctor's qualifications."

"I do not accept his concession," I responded. "I'd like the jury to know." This was the answer Mulligan should have given me about Dr. Vronsky a couple of days ago.

"Go ahead," said the judge.

So I proceeded to elicit in detail each step of Dr. Freerick's impressive career, including his education, publications, and teaching positions. It took about twenty-five minutes. From their glazed expressions I could tell some of the jury found this tedious, but I pressed ahead.

"And, doctor," I asked, "were you appointed as an independent evaluator by the court to offer a professional, unbiased opinion?"

"I was."

Independent evaluators are chosen arbitrarily from a list of qualified psychiatrists maintained by the Appellate Division of the Supreme Court of the State of New York. Relatively few of the doc-

tors on it are interested in and qualified for work in the forensic
area, though, and even this early in my career I already had a good
idea of which doctors would give what kind of testimony. Mac-
Knight had been lucky to draw Dr. Freerick. Most of the others
would not have been as willing to give him much support.

I asked Dr. Freerick about his work on this case. He had spent a
total of six hours looking at records and two hours with MacKnight.
He had spoken with Dr. Bernstein, MacKnight's treating psychologist, and, significantly, with Ms. Fish, Mr. Stafkey, and Mr. Bromley.

"Why these last three, doctor?" I asked.

"Because," he replied, "they see him all day every working day. If
something significant happens, they see it firsthand."

"What is your diagnosis?"

"On Axis One, schizophrenia, paranoid type, in full remission."

What followed was testimony about the changes since 1976 in
MacKnight's mental processes, including magical thinking, delusions, and hallucinations. Dr. Freerick found MacKnight to be currently free of those symptoms. He also found the patient's insight
much improved.

"Mr. MacKnight's understanding of his mental illness has
changed considerably since his admission to the hospital," Dr. Freerick told the jury. "Initially he did not fully understand that he suffers from a lifelong mental illness for which he will always need to
take medication, but now he does. He realizes he will continue to
need medication, even if he is feeling good, and even if he is not
having hallucinations or delusions."

"What did he tell you about his illness when he didn't take medication?" I asked.

"He told me he'd been hearing voices. He said he'd believed he
was Jesus Christ, that his father was God, et cetera. And I asked him
how he understood such beliefs today, and he told me, quote, I was
sick, and that such thoughts, quote, were absurd and must have
been the product of a mentally ill mind. What was important for me
to differentiate, to see if he understands, was that even if he recognized he was mentally ill at the time, does he recognize in the present he actually suffers from the same illness even though he doesn't
suffer from the same symptoms? He said he still has paranoid schiz-

ophrenia, and I think, to use his words, he said it was 'a perpetual illness' from which he will always suffer. That shows good insight.

"But there's also a different type of understanding which Mr. MacKnight has—what I call 'the reality principle,' in that he knows it's in his best interests to follow whatever rules that are imposed on him. He understands that he's already been involved with the criminal justice system, and that to break any rules would cause him further difficulties, and he does not want to put himself in that position. Furthermore, he is aware that his physical health is not good and that he might need medical attention at any time."

"Now, Dr. Freerick," I said, "Dr. Vronsky testified that Mr. Mac-Knight is psychotic; would you agree with that?"

"I strongly disagree with that statement."

"Now, doctor, if a patient were hearing voices and denied it, is there any way you could tell if he were lying to you?"

"When you have a prolonged opportunity to examine someone, their behavior as well as their statements give you information about them. I'll give you a telling example. If you see someone on the street mumbling to themselves, they may tell you, 'I am not hearing voices,' but obviously there is evidence they might be. Or if a person seems preoccupied, and you ask them to do something and they don't seem to respond, or if they're given instructions to do something and they don't follow the instructions appropriately, generally the assumption is that they are more preoccupied with some internal state, often with internal phenomenon of voices, rather than external reality. Oftentimes someone will tell you, 'No, Doctor, I don't hear voices,' but nevertheless right in front of you they are mumbling to themselves or they are looking up into the air, for example, as if the voices are outside their head. That someone may be hearing voices."

"Is Mr. MacKnight hearing voices at present?"

"No. Unquestionably not. He is not hearing voices at present, he was not hearing voices during the period of our interview, and, to a reasonable degree of medical certainty I can say he has not heard voices for a very substantial period, probably years."

Mulligan rose to his feet. "Move to strike that last part as not responsive to the question and beyond its scope," he said, somewhat half-heartedly. He wanted the judge to direct the court reporter to remove from the record the part of Dr. Freerick's answer that referred to periods other than the immediate present.

The judge declined. "I'll allow it," she said, nodding at me to continue.

Now we moved into the area of the other doctors' statements. I wanted Dr. Freerick to explain why he had not been swayed by them.

"Doctor," I asked, "when you came to your conclusions and made your report, did you use other doctors' reports as a basis in making your determination?"

"Yes, I did."

"Have you seen Dr. Vronsky's report?"

"Yes, I have."

"And have you used that in any way as your basis in what you're saying today?"

"Objection, Your Honor," said Berris without rising. I didn't see a basis for his objection, and neither did the judge. "Overruled," she said. But perhaps Mulligan knew where I was headed.

"I—I'll give you a bifurcated answer," said Dr. Freerick. "Prior to writing my written report I had not seen Dr. Vronsky's report. Now, in terms of my testimony today, Dr. Vronsky's report in no way causes me to alter or modify my opinions."

"Do you believe that Dr. Vronsky's report was an objective, unpaid, unbiased report?" I asked.

Mulligan jumped to his feet. "Objection again, your honor!"

"Objection," added Berris.

The judge looked over her half-moon glasses at me. "What type of question was that, anyway?" she asked.

"It was a bad one, actually," I replied sheepishly.

"It was terribly improper," said the judge.

"I'm sorry," I said. "I apologize."

In fact, though, my question was the result not of inexperience but of strategy. I didn't think it hurt to have the jury wonder about the answer. I believed that Dr. Vronsky had risen to his current position because he rarely had an official opinion that did not comport with that of Kirby's executive director. I was angry because earlier that week Dr. Bernstein said that she could not testify for Mr. Mac-Knight because of the negative impact it would have on her career. She noted how few jobs there were for psychologists and she told me that already she was being criticized by the hospital's upper echelon for having gone on record with her opinions in this case. I wanted the jury to know that Dr. Vronsky was not necessarily an objective witness, but a lawyer can antagonize a judge only so much. I moved on to the question of medication.

"Now, Doctor, Mr. MacKnight takes the medication now, five milligrams of Haldol by mouth?"

"That is correct."

"Is there any significance that he gets it by mouth as opposed to injection?"

"Yes, the significance is that the hospital staff trusts his compliance sufficiently that they feel that if he's given the medication, he will take it—as opposed to other patients who oftentimes spit out the medication or hide it in some way. No one really knows if they're taking the medication, and to make sure, they're given injections. Generally a person who is trusted and compliant with treatment will be given pill form."

"And, Doctor, has his dosage of antipsychotic medication changed since his first admission?"

"Yes, of course. As someone begins to improve and is no longer having symptoms of psychosis, then it's wise to decrease the dose, the idea being to expose the patient to the lowest dose necessary to control their symptoms in order to avoid side effects. You would not lower the dose if someone remained grossly psychotic; generally they would need more rather than less medicine."

Now I moved on to the crux of our case. "Dr. Freerick, what is your conclusion as to his suitability for transfer to a non-secure facility?"

"My conclusion is that since Mr. MacKnight does not currently suffer from a dangerous mental disorder, he should be transferred to a civil psychiatric facility."

"I have nothing further of this witness," I told the court. I didn't want to take a chance by pushing too hard.

However, the court was still curious. Some judges never get the lawyers-that-they-used-to-be out of their system. It is not easy to sit back and listen, hour after hour; talking is much easier. Although from a lawyer's point of view it is generally unwelcome and annoying, it's not uncommon for a judge to inquire of a witness. Judge Martinbrook-Rodriguez asked a series of questions that Dr. Freerick fielded better than I expected.

"Do you have any opinion," asked the judge, "as to whether Mr. MacKnight would be a danger if he were to be completely released?"

"Over the entire course of his lifetime, if he were not getting treatment and not receiving antipsychotic medication, there is the possibility that he would become psychotic again—but that's not a guarantee he would be violent again.

"Doctor," the judge continued, "if he were released and he received treatment, what would be your prognosis regarding his ability to survive in the community?"

"I would say that it is quite unlikely that he would become psychotic and even less likely that he would be violent. Generally, someone gets sick over time and gets better over time. His psychosis got better gradually, just the same way he didn't suddenly snap and become psychotic. The idea that people are fine one moment and suddenly go haywire, that's a misconception. It's all very gradual."

"Thank you, Doctor," the judge said. "Let's take an hour for lunch. The jury is to return at 2:15."

Dr. Freerick was unwavering during cross-examination by both Mulligan and Berris. Mulligan bullied him, holding a big pile of books and asking what literature the doctor relied on to keep current in the field. Dr. Freerick looked back calmly and said he had been mentor to many of the doctors whose books Mulligan was holding. Mulligan asked about the ability of psychiatrists to predict future dangerousness, citing several studies that the doctor recognized as authoritative. Dr. Freerick agreed it was impossible to predict accurately but he also noted—and here the judge wouldn't let Mulligan cut him off—that false positives (in other words, predicting dangerousness when it did not exist) were far more common than false negatives. Some of the jurors were clearly bored by the technical nature of this talk, but it seemed to me that Dr. Freerick's calm demeanor and Mulligan's increasing agitation was working well for my client. Mulligan's famous passion was backfiring. Berris was not any better and not any worse. Perceptions are everything in court, and he made Dr. Freerick look sympathetic, while he himself came across as somewhat nasty. At the conclusion of Dr. Freerick's testimony on Friday, the uncertainties I felt over lunch on Monday had slipped away. MacKnight certainly had a chance. The jury could compromise between outright release and retention in a secure facility by choosing transfer to (and retention in) a civil hospital. That was what we hoped for.

It would be a much simpler task to get MacKnight released from Manhattan Psychiatric Center, a civil hospital, than from Kirby. No one had ever been released from Kirby, and Kirby had no provisions for discharge planning, whereas discharge planning was a regular part of a civil hospital's function. If MacKnight were transferred to Manhattan Psychiatric Center, I could continue as his lawyer. And I knew from experience that doctors at MPC were less experienced in court matters and more intimidated by the prospect of testifying. Furthermore, because of his physical condition, I knew that MacKnight would probably end up on a ward that emphasized medical services as opposed to mere containment, and most of his fellow patients would be elderly individuals with overt, chronic symptoms of mental illness. Statistically speaking, they'd be patients with no history of violence or crime, so if their symptoms were not pronounced the state would have little basis to hold them. MacKnight would appear relatively sane in such a setting. If his mental condition didn't deteriorate, and he could contain his impatience, I thought he'd be a good candidate for eventual release.

Of course, tactically, we'd ask for release now rather than transfer. That would leave the jury with the maneuvering room that would allow them to compromise.

But before the jury members could approve even a transfer, they had to be ready to accept my client psychologically as a fellow human being. If MacKnight could hold up under cross-examination, we had a good chance of undermining the evidence against him. In any event, he badly wanted to testify. He was willing to take the risk that his own testimony could be his undoing, and so was I. I called him to the witness stand after lunch on Friday.

He was wheeling slowly out from behind our table when the judge spoke up. "Mr. MacKnight, we can take your testimony from there. I'll have the court clerk swear you in. No need to inconvenience you," she said.

"That's all right, judge, I'm used to it," he replied in his gravelly voice. "I want to give my testimony just like everybody else." He kept wheeling. "I don't mind the inconvenience. I don't want no special exceptions. Except for this wheelchair, I'm just like they are."

A couple of court officers helped him get into place, then he raised his right hand and he was sworn in. His chest heaved from the exertion.

"Mr. MacKnight," I began, "you've heard a great deal of testimony from several doctors regarding your mental condition. A number of doctors have testified that what has been referred to as 'the acid incident' was a sign of a mental disorder. In your own words, would you describe for the jury exactly what happened that day?"

"Well, to start with," he said, "it wasn't day, it was night. I was feeling pretty old and tired and I had a chill. These young fellas, they hang around on the stoop where I live, they's all spread out and didn't want to move to let me pass. I said 'Excuse me' a couple of times. I wasn't looking for no trouble, especially with young men like them, but they acted like they wasn't hearing me. My breath was hard—it was hard to breathe, and I needed to hold onto the rail just so I wouldn't fall over. I could see they was high, but they wasn't so high they didn't hear me or see me. They just didn't want to move. So after awhile it gets so I can't just stand there, I'm ready to fall down, so I step over one of them, holding on to that rail real tight so I don't fall on him. Well, I'm just about clear when he gets up suddenly and just about knocks me off my feet. But I'm past him now, I turn and grab the doorknob, and I hear him shout, 'Hey, old man, you stepped on me, motherfucker!' That's just what he said. 'Motherfucker.' I don't mean no disrespect to the court, but that's what he said. 'Hey, motherfucker, you stepped on me in front of my boys, and now I'm going to have to fuck you up!' Well, I seen him around a lot, this one, he's just a young punk hustling with a little street heroin, crack, whatever, the D.A. can tell you that, all about it. So I look at him and his friends and he's looking all scowly and mean but his friends, they's young and just about ready to bust out laughing. So I just turn and go in, and as I do I hear his friends ragging him about how he don't do shit.

"Well, this wasn't the first time he was fresh to me, and in the old days I would have slapped his face good, but kids—well, not kids, he must've been twenty-three or twenty-four—today, they're crazy. You can't fuck with them—excuse me—you can't mess with them these days because they'll do anything. If they get it in their heads, they spend their whole life getting even. A grown man got better things to do, but not kids. He must've been like this. I knew I'd be having trouble with him one day, but I didn't know that this was the day.

"A few hours later I'm sitting in the dark in my room waiting to catch my breath—it's one little room with a kitchenette and a private toilet that don't work all that good, but it's private. Lot of those places up that way don't have private toilets, you got to share, but this one has a private toilet. I need that. I'm too old to share a toilet. Too many junkies up that way anyway. But this toilet, like I said, was none too good, it's been clogging up, so I keep a jar of lye right by it to keep those pipes open—when I hear him banging on the door. I knowed it was him, 'cause he was calling out to me, 'Old man, old man, I'm gonna fuck you up!'

"Well, I couldn't call the police because I didn't have a phone, and the door was starting to shake real bad and I was starting to worry how many of them was out there, so I grabbed that jar of lye I told you about in one hand and a piece of broken lead pipe in the other, just in case the door gave way.

"Which it did in another five minutes. I knew it was about to by the way those hinges was crying, but it was still kind of sudden, it just came down off the top hinge and hung there just from the bottom, and he was in my room. I was scared for my life. I didn't have nowhere to run, so I just heaved that jar at him and he got himself a good splash of that stuff, a real good splash, and he went running out of there screaming with his hands over his face. Of course, now the police come—not fifteen minutes earlier—and they take me down to the station, which was probably a good thing because I don't like to sleep in no apartment that don't have no door."

MacKnight kept the stand for the rest of the afternoon and part of Monday morning. The weekend break did us good; it meant the jury's recollection of the prior week would be less fresh, and MacKnight's testimony would get greater weight. He would tell the story of the break-in twice again in detail for Mulligan and Berris. Each time he sounded more convincing than the last. His language wasn't stilted; the facts never changed, but his way of telling the story did. It was clearly unrehearsed. His self-portrait as a victim of circumstance was complete.

MacKnight discussed his need for medication with the understanding of a medical school graduate and the demeanor of a mortician. He spoke about his impending death and implored the jury not to sentence him to live his final days behind cinder blocks and razor wire.

He was unflappable. He showed remorse, he blamed himself, he took moral responsibility despite having been found legally not responsible for his crimes. He was not the raving monster Mulligan had promised the jury. He was an old man at fifty-one, with only a short time left. He coughed a lot. When Mulligan was finished, Berris took over with the classic questions that most patients get wrong because they tend to reason that they cannot be released until they are cured.

"You, sir, are you mentally ill?"

Most patients fall into the trap of saying, "Not anymore." But not MacKnight. "Yes," he replied.

"Don't you suffer from the same disease today that you did in 1976?" asked Berris. This was another standard inquiry in mental health cross-examination.

"Yes."

"And what happened in 1976?"

"I was having trouble breathing in my apartment, and suddenly I heard God's voice telling me I must be Jesus. The voice said that the evil neighbors was pumping poison gas into my apartment through a hole in the wall, and to take a knife and pay them a visit.

"When they opened the door, they was both standing there with baseball bats. They was entertaining two lady friends in the kitchen—neither was the boy's, ah, the younger man's, ah, mother—and these fellas wanted to show off, I guess. As a man I realized that two guys with bats were more than a match for one man with a little knife, but as the son of God I 'knew,' again in quotes, that I was invincible. I made the first move, and before either of them could raise their bats I stuck that young man in the chest. He went down. His father began beating me around the head and shoulders, and the voice kept shouting 'That's enough.' These two ladies started screaming and I was trying to back out, but the father kept swinging, so I had to move in on him and cut him too. Then I went back to my apartment, and the air was fresh and pure. 'Good work,' said the voice. I realize now that my tuberculosis was acting up."

"This mental disease you have today, it's the same disease you had then, isn't that so?" asked Berris.

"Yes."

"It's the same disease you had in 1981, when you escaped, right?"

"I guess so."

"You were getting treatment before you escaped, weren't you?"

"I was taking medication."

"Did you take that medication after you escaped?"

"No, I couldn't get it. I took heroin."

A smile flickered across Berris's face. "Heroin," he repeated. "Does that alleviate your symptoms?"

"I had no symptoms at the time. The voice didn't come back. I lived on the street for four years without hearing any more voices. I wasn't sick. . . ."

"Thank you, Mr. MacKnight. You say you weren't sick—"

"Objection, Your Honor," I cried, rising. "Mr. Berris is interrupting the witness without allowing him to finish his answer."

"Sustained. Finish your answer, Mr. MacKnight."

". . . I wasn't sick in that I wasn't hearing voices," MacKnight continued. "I was still schizophrenic, but in remission."

"You didn't think you were sick at that time, did you?"

"No, I didn't."

"What about now?"

"Objection," I said. "The question is ambiguous and unclear."

"Do you understand the question?" inquired the judge.

"Yes," MacKnight said, looking at the judge. Then he turned and faced the jury. "I now believe that I was mentally ill back in 1981, but I didn't think so then because I had no symptoms. Now I realize that just because I don't have symptoms doesn't mean I'm better. I'll never be completely better."

"Are you a paranoid schizophrenic?"

"Yes."

"What is the meaning of the word *paranoid?*"

"Objection. That's a medical term, a question for a doctor."

"Sustained."

"Your Honor," protested Berris, "he says he's mentally ill. The question goes to his understanding of his illness."

"Then ask him in appropriate language," she replied.

"Do you feel that people are after you?" asked Berris.

"No."

"Did you feel that someone was after you in 1981?"

"Someone *was* after me in 1981. It reminds me of a joke: Just because you're paranoid," MacKnight said, flashing a rare smile, "doesn't mean they aren't out to get you."

"So you were paranoid in 1981."

"Objection," I said.

"Sustained as to form," said the judge.

And things went on that way for some time, with Berris trying to pin MacKnight down, and me frequently objecting to what I felt were improper questions. But MacKnight was not to be pinned. He fielded questions far better than someone who had never been mentally ill could have.

Berris began to look very much the bully as he tore into MacKnight about his escape and return to the world of drugs. MacKnight had already explained his misbegotten motives, but Berris continued to pound at him. Once again MacKnight, rather than minimize what he had done, blamed himself and his own failure to recognize his need for treatment. I could see by the jury's response that he was making a favorable impression. When Berris asked him about his brother's death, MacKnight's expression dropped to a dark unhappy stare, and his voice cracked as he began to speak. Then, suddenly, he began to cough uncontrollably. The court declared a ten-minute recess that ended up lasting an hour. When the session was reconvened, Berris decided to let the matter rest.

And so the case was concluded. We lawyers made our closing statements, and then MacKnight's future was in the jury's hands.

One event followed that is difficult to understand outside of the numbing repetitiveness of an actual trial. The jury, after listening to four different doctors over a week of testimony, were confused about who had said what. They asked to have a certain portion of Dr. Wu's testimony—regarding his position on transfer in light of Mac-Knight's self-acknowledged need for treatment— read back to them. The court reporter proceeded to read some testimony, and suddenly it dawned on me that he was reading not Dr. Wu's testimony but Dr. Freerick's. Were my ears failing me, or my memory? Dr. Wu had not recommended transfer, but Dr. Freerick had. I couldn't believe it! I looked over at Mulligan and Berris, and they were smiling amiably over some private joke. Other than MacKnight, no one else seemed to be paying any attention. Our eyes met knowingly. As an attorney, I was an officer of the court. Was it my role to stop the proceeding and correct the reporter? Wouldn't that be betraying my client in open court? I felt sure that whatever I did would be a horrible blunder. I lost my courage. So I did nothing.

The jury retired. After deliberating the rest of the day and returning on Tuesday, they reached a verdict before lunch.

"We find," said the foreman (a woman, actually), "that Mr. Mac-Knight suffers from a mental disease but not a dangerous mental disorder." And MacKnight was ordered transferred pursuant to this finding.* We had won.

---

* Since MacKnight's trial there have been numerous legal motions by the Office of the Attorney General to remove transfer as an issue for the jury to consider and have them deliberate only regarding retention or release. And at times that office has lived to regret making such maneuvers, because it has forced lawyers like me to go all out for release—a harder case, I'll grant, and one I'd rather not have to make. To my mind, a transfer for further treatment is an appealing option.

"You know," I told Mulligan over egg rolls and Chinese tea, "Mac-Knight was very pleased that they never traced the knife back to him. Now he'd like to have it returned." Mulligan's face turned ashen for a moment and then he gave a laugh. I never told him the court reporter had read the wrong testimony, deciding it was all for the best—but within a year something happened that made me doubt this conclusion.

Because of his poor physical health, MacKnight was transferred to a geriatric ward where medical care was more easily accessed. He found his fellow patients there intolerable: regressed, stupid, and in poor mental health. As I had expected, MacKnight was easily the most lucid on his ward. He had no one to talk to other than the doctor, whom he nearly drove crazy. Within a year Dr. Aquinesartro had established a discharge plan for my client, and I was on the verge of negotiating his release.

I had expected a fight because the hospital almost always takes the conservative position in order to minimize its legal liabilities. If the hospital goes on the record as opposing release and loses in court, then at least it has protected itself from a subsequent lawsuit should the patient go out and kill or injure some individual who might have been foreseeably at risk. But this time the hospital forensic committee did not overrule the judgment of MacKnight's treating psychiatrist, and there was little opposition from anybody else, even up to the director of the Office of Mental Health for the State of New York.

And although we did appear before a judge on this matter, the hearing was a simple affair because the application for release had been initiated by the hospital's doctor. Berris, of course, supported his client, the hospital. Mulligan was off the case, and the new assistant district attorney was willing to accept this doctor's findings. It was practically a negotiated settlement. Due to his poor health, MacKnight was unable to attend the hearing. The matter was heard downtown by a judge who had taken an interest in the case, and he signed an order directing MacKnight's release.

The following morning, a bright, hot day in August 1987, I looked for MacKnight in the hospital infirmary, but he wasn't there. His condition had improved over the course of the night. I thought I knew where else he might be.

As I walked outside, two whining tractor-mowers crawled over the hospital lawns in the distance, and the fragrance of newly cut grass wafted through the air to linger with heavy sweetness. The trees drooped in the heat under the weight of their late summer leaves, and in their shade I found MacKnight keeping his usual vigil by the river's edge.

He had long since been granted privileges to leave his ward—it was the only way Dr. Aquinesartro could get any peace—and Mac-Knight had found the shade along the riverbank offered him more relief, and privacy, than anywhere else. Because of his poor health he was not required to attend hospital programs, but when other patients wandered too near he still had enough tough talk left to make them move on. He enjoyed being alone.

Fortunately, he always seemed happy to see me. As I approached, I marveled at his attire. Wrapped in a winter coat and in dark glasses, a hat, and gloves despite the warm weather, he reminded me of those people who wear all they own because they live on the street, where the phrase "use it or lose it" means if you put something down and turn your back, it will disappear. Even the wheelchair contributed to this association, wheelchairs being valuable tools for street beggars (disabled or not) who are soliciting contributions. And perhaps that's what MacKnight wanted—the freedom to beg on New York City streets. But the judge had another idea.

In my pocket was a copy of an Order of the Supreme Court of the State of New York releasing MacKnight from inpatient status, directing that the hospital make every effort to find suitable shelter where MacKnight could get medical assistance for his tuberculosis and AIDS-related conditions, and that MacKnight reside informally at the hospital "as a free man" until a suitable group residence could be found.

I told him the news, but it didn't make him happy. He began to cough, and I stood up to avoid the spray. Leaning forward in his wheelchair, he wheezed, spat, and whispered through his teeth that he was going to kill his roommate if he wasn't released—physically released—by the end of the month, that he didn't give a damn about being a free man if it was only on paper. Then he lowered his voice. He said his roommate had been making threats, bugging him, buzzing in his ear, not letting him sleep. In fact, the man was whining to him right that second, demanding sexual favors, or else. "Don't you hear him?" he cried. "I don't think I can wait until the end of the month! I want my own apartment. Now! I don't want to live with no faggots and no junkies. I can't stand the smell of death. And I can't stay here. I can't. They got me in a room with this stinking old man who don't take showers, don't wipe his ass. I don't think I can wait until the end of the month!

"Shut up, Romero!" he screamed over his shoulder. "He's threatening me! Don't you hear him?" he cried, turning back to me.

My skin crawled at the back of my head as I looked around. Just us two; no one else was near. I heard the mowers whine in the distance, nothing else. I got that sinking feeling in my guts.

"It's either kill or be killed!" declared MacKnight.

It sounded unpleasantly familiar.

The last time he had killed, he was sure his neighbors were pumping poison gas into his apartment—and it was kill or be killed. The time before that, his own brother had threatened him with a knife—it was kill or be killed—although the only knife that was found was his own, embedded in his brother's heart. Even when he had escaped from the hospital and spent a few short years on the street before his arrest on the charge of attempted murder for throwing acid into another man's face—it was kill or be killed. Classic paranoid schizophrenia, just as Dr. Vronsky, supervising psychiatrist at Kirby Forensic Psychiatric Center, had said on the witness stand.

To believe in MacKnight and his continued remission, I suddenly realized, had been wrong. It didn't matter whether he'd decompensated because he'd stopped taking his medication, or for some other reason. He was sick again.

"Shut up, Romero!" MacKnight screamed hoarsely once again. "I don't got to take this," he said, his eyes imploring mine. "Get me a place now, or I'll kill him. I'll have to. It's him or me."

I knew Romero to be so mentally disorganized that his language was referred to psychiatrically as "word salad," a term that conjures up an accurate picture of the lack of discernable meaning that was characteristic of his speech. I didn't think he was capable of threatening MacKnight, but for an old man with a bleeding stomach ulcer, he was remarkably quick on his feet. My dilemma was whether I should act on my recent discovery of MacKnight's *current* mental condition—or, more accurately, in view of the particularity of MacKnight's threat to kill him, did I have any responsibilities to Romero? I had an ethical obligation (if not an actual legal duty) to exercise some care to protect Romero as a foreseeable victim, but only if I had reasonable cause to believe that MacKnight was a danger to him. On the other hand, I was MacKnight's attorney, not Romero's, and MacKnight's communication to me was confidential. To tell what I had learned would be a betrayal of my obligations in that role and in conflict with my professional ethics. Furthermore, my allegiance to MacKnight required my best efforts to get him outside the hospital system, not turn him in.

And that would have been an immediate solution: to get MacKnight outside the system, thus relieving him of the opportunity to act on his threat.

However, the circumstances did not present this as an option, and I made my own decision. I felt that although MacKnight might in fact have intended to act on his paranoid ideation, I did not believe he was physically capable of carrying out his threat. Thus Romero was not a foreseeable victim, and my duty was to keep my mouth shut. I could have been wrong, and to this day I am not comfortable with the choice I had to make. I'd been wrong before and I've been wrong since. I've had to acknowledge my part in getting patients released who later reverted to dangerous behavior. But as it turned out, in this instance I was right. Whatever MacKnight intended, he never did anything about it. Romero was never hurt.

After having grown successively weaker, more debilitated, and sicker with each passing day, MacKnight finally succumbed to the ravages of his body. It was what we call Indian summer, that last great wave of warm weather before cold December, when I heard the news. He died on a Sunday. He finally got to leave the hospital grounds.

Land of Opportunity

In the middle of the journey of our life I came to myself within a dark wood where the straight way was lost.—Dante's Inferno, canto I

According to the papers that were forwarded to me along with my new assignment, Mtumbo Balinka had come to the Manhattan Psychiatric Center (MPC) from Rikers Island prison, where he had been held awaiting trial on several misdemeanor counts, including menacing, resisting arrest, and fourth-degree criminal possession of a weapon. While at Rikers, two psychiatrists had examined him and found that he didn't understand the nature of the charges against him and/or could not assist legal counsel in his own defense.

Had he been charged with a serious felony, particularly a violent felony, he would have been sent to Kirby, the maximum-security hospital—and though it might have taken years, he almost certainly would have been held there until he could regain fitness to stand trial. But since misdemeanor trials are legally required to begin within ninety days of charges being filed, and because psychiatrists are virtually never willing to deem patients fit to stand trial after only three months of observation and treatment, patients charged with these lesser crimes wind up serving a kind of equivalent sentence at the mental hospital. If they haven't been overtly dangerous since arrest, they will then be sent to a civil psychiatric hospital. Balinka was sent to one of the two high-security wards at MPC because he was accused only of misdemeanors, and after ninety days the charges were dropped. He thus became a civil patient by operation of law.

Most patients on Meyer 10, the floor at MPC to which Balinka was assigned, had transferred either from maximum-security hospitals such as Kirby or from jails or prisons such as the Rikers Island facility. Meyer 10 was also home to purely civil patients who had been transferred from other wards because of violence. Many were big, young fellows with a street-drug habit.

Patients often attacked each other. On a day-to-day basis, in fact, Meyer 10 was much wilder than Kirby because the MPC staff had no special training to deal with outbreaks of violence. The physical condition of Meyer 10 also made its contribution. The blue walls, unwashed during my tenure, were grimy with the grease of thousands of handprints made over the years. The floors, although washed occasionally, always looked dirty and were often sticky underfoot.

To new arrivals, the apparent wildness of the other patients and the indifference of the hospital to its own physical surroundings sent a message. I like to think that message was about the importance of self-control. When my clients from Kirby were about to be transferred to Manhattan Psychiatric Center, I prepared them for life on Meyer 10 by describing it as a descent into a lower ring of hell with the hope that they could perhaps emerge someday to a better world. I had Dante's "Inferno" in mind. But they knew more about hell than I did.

The papers on my desk indicated that Balinka had been held as a civil patient on a locked (high-security) ward for an additional eighteen months after the criminal charges against him were dropped. His treating psychiatrist had continued to find Balinka needed further in-patient treatment, and now these new papers asked the court (1) to approve twenty-four more months of hospitalization, and (2) to order Balinka to take medication. The diagnosis given in the doctor's report was "atypical psychosis, in partial remission." He cited delusions, hallucinations, incoherence, and illogical thinking as the principal symptoms of his illness without enumerating the particulars. Though he was supposed to specify the basis for his conclusions by explaining the nature of each of these symptoms, he did not, and it seemed to me he might have been merely copying words from the standard diagnostic manual. He did specify the criminal charges as evidence of a pattern of violence, supported by a number of documented fights on the ward. And Balinka's refusal to take medication indicated to the doctor that he did not realize he had a mental disease.

The diagnosis of "atypical psychosis" indicated to me that Balinka's condition had some confusing features and that this catchall diagnosis was the best the doctor could do with the information he had. As a lawyer, I knew I'd be looking at this closely. *Partial remission* in this case indicated that full-blown symptomatology had disappeared. The doctor's report seemed to emphasize some residual delusion—and that could present a problem for us in court—but the precise nature of that delusion was unspecified.

The irony was that if Balinka had been convicted of every criminal charge against him, his sentence would have been counted merely in days rather than years—if he indeed served time at all, since he had no prior criminal record. And because incarceration, even in the mental hospital, is counted as time served, the criminal justice system really had no more interest in him. The doctors at MPC, though, could keep Balinka forever if they could show the court that he needed continued in-patient treatment. Sick people need hospitals. I briefly spoke to the doctor on the telephone; he told me Balinka had gone berserk earlier that week, attacking a much larger man. The doctor made an application to medicate him so that hospital staff could get him under control, and he wanted to go to court right away.

So with Balinka's papers in hand, I left my quiet office and entered the teeming corridors of Manhattan Psychiatric Center to pay him a call. Heading for the elevators on the first floor I passed two young men, one black and one white, shuffling around in tight, separate circles. Both had a glazed and medicated look, and each seemed oblivious to the fact that the other was doing exactly the same thing a few steps away. The white man wore red plaid bell-bottoms and a black buccaneer shirt with billowy sleeves, the black man a polyester baby-blue leisure suit. In these decades-old cast-offs that had finally found their way to the Good Will Shop donation center, fashions that had been "out" for so long they were "in" again, the men swirled counterclockwise, their arms held tightly to their chests.

I turned the bend in the hall, passing several more patients huddled quietly in corners. Some shook involuntarily, their tongues wandering out from their mouths as though they had minds of their own. Other patients were screaming or crying; just down the hall, still others slept on the floor or stood near the commissary begging for loose change. A few went about their business quietly, perhaps on their way to attend a day program in Manhattan, waiting for the bus that stopped at the main entrance every half hour.

This was a civil hospital, and these were all "good" patients. They all had earned grounds privileges and were free to move about the hospital complex. Other patients—the escape risks, the wild ones—were not allowed such freedoms. My clients, for example, were all on locked wards.

I stepped onto the institutional elevator with twenty or so patients and a social worker and pressed the button for the tenth floor. We stopped on every floor; on two occasions the elevator doors were held open while conversations were concluded. I emerged on the tenth floor perhaps twenty minutes later to meet my new client.

I had no preconceived notion that Mtumbo Balinka was anything other than what the doctor's report had said—a psychotic man in need of medication—but I don't rely on doctor's reports, both as a matter of policy and because I have learned not to. Still, it is prudent to be careful. I used my passkey to unlock the first heavy metal door and then lock it behind me, then repeated the procedure with the second, mindful as I did that this ward—like Balinka himself—was noted for violence.

I asked the staff to provide me with a space to meet with my client, and I asked that Mr. Balinka—who was only a name to me at that time—be brought in to see me. The man who walked into the office a few minutes later was tiny, five foot five inches and a hundred and twenty pounds at the most, with delicate African features and a blood-caked gash on his open brow. I knew him to be twenty-one years old, but he could easily have passed for a high school student. He wore low white canvas sneakers without socks, blue jeans that were two inches too short, and a white T-shirt with Michael Jordan's picture on it. I was stunned to realize I had previously seen him lying around the ward in a stained and tattered sweatsuit, doped up on Thorazine and sleeping on the floor. But the man before me was not the dazed fellow I remembered.

"I'm here to help you, " I said, not feeling confident that I could.

"To help me?" he asked blankly. I knew he'd heard that before. From psychiatrists who had always decided to keep him locked up to lawyers who had given him bad advice, everybody offered him "help."

His criminal attorney had helped him by allowing him to be sent to a mental hospital when he was facing only misdemeanor charges; even if he thought Balinka were genuinely crazy, he might have arranged a voluntary admission along with the dismissal of the criminal charges. Michael Zabinsky, his prior mental health attorney, had similarly helped him by not subjecting him to the rigors of court. After Balinka was at MPC for six months, Zabinsky suggested that Balinka consent to the hospital's wish that he stay for another year. I knew Michael quite well, and though he was really a nice person to me, he was not much of an advocate; he seemed to accept the doctor's stated position as established fact and work from there.

"I'm your new lawyer," I told him. "I've taken over Mr. Zabinsky's assignments. He's been transferred to another location. My name is Denis Woychuk.

"I'm not here regarding your criminal charges; they have been dropped. The doctor says you need to stay here at the hospital for two more years and take medication. That's why I'm here. If you don't agree, I'll help you fight it. You have a right to legal representation if you are being held at the hospital against your will. Now, where'd you get that nasty cut?"

His big eyes grew moist. He rubbed his face. "I can't take those drugs no more, man," he said plaintively with an accent. "I sleep for years too much. I don't want to stay here no more." He looked at me suspiciously.

Medication has done amazing things for a huge percentage of mental patients, letting many live successfully outside of institutions during the last twenty years. But even if it had seemed obvious that Balinka needed drugs, my duty was to act based not on what I thought was best for him, but on what *he* thought was best for him.

"That's okay," I said. "If you don't want to take medication, I don't want you to take it. But we are going to have to work together, and since that's the case and I'm the lawyer, I'm going to ask you to do this my way. You will have an opportunity to tell me whatever you want—in fact, many opportunities—but since we may be going to court in the near future, we might as well begin good habits now. Please, Mr. Balinka, when I ask you a question, listen to the question asked, then answer that question and no other. It's not exactly the give-and-take of conversation, but I'm a little pressed for time right now. If you work with me, maybe I can help you."

I could see he didn't believe that last line, but he had to take a chance. I was all he had.

"If you want to know," he said, "Robinson slap me in my face so I punch him in the eye. Then he hit me with a chair."

"Why did this happen?"

"Last week I give him my cigarettes because he promised to leave me be. But I can see now he greedy. He always want something. Cigarettes, candy, money. He won't fuck with me no more, though. I popped him good."

Robinson, a gorilla of a man, was well known for shaking down the smaller patients. I heard the ring of truth in Balinka's remarks.

"How did you become a mental patient?" I asked him next. "You can take your time with this one. Just start at the beginning, go on to the middle, and finish up at the end."

And so he began, and as I listened to his story, I was amazed, more than anything, by the clarity of his account.

Before I recount any part of Balinka's story, I want to make clear that whether he told me the truth was irrelevant to me as his attorney, and in many ways would be irrelevant to the court. At issue was his mental condition—his need for further hospitalization and for forced medication. True or not, his remarkable account belied the doctor's description of a mentally disorganized individual whose condition had remained unchanged since admission. This young man, no longer drugged by psychotropic medication, seemed normal to me.

Balinka told me he had been arrested at his job at a subway news-stand for protecting his boss's stock of girlie magazines from plain-clothes police officers. He said he didn't know they were cops. He thought they were thieves because they weren't in uniform—be-cause they acted like thieves. His uncle, his only blood relative in all of New York, had told him he didn't believe in bail and refused to post the money, almost nine hundred dollars, needed to keep him out of jail. Balinka had no money of his own.

When I asked him how it came to be that he was found unfit to stand trial, he told me about his arrival at prison on Rikers Island, where he was herded along through the cinder-block corridors amid a ragged group of other men who could not make bail. Two of the big fellows, perhaps used to this routine, had bumped him between them with their swollen, sweaty bellies. One, with bad teeth, bent over him to whisper, "You going to be my girl. Tonight I show you the rope. I protect you, honey, so you don't get hurt."

"*Our* girl," whispered the other, flashing a grin. "You so young and delicate. I know this your first time. You need extra protection. We teach you to live. *Mmmmmmm.* We teach you."

The entire group was herded into a tiny holding cell, and the iron door slammed shut behind them.

It was Balinka's first time in prison. He was eighteen years old. He heard the men's whispered words echoing loudly inside his skull. He tried to calm himself, to tell himself it was just a bad dream, but he knew it wasn't.

Balinka imagined that after they'd raped him and passed him around to the others, his lies would be discovered—he'd lied to the police about his immigration status—and U.S. Immigration would send him back to Sudan. He didn't want to go back. He felt his fear rising like vomit in his throat.

"Please, God, please!" he had cried to the heavens, falling to his knees on the concrete cell floor. "Don't let this happen! I work too hard. I struggle to get to this country in the boiler room of that stinking boat. Here I mop floors, wash dishes, deliver groceries, do anything, anything. I want to work. If they send me back my family will die of shame. I want to stay. Please, God!"

And so Balinka spent his first few days at Rikers Island crying, or screaming, or huddled on his cot with his arms wrapped around his knees. After a few days one of the guards reported this as a matter of concern. His own lawyer, from Legal Aid, also noted what he called "hysteria," and he informed the appropriate officials. A harried prison psychiatrist finally took a few moments to speak with Balinka at the end of the week.

"You look nervous," said the psychiatrist as he reviewed the district attorney's recommendation on the charges, jotting down notes on a yellow pad. "What do you think is going to happen?"

Words tumbled out of Balinka's mouth, and he began to scream—of rape, of U.S. agents tracking him down. That was all the busy doctor needed.

"Dr. Beeb!" he called to his colleague in the adjoining office. "Come in here for a second. Take a quick look at this guy."

"Paranoid psychosis, delusional; disorganized thinking," said the first doctor's report. "Lacking legal competence to stand trial at the present time." Within two and a half weeks of his arrival at Rikers Island, Balinka was sent to the mental hospital.

Anglo-American jurisprudence has long recognized that a person who is mentally incapable of making a defense—"disabled by an act of God," as one case put it—cannot be subjected to trial and conviction without violating certain immutable principles of justice. The truly incompetent defendant can be so unaware of what is happening that he might not even know he is being criminally prosecuted. Furthermore, he might have information that could establish his innocence but be unable to relate it to his attorney. Prosecuting a mental incompetent has been likened to allowing a small boy, unable to dodge or return blows, to be beaten by a bully.

Fairness is the underlying ideology. But both sides, defense and prosecution, abuse it. Defense lawyers may request an incompetence evaluation of their clients as a stalling tactic. Prosecutors may try to incapacitate a defendant when they lack sufficient evidence for a conviction. However statistically irrelevant, this abuse only adds to the ten thousand criminal defendants found unfit to go to trial nationwide every year, most of whom will be either returned to trial once their competence is restored, or, like Balinka, have the charges against them dropped. Very few will ultimately raise the insanity defense. Fewer still will be found not guilty by reason of insanity.* Those defendants who proceed to trial need only possess a basic understanding of the criminal court system and the ability to work with their attorneys; a finding of competence thus is necessary before the issue of sanity ever arises.

In all fairness to Dr. Wong, the staff doctor for this ward, the application for Balinka's continued retention and forced medication had been submitted by his predecessor, Dr. Denbar. In the two years that I'd been working at Manhattan Psychiatric Center, six or eight doctors had worked that ward. This was a lot of turnover, especially considering the importance that psychiatrists attribute to continuity of treatment.

Although he was in his early forties, Dr. Wong had been a psychiatrist only a few years. He'd been trained as a heart specialist in his native Korea, but was admitted to this country as part of a program designed to help alleviate a shortage of state hospital psychiatrists in the United States. Even before coming to the United States, he had knowledge of pharmaceuticals, and it was this knowledge that made him desirable. In recent years psychiatry in America, particularly in state mental hospitals, had moved sharply toward a pharmobiological approach, and the state needed people who could write prescriptions. After two years of psychiatric training, Dr. Wong was put on staff at MPC.

He lived in a comfortable home in a New Jersey suburb and came

---

* For example, New Jersey, which handled more than 32,500 criminal cases in one year, had only 50 NGRI pleas entered, and only 15 of those were successful—approximately one twentieth of 1 percent.

to work every day determined to develop the knack for treating his patients. He was sincere and well-intentioned. He told me he was familiar with immigration problems, and his heart went out to Balinka. But he seemed remarkably unfamiliar with urban New York street culture, as though he could not even imagine a part of New York City that wasn't intended for tourists. Furthermore, his English was terrible.

Having relatively little training in therapeutic modalities other than psychopharmacology and almost none in psychotherapy, he appeared to make little attempt to reach patients by language and thought. He didn't have the time or the language skills. He strongly believed that the doctor knows best and was accustomed to patients' doing what he asked without a lot of discussion. He took Balinka's refusal to follow his recommendations as a personal affront.

Because the hospital record indicated no change in Balinka's behavior, Dr. Wong believed that he continued to suffer from the same mental disorder he had upon admission—which the admitting doctor had diagnosed as "atypical psychosis," as opposed to any paranoid disorder, because by the time Balinka arrived at MPC there were no persistent manifestations of any persecutory delusions. Yet after a brief discussion with Balinka himself, he noted in Balinka's chart that at least one residual delusion persisted: "Patient has delusions of arriving at the hospital by train."

In fact, what he'd said was, "Doc, I was railroaded in here." What we had here was a failure to communicate.

Poor Balinka had encountered bad luck, but he was not as unfortunate as most of my clients. He really wasn't crazy, for one thing. Perhaps his worst luck was that he was black. It is extremely unlikely that a white kid, as a first-time offender, would have been sent to Rikers at all. White kids, especially first-time offenders, also have a higher suicide rate in jail than other groups—and a higher victimization rate in Rikers than other groups. A white boy's panic at his first time in prison thus would have seemed understandable, even sensible, to the Rikers psychiatrists. The population at Rikers Island is 65 percent black, 25 percent Latino, and only 7 percent white. A white boy, especially one so young, would stand out, and he'd get a different kind of attention from the prison doctors. But a black kid is supposed to do his time "standing up." The presumption that he is violent is, unfortunately, also implicit. It's entrenched systemic racism; the doctors have such a crush of new inmates every day that there isn't time to give much thought to individuals.

That crush exists on every level, and criminal justice in New York City is not generally a matter of careful consideration. There are enormous pressures on the system to dispose of cases as quickly and as easily as possible. Fifty criminal court judges have somehow to get rid of 17,000 felony indictments every year; the numbers just don't allow for long and profound thought about each individual case. It's no surprise that 95 percent of these cases never get all the way to trial, and that 80 percent are hastily disposed of by plea bargains.

The racism that is a fundamental part of the system is, incidentally, supported by statistics. At any given time, 25 percent of all black men are somewhere in the continuum of the criminal justice system. Seven out of ten have been arrested before age thirty-five. A young black man is twenty-three times more likely to go to prison than a young white man. (A young Latino is eleven times more likely.) Society treats crime as an individual problem and professes to be color-blind, but many young black men have no future and they know it.

The presumption that blacks live in an actively violent criminal culture is not lost on foreign-born psychiatrists. They may find American culture violent overall, as evidenced by its movies and other media, but view violence in white America as being for entertainment purposes and mostly passive, like watching football or baseball. The poor—whom they know as the blacks, the Puerto Ricans, and other minorities—are more prone to become mental patients through the criminal justice system because it is they who live with and in that system. But mental illness, including dangerous mental illness, knows of no class or racial distinctions. Every race and every socioeconomic group has members who are afflicted. Some just get a greater benefit of the doubt.

Balinka did not.

His case became very special for me. To my admittedly untrained eye, he had no discernible mental illness, yet his treating psychiatrist insisted he was deeply ill. I saw a tiny man, almost a boy, lost in a system he couldn't even dream of understanding. I don't know what his doctor saw. I tried to picture myself suddenly a prisoner on Rikers Island and imagine how terrified I would be when the hot breath of much larger men enveloped my senses. I concluded I'd quickly go mad.

The psychiatrist's supporting evidence did not convince me that Balinka was crazy, however, and I didn't think it would convince a judge. The hospital—represented by the attorney general's office because it was a state facility—thought differently. Because the criminal charges had long since been dropped, the district attorney's office was not involved, and there were no other parties to this proceeding. It was Balinka versus the hospital. Already I could taste the thrill of a real courtroom contest, the excitement of a case where not all of the facts were lined up against me. We had a fighting chance.

The issue at his trial was his current mental condition. Did he need to be in a hospital?

The day Balinka was scheduled to go before the judge, we had some luck. For the first time since Balinka's hospitalization, his uncle showed up. And he was willing to testify. This might not sound like much, but the appearance of any family member is looked upon favorably by every judge before whom I've ever appeared. Still, the quality of his testimony could be crucial.

"How come you never showed up before?" I asked him.

"I had to drive," said the uncle, with the same accent as Balinka. "Sometimes I drive my gypsy sixteen to twenty hours a day. Good business, taxi. That why I no come. Beside, Mtumbo is man. If Mtumbo get himself in trouble, he should get himself out. But finally I see he need my help."

This was not a very satisfactory answer; I would have preferred a doting uncle who took an active and regular interest in his nephew's life. But as an attorney I have to make do with the facts; though I may put my own slant on the evidence, I do not manufacture it.

As always, my courtroom approach to the case recognized that we'd have to persuade the judge that my client was not to be feared if met by accident some dark night on a quiet street. In our favor was Balinka's small size, which could overcome his blackness. My additional strategy in this case was threefold: first, to demonstrate that Dr. Wong's inability to communicate with Balinka was a function of his bad English and not of Balinka's poor mental condition; second, to reveal that Balinka's panic at Rikers Island was misdiagnosed at that time and was the basis for his current misdiagnoses; and third, to portray his documented violence in the hospital as merely self-defense.

There were no juries at this level. Today's proceeding was not a trial but merely a hearing, and it would last at most several hours. The courtroom was down the hall from my agency's legal offices in the basement of the Meyer Building of MPC. It had painted blue walls and a worn linoleum floor, an old table functioning as the judge's bench and four rows of pews as public seating (the "public" consisting of lawyers, hospital staff, a few students, and family members, if any). Originally a patients' dayroom, it had none of the grandeur that many people associate with courtrooms, but it was conveniently located. Because the judges, all from the state Supreme Court, came to the mental hospital to hold their hearings, patients did not need to be shipped downtown by the busload.

Court was about to begin, and I still didn't know who the judge on our case would be. My spirits rose, though, as Judge Wight entered the room. Like a dozen or so other judges, she was a regular on the mental health circuit, and she was familiar with the issues that would come up before her. I had appeared before her many times, and she conducted her courtroom with fairness and dignity. And it didn't hurt that she was black.

Assistant Attorney General Curtis Liebling called Dr. Wong to take the stand as the first witness.

"Will counsel stipulate that the doctor is an expert in the field of psychiatry?" Liebling asked me.

"No, I will not," I replied.

"Doctor," he asked, "when were you licensed to practice medicine in the state of New York?"

"Yes, I am," he replied.

"When, Doctor, when?"

"Yes, I am practice."

My first point had been made, and I had barely opened my mouth: Dr. Wong's English was far from perfect. I didn't want to be cruel or make the doctor suffer, but I felt it important that the court observe his poor command of the language. If he couldn't clearly understand and be understood in court, what hope did a mental patient have of communicating with him successfully? His English, however, improved as he discussed my client's alleged criminal act, his recent fight on the ward, his refusal to take medication, his mental disorganization, and his history of paranoid psychosis.

When it was my turn to cross-examine Dr. Wong, I first questioned his education. Although he had already been qualified as an expert, I suspected that he had not been certified by the Board of Psychiatric Examiners; it is not required, or unusual, for a doctor at Manhattan Psychiatric Center to be certified. I wanted the judge to know that Wong was not the perfect doctor, even though he was licensed in New York. Then I questioned the doctor about the testimony he had given regarding my client's propensity for violence.

"Isn't it true, Doctor, that Mr. Balinka was recently cut badly on the forehead?" Dr. Wong nodded.

"Doctor, please speak up," I admonished him. "It is not enough just to shake your head in the affirmative."

"Yes."

"And that cut resulted from a fight he had with another patient, Willy R., isn't that so?" I continued. (As a matter of convention and to protect privacy, last names of other patients are not used in court.)

"Yes."

"Willy R. hit him with a chair, isn't that so?"

"Yes."

"And isn't it a fact that this other patient is over six feet tall and close to two hundred pounds?"

"Objection," called Liebling. "Not relevant."

"I'll allow it," said the judge. "Go on, Doctor. Answer the question."

"Yes."

"And how many other fights did my client engage in over the last six months?" I asked this question because I knew the answer.

"I don't know," answered Dr. Wong.

This was an even better answer than the truth, because it allowed me to show the doctor as less than fully prepared. I could establish later that Balinka had been in only this one fight within the last six months.

"Doctor, as a psychiatrist, is it important to know a patient's history in the hospital?"

"I don't understand the question."

I repeated the question again, because the answer was so obvious. Of course it was important, and there was no way the doctor could answer this question without giving me points. I went on.

"And isn't it a fact, Doctor, that Mr. Balinka was injured because he refused the other patient's demands for goods?"

"I don't understand."

"That Willy R. was demanding that Mr. Balinka give him money and cigarettes?"

"I don't know."

"How many fights has Willy R. been in over the last six months, Doctor."

"I don't. . . ."

"Objection!" shouted Liebling, jumping to his feet. "What another patient did or did not do has no bearing or relevancy to this proceeding."

"Sustained," said the judge. "The witness is to ignore that last question. Please go on, Counselor."

I knew that Robinson was often in fights, but I respected the judge's ruling and continued my cross-examination. It went on for over an hour, during which time we examined a great deal of material from the hospital record. Much of it was not readily familiar to the doctor. I was making him look bad, but that was my job. Now that I'd softened him up, I questioned him at length about his predecessor's opinions; I told him that he had relied on the earlier diagnosis without coming to any independently verifiable conclusion based on his own observations, then made my statement a question by adding, "Isn't that so?" I was also implying that Wong's predecessor had done much the same thing with *his* predecessor: that once a diagnosis had been reached by any doctor, each psychiatrist who followed presumed it was valid, no matter how long the chain. That was how the business of psychiatry was conducted on the tenth floor of the Meyer Building.

Dr. Wong didn't deny any of it. He seemed to understand the English of what I was saying, but not the implications or intent. He nodded along dutifully, in any case.

Psychiatrists I know tell me that lawyering is one of the few jobs where an antisocial personality is considered a professional asset. (Personally, I can think of several others.) I didn't want to hurt Dr. Wong's feelings or self-esteem, but a man's freedom or continued incarceration depended on his testimony.

The state called no other witness, choosing to rest its case. Although Dr. Wong's written application, if taken at face value, would have condemned Balinka to another two years at MPC, to me the doctor had not *sounded* convincing as a witness, so I made a motion to dismiss the hospital's application on the basis that the hospital had not put in sufficient evidence.

As I expected, the judge ruled against me, so I called my first witness, Mr. Balinka. I asked him to testify to his version of the underlying crime. The assistant attorney general objected on the grounds of relevancy.

"Your Honor," he said, "Mr. Balinka's version of the crime has nothing whatever to do with his current mental condition."

"Your Honor, I . . .," I started to say, but Judge Wight cut me off.

"This is highly unusual, Counselor," she said, looking at me. "Usually you're the one fighting to keep the underlying incident out of evidence as irrelevant when Mr. Liebling is trying to introduce it. But since Dr. Wong already testified to his understanding of why Balinka was arrested as a part of the patient's history, it wouldn't be fair not to let Mr. Balinka give his version. I'll allow it."

And so Balinka gave his version. While working the late shift as a newspaper vendor in the subway station at Forty-Second Street, he had been approached by two burly fellows who demanded free pornographic magazines. They claimed to be undercover police officers. Balinka told them that even if they were cops, he did not have the authority to give away inventory, only his boss did. When one tried to grab him, he ducked and ran. They cornered him, cuffed him, and charged him with menacing, possession of a weapon—the weapon being the cutter that newspaper vendors use to open the cord that binds their newspapers—and resisting arrest.

He told the court that he had never had the opportunity to confront his accusers, that they had never testified against him or pursued their legal charge in any way. But they didn't have to; he had been locked away in a mental hospital.

He also testified that he punched Robinson in self-defense. Finally, in a logical, coherent manner, he testified that he wasn't hearing voices and didn't have delusions. He said that his command of English was less than perfect; as a result, he was sometimes misunderstood. He thought that being railroaded had nothing to do with transportation systems. Then he said he didn't want to take the medication that Dr. Wong prescribed because all that it did was make him sleepy. He'd tried it to make Wong happy, to get him to release him from the hospital, but if he wouldn't do that then there was no point in taking it.

On cross-examination Liebling made Balinka look dumb and possibly confused—ignorant of the role of the police, and unfamiliar with medication and how it relates to alleviating psychosis. But he didn't make Balinka seem crazy.

"Sir," Liebling eventually asked, "do you suffer from a mental illness?"

Balinka said, "No." I'd tried to make him understand that when a mental patient denies having a mental illness it makes him appear to lack insight into his mental condition. I spent hours explaining how much better an impression a mental patient makes when he admits to having a mental illness than when he denies it. But I hadn't specifically told him to say the magic words, "Yes, but I'm much better now." I was kind of proud of him, actually. I didn't think he had a mental illness either. I could see Liebling almost snickering, however, and I knew he intended to make the usual "lack of insight" argument at the end of his case.

He asked Balinka, "Sir, are you a legal resident of this country?"

Balinka froze.

"Objection!" I shouted, jumping to my feet. "That is completely irrelevant to his mental condition!"

"Objection sustained," said Judge Wight. "Don't answer that question, Mr. Balinka," she said.*

"No further questions," said Liebling.

Then Mr. Balinka stepped down and I called my second witness, my client's relative, Mr. Gantu.

"Mr. Gantu, what is your relationship to the respondent, Mtumbo Balinka?"

"I am his uncle. His mother is my sister."

"How long have you known that Mr. Balinka has been in this hospital?"

"A long time. Maybe from beginning."

"If he were to be released today, would you be able to help him find a place to live?"

"Yes."

"Would you watch out for him?"

"Yes."

"Do you care for him?"

"I am his uncle."

"But do you care for him?"

"Yes. Yes. Of course. I am uncle! He is of my blood. I am of his blood! Uncle!"

"Then why, Mr. Gantu, have you waited almost two years to appear? If you care so much, why has he sat alone in a hospital without your help or support?"

"He was arrested. They send him to jail. They send him here. He

---

* Although the question of an undocumented alien's status might be of great interest to federal authorities, New York state and city authorities seldom make a great effort to share such information with their federal counterparts. Part of this is due to turf battles and the reluctance of the various law enforcement agencies to cooperate, and another part of it is due to the sheer volume of criminal cases that go through New York City each year. Yet another part of it is doubtless due to an unspoken understanding that a close look into the immigration status of non-felony accusees might deprive the underground economy of its wellspring of restaurant, domestic and child-care workers—jobs that, because of their low wages and low status, are difficult to fill with American citizens.

get himself into trouble. If someone get into trouble, someone should get himself out of trouble; that was my belief. I thought this was like jail. But it is enough. Even if he do what they say he do, it is enough."

"Will you take custody of him, if the court grants his release, take responsibility for him?"

"Yes. He can live at my house until he get his own apartment. That should not take long. I have small apartment, but for a month or two, it's okay. I will give food. A bed in kitchen. He be okay."

"No further questions," I told the court.

Then it was the assistant attorney general's turn. He opened his cross-examination.

"Mr. Gantu," he said, "you say he can stay with you for a month or two, until he finds a job?"

"Yes."

"You've told the court that you would take custody of the patient, that you would be responsible for him?"

"Yes."

"But he's been in the hospital almost two years and you've never been to see him, isn't that right?"

"Yes."

"And even if you give him a place to sleep and food, you're only offering that for a short time."

"No."

"Didn't you just tell the court that he could only stay with you for a month or two?"

"Yes."

"That's it. A month or two. Isn't that a short time?"

"No. That is not short time. Short time is week. Month is long time."

"Mr. Gantu, isn't it true that after the patient stays with you for a month or two, he would no longer be welcome to live with you?"

"I have very small apartment. I live with wife and two children."

"Please, Mr. Gantu, answer the question. You just testified that you never came to visit the patient during his entire hospitalization. Do you expect this court to believe you are committed to taking care of him in your own home?"

I quickly stood up. "Objection as to form."

"Objection sustained," said the judge. "Proceed with your next question."

"Isn't it a fact that you would throw him out if he is still living in your home in, say, two months?" asked the assistant attorney general.

"He will not be there in two months," replied Mr. Gantu. "He will not be there even in one month. He will get job and have money for own place."

"But suppose, Mr. Gantu, he doesn't get a job. You are not ready to take him into your home for as long as it takes, are you, Mr. Gantu?"

"It doesn't take long."

"Mr. Gantu, suppose he doesn't get a job. Suppose two months have gone by and he hasn't found work. He's sleeping in your kitchen. He's eating your food. You will want him to leave, isn't that so?"

"Of course he get job. Right away he get job. He always have job. Even as a boy he have job."

"But suppose he doesn't, Mr. Gantu. Then what?"

"Of course he get job. This is America!"

And Mr. Gantu went on to tell the assistant attorney general that anyone who wants work can find it. That immigrants can always get work in America because, although Americans are lazy, America is great! What a country!

Dr. Wong, who had retired to the public seating after his testimony, seemed to be nodding in agreement. What a country, indeed!

Balinka was ordered released to his uncle's care and custody within twenty-four hours and without an order for outpatient medication. I shook Balinka's hand and then his uncle's, and I was pretty much sure I'd never see either of them again.

Three months later, though, on my way through the hospital corridors to visit a new client, I looked up and saw Balinka. My heart sank. He smiled up at me.

"Mtumbo," I said, "you promised me I'd never see you back in the hospital."

"Oh, no, Mr. Woychuk, I have back my old job, and today is my first day off. I only visiting friends."

Dangerousness is always an issue at the mental hospital, and I think about it all the time. I think about it when I meet a new client with a history of violence. I think about danger when I see photographs of a corpse with the face pulled off. I think about it when my life is threatened. But for the most part, in the hospital, I feel very safe. Unlike psychiatrists, lawyers in the mental health system are almost never attacked by the patients, perhaps because they are rarely the bearers of bad tidings and generally know which side they're on. Doctors, in contrast, may have to "tell the truth." It's part of the system.

For example, if my client wants to be released, regardless of who he is and what he has done, I can tell him honestly that (1) I will do my best to get him released; (2) I will ask the judge in court to release him; (3) he can be present to see that I do what I say I will do; and (4) subject to my recommendations as his attorney, he will have an opportunity to testify on his own behalf. And if my client doesn't want to take the medication that the doctor has asked the court to order him to take, I will review with him why he doesn't want it and try to convince the court that the medication is not needed.

Psychiatrists, though, often must tell a patient (1) why he is not ready for release; (2) why they still consider him dangerous and in need of further hospitalization; and (3) why he may need to take medication that makes him feel physically ill. This frustrates the patient, who is often asked to take the medication precisely because of his inability to tolerate frustration.

Sometimes the psychiatrists are right. But that doesn't make it any easier. And the psychiatrist may have to go before a judge and—with the patient, whom he sees every day on the hospital ward, watching and perhaps praying for release—tell the court in great detail why he believes the patient must stay. It takes a special individual to maintain a successful therapeutic relationship under this kind of pressure. As a result, at least in part, the state hospital system has difficulty recruiting good psychiatrists. And while some of the best may go into the profession as a matter of interest and choice, many others become psychiatrists by "necessity" and without the burning commitment to make the best possible medical decision on each case every time.

Poor Dr. Wong may have felt as safe at the hospital as I do. But one day Willy Robinson, the patient with whom Balinka had fought, broke Wong's jaw with a telephone receiver during an interview to consider him for ground privileges. Unfortunately, they were alone, and Dr. Wong was being a little hard on him (stressing him, so to speak), to see how he'd react. Robinson felt betrayed, and he reacted with anger. When Dr. Wong returned to the hospital two months later, he went to work on a geriatric ward.

At least Dr. Wong was trying. I was partly sorry to see him go, and I wondered whether some of my own latent racism had played a role in our adversarial scenarios. Certainly lawyers have been accused of racism in their dealings with the hospital staff. In fact, after the news media discovered that our agency had brought suit against the hospital to require better professional care for the patients, the president of the local chapter of the hospital workers' union denounced our acts as unmitigated racism: white lawyers attempting to discredit a primarily minority staff.

At least one prominent black psychiatrist, Alonzo Jones, contends that Afro-American therapists can be more effective than white ones in treating Afro-American patients because they have the bicultural skills to understand both black (patient) and white (administrative) perspectives. Furthermore, Dr. Jones says that what white therapists might see as paranoia regarding the power structure of society is often a legitimate viewpoint for the Afro-American. He insists that, just as patients could not be expected to receive therapy in a language foreign to them, they shouldn't be expected to receive it in a culture other than their own.

But what do you do when mental patients come from every culture on the globe? Balinka traveled half the world to arrive in New York. Although he may be black, his worldview is distinctly not Afro-American, but African. Furthermore, in my experience, most black doctors, lawyers, and judges are drawn not from the urban poor (the primary pool for patients) but from either the suburban middle class or countries outside the United States. Neither is closely related to the black inner-city experience.

Perhaps in an ideal world Dr. Jones is right. But in an ideal world people do not suffer from mental disease. He seems unaware of how little psychotherapy is actually performed by psychiatrists in today's state mental hospitals. And if each patient should have therapy and perhaps legal representation provided by people of his own cultural background, what about the judge's background? Isn't that at least as important?

Balinka's case was not of interest to the press. He didn't kill, cannibalize his victims, or do anything else to make headlines. But his case was and is important to me. I did not do anything another lawyer couldn't have done, but I probably saved this man's life because I was there.

Most of my clients are clearly in need of hospitalization. The vast majority of patients at Manhattan Psychiatric Center are people for whom I can do nothing. Most have mental problems so severe that they are fortunate to be wards of a benevolent state. But sometimes I discover a poor soul like Balinka who has fallen through the cracks of the system. As a result of being in the wrong place at the wrong time, he had been held against his will at another wrong place—the state mental hospital.

I helped Balinka get released from the hospital so that he could again earn his own living. I changed his life. The satisfaction of helping him made up for some of the frustration I'd experienced representing patients who would never be well enough to break free of institutional living. It seemed to make the job worthwhile.

Psycho-Killer,
Qu'est-Ce Que C'est?

The heart has its reasons that reason cannot know. —Pascal

Nineteen years before we met, a young man named Hugh Kelly*
physically destroyed a woman with unimaginable brutality. Shortly
thereafter he was apprehended by the police. Then the psychiatrists
took over. At trial he was acquitted by reason of mental disease or
defect—Not Guilty By Reason Of Insanity, as the verdict is com-
monly known—and he spent the next two decades in one mental
institution or another. Today he is back on the street, living anony-

---

* Mr. Kelly requested that I use his real name. Initially I resisted, to protect his identity; but
ultimately I honored his request. However, certain identifying characteristics regarding Mr.
Kelly have been changed. The names and identifying characteristics of other people in this
chapter have also been been changed, and in certain instances the people depicted are composites of people I have met over the years.

101

mously in a community that is partly blue-collar and partly aspiring middle-class, and married to an attractive young woman who herself was acquitted of a killing by reason of mental disease or defect.

I'd heard about Kelly in 1986, when a hospital social worker slipped me a photocopy of an old newspaper clipping and said, "They say he ate a woman's heart." Perhaps the social worker was trying to rattle me, to make me less willing to do my job. Sometimes members of the hospital staff see lawyers as the enemy because we question their judgment, often in court. But more likely he was trying to be friendly and share some gossip about the job. He seemed nice enough.

The headline, from a 1969 *Daily News*, read as follows:

STOP ME BEFORE I KILL AGAIN, KILLER WROTE; SUSPECT HELD.

The suspect was Hugh Kelly, nineteen years old, six feet three inches. What followed was a concise account of the criminal investigation and the clues leading to Kelly's arrest at Kings County Hospital while he was being treated for injuries; after what the paper suggested was a botched robbery attempt, he had leaped from the burning steeple of a church in Brooklyn. The *News* reported that where the body was found, he had scrawled in lipstick on the wall and the mirror, "I done it because my love left me. I will kill again for her, as you can see, but I would never hurt her again as long as I love her." The story ended with a warning that although Kelly remained in the hospital under maximum security, he had remarked to another patient that "he was going to escape as soon as he could get around better."

Kelly became my client in 1988 when I was assigned to handle the legal cases coming out of the high-security wards at Manhattan Psychiatric Center (MPC), a civil hospital. Rebecca Paul, the lawyer who preceded me, told me that she really only felt comfortable representing the relatively harmless types, the classic civil patients who were the vast bulk of the patients at MPC. She found it easier to fight for them because they hadn't done anything wrong. Aside from making her nervous, representing men of past violence created for her an ethical conflict that she did not experience when she was representing purely civil patients, so it was with relief that she passed her clients on the tough wards to me.

The patients on both Meyer 10A and 10B were either transfers from maximum-security hospitals such as Kirby or, like Balinka, transfers from jail. About the only patients on Meyer 10 who were not connected to the criminal justice system were those who, due to their predisposition to act out violently, could not be controlled on regular civil wards. Meyer 10A and 10B were both young men's wards, with double-locked doors that served two purposes: to stop patients from getting out, and to stop street drugs from getting in. (Although neither goal was fully achieved, the former was more successful than the latter.)

I met Hugh Kelly for the first time when he called one day on the telephone, asking to see me. He had come to MPC not from nearby Kirby but from Mid-Hudson, Kirby's upstate equivalent. When I arrived at Meyer 10A at the appointed time, he was waiting. He looked fit and trim, about forty, with closely cropped black hair. He wore a dungaree jacket, jeans, and black cowboy boots with ornamental spurs. I supposed the hospital could have taken those boots from him, given those spurs, but they weren't more of a potential weapon than a pen or even a paper clip. (Both were restricted at Kirby because they could be used as lethal weapons. He wouldn't have been allowed to wear boots like that at Kirby, either.)

Kelly's hands were covered with tattoos; h-a-t-e spelled out across the knuckles of his right hand in the poorest penmanship, l-o-v-e across the knuckles of his left. The name Christine crawled up one arm. He had none of the tics or involuntary movements often associated with mental patients, because he was not taking any medication. Although he was missing his four upper front teeth, the poorly fitting replacement bridge that he wore softened the impact that such a gap would have had on his appearance. As mental patients go, he was a good-looking man.

Together we entered a large private room where patients sometimes read, engaged in other quiet activities (such as smoking cigarettes, judging from the burn marks on every inch of the plastic furniture) or met with their families. Rebecca Paul had warned me about this guy, so I took a seat next to the door and directed Kelly to take a seat three or four chairs away. The door closed behind us.

"Do you know who I am?" he asked me.

"Yes."

"Good. I know who you are, too. I saw what you did for Balinka—he used to be on this ward not too long ago. I heard what you did for MacKnight, too. I'm as good as those guys mentally. In fact, I'm better. And I know the law. The law says that when a patient is ready to leave the hospital without danger to the public, he must be freed. Look—I'm thirty-eight years old; I been in the hospital almost twenty years. I'm ready to get out. I want a writ of habeas corpus."

I was a bit surprised. A writ of habeas corpus, an application to the courts for "the release of the body," is an age-old Latin expression that comes down to us from ancient English law. Essentially, the writ expresses the position that the individual in question is being held illegally. It is technically a lawyer's duty to accede to a request for a writ if there is a reasonable basis for one. This is true for all incarcerated individuals, not just mental patients, and it is the duty of the lawyer to try to find such a basis.* Although Kelly appeared to be perfectly sane (aside from looking scary), I knew that patients who are held due to violent criminal acts can often go days or even months without showing overt signs of a mental disorder. Without much hope for him, I nevertheless resolved to determine his prospects. After all, he was my client.

According to a quick initial review of the hospital chart, Kelly had been in psychiatric centers since childhood and had been released just a few months before his violent, horrific act. He had killed and dismembered a woman old enough to be his mother, then cooked and eaten her heart. My stomach turned; I was disgusted and saddened. I assumed that Kelly would be a lifer, born to die in an in-

---

* Of course, some clients ask for a writ every month without any change in their mental condition, and neither I nor my fellow mental health attorneys have time to bring a writ for anyone on a monthly basis. There's too much other work to do. However, I often will bring a writ regardless of my belief as to the merits. I recently brought a writ, for example, for a man who claimed that his detention was improper in that, as an ambassador from the City of Saul, on the Lower East Side of New York City, he was not subject to the courts of New York State, only to federal courts, and in any case had diplomatic immunity. No one laughs at these applications. They are treated by the courts as serious matters, which indeed they are.

sane asylum. Rebecca Paul, a woman with years more experience than I, had made it plain that she considered such an ending appropriate. "He's a malcontent," she told me. "He's constantly complaining about staff, always looking for trouble. He appreciates nothing they do for him. Maybe he's not psychotic anymore, but the guy's a total asshole. Read the confession."

Still, my duty as Kelly's attorney was to see if a case could be made. My first strategy would be to find someone responsible for treatment, a psychiatrist or other member of the clinical staff, who was willing to take the patient's view. I conducted a series of interviews. By custom I can do these interviews without the presence of the hospital's attorney, so I get more information more easily than one could expect in ordinary civil litigation. My attitude at this stage is friendly and sensitive. I want potential witnesses to understand that I appreciate the courage it takes to make a finding that will be unpopular not only with the public but with their employer—the hospital, which prefers to be conservative when it comes to releasing patients who have a history of violence. I conducted my initial interviews with Kelly's treatment team on Meyer 10A: Dr. Bayberry, the treating psychiatrist, Dr. Blau, the ward psychologist, and Ms. Hernandez, a psychiatric social worker.

Dr. Bayberry, a tall, garrulous man with wiry gray hair, said that Kelly unquestionably needed continued hospitalization. He cited Kelly's hostility and his recent misadventure with a stolen television as indicative of his poor judgment and his personality disorder. "He doesn't want to be released," Dr. Bayberry told me as I sat across from him in his office. The office door had a little window, and once in a while a patient would press his face against the glass. "Every time we get ready to move him along—excuse me, Mr. Woychuk— Get away from that door, Mr. Gillis, or I'll write you up!—I'm sorry, where was I? Oh, yes, Mr. Kelly ruins it for himself every time. He's quite afraid of release. His whole life has been lived in institutions, except for a few years of his childhood and a few months preceding that brutal murder, and the prospect of release is truly terrifying for him. Men like that rarely can make it in free society. Institutional life is all they know.

"Immediately before his transfer back here, to Meyer 10A, he was on an open ward and almost as free as a forensic inpatient can get. He could walk unescorted around the hospital property; he was able to come and go without supervision. In response, what does he do? He steals the television set from his ward, carries it over the foot-bridge into Manhattan, and sells it on the street. Then he uses the money to buy cocaine.* Another big step backwards.

"He's an intelligent man, Mr. Woychuk. He knows we have mandatory drug testing. He's crying out for structure, for supervision. 'Don't let me go!' That's what he's telling us. And that's why he was sent back to Meyer 10. He's far from ready for release. He may never be ready.

"Aside from which, he's a tremendous troublemaker. He's one of those patients who's always trying to pit one clinician against the other, attempting to manipulate those who take care of him. But he's really no good at it and only ends up hurting himself. It shows very bad judgment. He's not the sort of patient I'm looking to release. Have you read his confession? A man with his history has to go out of his way to avoid trouble. But Kelly seeks it. I'll grant you that his willingness to confront, to make demands, to stand up to others at obvious cost to himself belies a conscious attempt to manipulate the system. I told him he should make friends, be good, learn to make the system work for him, but he persists in rabble-rousing at every turn.

"It's not *all* his fault, I'll concede. He has problems with night staff that result from his feeling singled out, treated as a freak, a legend, a monster. And while I don't believe it is true to the degree that he does, there has been some evidence that what he says is so. You know what trouble the hospital has finding good support staff. I myself heard rumors that a therapy aide had sneaked in a camera to get Kelly's photograph. I'm certainly not condoning such behavior, but our staff is undertrained. Although he was being unprofessional,

---

* Although they feature drug-testing programs and patients with a history of drug abuse are regularly tested, the state-run civil mental hospitals in New York City have as great a problem with street drugs as any other part of a free, urban society. With the right connections and money, a patient can gain access to just about any kind of drug he wants.

this fellow was only being human. When Kelly complained to me, I told him to cooperate more, to stop trying to force the treatment team to take sides. No one likes a stool pigeon. I cannot allow a patient to divide the team; life here is difficult enough. But Kelly continues to complain.

"He demands a tremendous amount of attention. I have thirty other men I need to treat. Last month he told me that confidential portions of his hospital chart had been copied and circulated. Four months ago he complained that three black staff members had threatened him for killing a black woman. I know one of them came at him with a knife, and that fellow was fired, but Kelly's problems with the late shift will persist as long as he insists on confronting authority whenever possible. You know, of course. . . ."

Suddenly something slammed against the door and a fit of cursing broke out, followed by another voice issuing threats. Dr. Bayberry jumped from his seat. "Excuse me, Mr. Woychuk, but duty calls. Just look at the record; the recent notes should be enough." He left me sitting in his office with Kelly's hospital chart on my lap. I'd have to get around to reading it thoroughly in order to prepare my case, so I sat and browsed through the record.

Dr. Bayberry's recent entries made much of Kelly's ongoing confrontations with minority staff, but did not note any persistent persecutory delusions or other paranoid features. That was significant because it indicated that the doctor recognized that Kelly's complaints were not merely in his mind; they had some basis in fact. According to the doctor's professional opinion, Kelly's confrontations were a symptom of a deep-seated racial antagonism. But it was also a tough-guy thing. Once it had become clear to Kelly that he would always be singled out by at least some members of the staff as a freak, he waved his twenty-year-old crime like a flag. Violence as a badge; pure *machismo,* not psychosis. That was how I understood it, having Brooklyn roots myself, but Brooklyn was a foreign culture to most of the professional clinical staff. However, the therapy aides, who were almost entirely from the streets of Manhattan and the Bronx, shared some common culture with Kelly and understood his behavior for what it was.

Some therapy aides felt they were there to give orders, and Kelly was there to obey. After all, *he* was the sick one. They talked in military jargon, issuing orders or even threats as though they were drill sergeants. And if Kelly talked back, they'd write him up as difficult, hostile, or worse. His treating doctor had never actually witnessed any confrontation between Kelly and the therapy aides, but as a matter of professional necessity he supported the members of his staff.

Although it didn't make a conclusive case for serious mental illness, the racial issue loomed as significant in our courtroom horizons. After all, Kelly's victim had been African-American—and now he had an African girlfriend, another MPC patient recently transferred from Kirby. Kelly hadn't mentioned her to me at all, but the record was replete with reference to her, stressing the danger of this relationship.

Later that week, still looking for someone with anything good to say about Kelly, I had an interview with Dr. Blau and Ms. Hernandez. We met in Dr. Blau's office, which was more tastefully decorated than almost any I'd seen at the hospital. The room had curtains (no other MPC office I'd seen had them) that obscured the escape-proof security windows, and it was furnished with what seemed to be antiques. To break the ice I complimented her on creating an environment that disguised the institutional atmosphere, and I asked her if she found such a setting helpful when she worked with patients.

"They're not real antiques," Dr. Blau told me when she saw me eyeing the furniture. "You can pick up terrific pieces in secondhand stores all over Manhattan. I think it helps my patients to understand I care about them when they see I'm willing to take the trouble to make my office nice for their interviews." I agreed but I secretly thought she took it too far in her manner of dress. She was a short woman in her early thirties, quite voluptuous, and she wore a short, tight-fitting floral print dress and high heels to give her height. Her navy blue blazer didn't conceal her cleavage even when she was wearing it. Without it, she looked like she was on her way to a cocktail party—a sexually provocative look that was especially inappropriate on a ward of young men noted for poor impulse control. Her appearance contrasted sharply with that of Ms. Hernandez, who dressed with a nun-like austerity.

When I explained my mission, the two women looked at me pointedly and explained that Kelly's refusal to back down from confrontation was a sure recipe for fights. "And his girlfriend is the spitting image of the woman he killed!" said Dr. Blau, who saw serious trouble ahead (although how she knew what the victim had looked like is still a mystery to me). Ms. Hernandez just nodded in moral support. "How do you lawyers sleep at night?" asked Dr. Blau.

And so the treatment team was unanimous. No one would say that Kelly was ready for release. That's usually enough to bury anybody.

"But I'm telling you, I'm not crazy," Kelly insisted. "And I'm not dangerous."

And surprisingly, he had a point. By now I had examined the record in depth, and nowhere did it show that Kelly had current signs of psychosis or any other serious mental disorder. This indicated that his illness was in remission, or what a layperson might call "cured." The forensic psychiatric hospital system is supposedly set up to function so that dangerously mentally ill people can recover and eventually be released. That, purportedly, is the result that society wants. But the public, as a whole, finds it more convenient to believe the system doesn't actually work. They doubt that dangerously mentally ill people can get better. And if someone seems to have gotten better, they doubt that he was ever sick at all; therefore, he must have been scamming, so he should be punished.

It was easy to keep someone like Kelly locked up, regardless of his actual mental condition, because his act of violence was so infamous; to release him would be fraught with political risk. That is why guys like Kelly need lawyers—because, despite the treatment team's unanimous position, there was in fact a basis to set him free.

As I'd been told, the record contained a remarkable confession. It did not ramble, nor was it incoherent, as are so many confessions by mentally deranged perpetrators. It was about the incident I would be dealing with, one long horrid moment of psychotic reaction. It is presented here in a somewhat abridged form. (Except for Kelly, names and other identifying characteristics have been changed.)

After being read his Miranda rights by detectives, Kelly described in straightforward if somewhat laconic fashion leaving his apartment after a fight with Christine Solieri, his common-law wife, registering at a Times Square–district hotel in Manhattan, and then meeting and having drinks with Lola Freeman, a black woman almost twice his age who was registered at the same hotel. Then, in chilling detail, Kelly responded to the detectives' questions about the woman's death and disfigurement:

Q: Now, in addition to drinking with her in the room, did you or she have any kind of physical contact at all?
A: Yes.
Q: What kind of contact? Was it sexual in nature?
A: Yes.
Q: Was that the first time you had any sexual relations with her?
A: Yes.
Q: And what did you and she do?
A: Well, what men and women usually does when they're together.
Q: Did you have sexual intercourse with her?
A: Yes.
Q: And what happened after you had sexual intercourse with her?
A: I went out and got a chicken, I think.
Q: You got chicken to eat?
A: Yes.
Q: And you brought it back to her room?
A: No. I ate it before I got upstairs.
Q: Well, did you then go back to her room?
A: Yes.
Q: What was she doing at the time?
A: She was still up.
Q: And did you speak to her, did you have a conversation?
A: Yes.

Q: And generally what would you talk about?

A: She wanted to marry me.

Q: And did she make any remark about the cut on [your] arm?

A: Yes.

Q: What did she say about it?

A: She asked me how I got them.

Q: And what did you tell her?

A: I told her—well, first I didn't want to speak about it. Then she says, I won't press it; I won't press you. Then she said later, couple hours later, well, ain't you going to tell me how you got the cuts on your arm? I told her I cut myself because of what I did to Christine. And she said, who's Christine? I said the mother of my child.

Q: What happened between you and Christine?

A: I hit her and felt bad about it. Gave her a black eye by mistake.

Q: Then you cut your arm?

A: Yes.

Q: Now, after you explained this to Lola, did she say anything?

A: She said everything about Christine.

Q: What did she say about Christine?

A: I don't know if I can say the words in here.

Q: Yes, you can say any words in here. We're all men, there is no problem. We've heard all those words.

A: She said she was a tramp. She's no good. I guess she was drinking, that's why. She was a little drunk. She kept on saying it. I ignored her. I didn't let her know it hurt me until she kept it up. Not in the sense she was screaming at me—she was just holding a conversation. She said anyone who do that to a man is no good.

Q: She said anyone who do that to a man is no good?

A: Yes.

Q: Did you ask her to light your cigarette?

A: I don't remember.

Q: All right. Now, after she was making all these disparaging remarks about Christine—it was Christine?

A: Christine.

Q: Did you then do something to Lola?

A: Yes.

Q: All right, would you tell us in as great detail as you can what you then did?

A: I strangled her.

Q: Now, how did you strangle her?

A: With my hands.

Q: You used both hands?

A: Yes.

Q: And did you put them around her throat?

A: Yes.

Q: And did you use a great deal of pressure on her throat?

A: All I did. (indicating)

Q: And as you were doing that what was she doing?

A: Choking. She couldn't say any words.

Q: And did a time come when her body went limp?

A: Yes.

Q: Do you know approximately how long you kept your hands on her throat?

A: No.

Q: Now, what happened after her body went limp?

A: I started to throw things around the room. I just went out of it. I started . . . I just snapped after that.

Q: Now, did you do something else to her body?

A: Yes.

Q: Would you tell us what else you did to her body?

A: I cut off her arm.

Q: Which arm was that?

A: The left one, I think.

Q: What did you use to cut her left arm off with?

A: I had a knife.

Q: And what part of her left arm did you cut off?

A: From the elbow down.

Q: How was she dressed at the time you strangled her?

A: She had a sheet over her.

Q: Was she nude otherwise?

A: Yes.

Q: Now, after you cut her left arm off, did you do something else?

A: I stabbed her in the chest. I don't know how many times. I just kept on.

Q: Was it many, many times?

A: I guess so.

Q: And do you know how long you were stabbing her in the chest?

A: No.

Q: And did you use the same knife to stab her in the chest?

A: Yes, sir.

Q: Was there a hot plate in the room?

A: (Nodding)

Q: You nodded your head up and down?

A: Yes.

Q: And did you do anything with that hot plate?

A: I guess I burned her face. I think I did.

Q: Well, did you first have to plug the hot plate in to make it get hot?

A: Yes.

Q: And did it take a while before it heated up?

A: Well, I lit a cigarette off of it. That's why I put on the hot plate. I didn't have matches in the room.

Q: Did you eventually plug the hot plate in and bring it over to Lola's body?

A: I think so. Yes. I don't remember taking out the plug. I guess, I could not bring it over to her body. I took out the plug.

Q: Where was her body at this time, in the room?

A: It was on the bed.

Q: And where was the hot plate in relation to Lola's body?

A: You mean where it was at when I picked it up?

Q: Yes

A: It was on a dresser.

Q: And approximately how many feet away was the dresser from the body of Lola?

A: Maybe two feet.

Q: And what did you do with the hot plate after you brought it over to her body?

A: Put it on her face.

Q: Did you put it over any other part of her body?

A: Not as I can remember.

Q: Do you recall putting it on her breasts?

A: No.

Q: Did anything happen to her skin when you put the hot plate on it?

A: Well, it was up around her hair, and it started to smell as I took it off.

Q: And did you do anything else with the knife to her body?

A: Yes, on one leg. I forget which one it was.

Q: What did you do to her leg?

A: I cut part of her leg.

Q: Did you cut a piece of the flesh completely off the leg?

A: Yes, sir.

Q: Was that in the thigh area?

A: I think so.

Q: Did you put that piece of flesh somewhere?

A: I don't remember. I might have. Or else I put it in the sink. I don't remember.

Q: Now, did you also cut open part of the calf of her leg, one of her legs?

A: I don't remember.

Q: Do you recall whether you put a cigarette right into the calf of her leg?

A: Yes.

Q: Then you put the cigarette into it after you cut it open.

A: Yes. Now I remember.

Q: Did you have a frankfurter with a roll in the room at that time?

A: Yes.

Q: And did you do something with that frankfurter and roll?

A: Yes.

Q: What did you do with that?

A: I put it between her legs, I guess.

Q: Did you insert it in her vagina?

A: Yes.

Q: Now, is there anything else that you did to Lola's body that you haven't mentioned?

A: I think I might have cut her stomach, I'm not sure.

Q: Now, after you did these things to her body what did you next do?

A: I sat down for awhile, smoked another cigarette, then I got up.

Q: What type of cigarettes do you smoke?

A: I must have been smoking Winston, I am not sure. I smoke Marlboro and Winston, but I'm not sure. I don't remember what I was smoking that day.

Q: Now, you were sitting down smoking a cigarette, you said?

A: Yes.

Q: Then what did you do?

A: I got up, went to my room. I took a radio into my room.

Q: Did you also take the knife with you?

A: No.

Q: Did you recall at all what you did with the knife?

A: I dropped it on the floor, but I didn't find it. There was so much junk on the floor.

Q: Approximately how big a blade did the knife have?

A: About this long.

Q: Indicating about seven inches?

A: Right.

Q: Now, what did you do when you were in your room?

A: The radio didn't play. I threw it under the bed.

Q: Then what happened?

A: I just put on my coat and left. I never came back.

Q: Now, before leaving Lola's room, room 609, did you write anything on the walls, the mirror, or behind a door?

A: Yes.

Q: And do you recall what you wrote on the wall in Lola's room?

A: No.

Q: Do you recall what you used to write on the wall?

A: Lipstick.

Q: Could it have been a red pencil?

A: No, it was red lipstick.

Q: Do you remember what you wrote on the wall?

A: No. I just remembered it now when you mentioned it to me.

Q: In other words, by me mentioning it?

A: It just came to me again.

Q: Well, I believe that on the wall there were the words to the effect of—"Somebody please stop me, I'll kill again"—with the initials "C.K." Do you recall writing that on the wall over the bed?

A: Well, yes, I wrote that. I put that there. I was so drunk.

Q: And whose initials were C.K.?

A: The last initial is mine, and the first one is my girlfriend.

Q: You mean Christine's?

A: Yes.

Q: Did you then begin to write something on the mirror?

A: Yes.

Q: What happened?

A: The lipstick had run out. There was no more left.

Q: Did you write something on the back of the door?

A: Yes.

Q: Do you remember what you wrote on the back of the door?

A: I can't remember that.

Q: Was it something to the effect—"I done it because my love left me," or something of that nature?

A: I may have. I don't remember. If it's there, I guess I did it.

Q: Do you recall also writing something to the effect—"I would kill for her, as you can see, but I would never hurt her as long as I love her?"

A: Yes, I think I wrote that, yes.

Q: Mr. Kelly, did you kill Lola Freeman because of the bad remarks she made about Christine Solieri?

A: Yes.

Q: And did you know you were killing her when you were strangling her?

A: Yes.

Q: Do you know what happened to her right eye?

A: No.

Q: Do you know how her right eye came out?

A: I took it out with the knife.

Q: Now, you've been smoking while we've been talking; is that correct?

A: Yes.

Q: And have the police officers treated you properly?

A: Yes. In fact, this officer, he bought me cigarettes.

Q: Indicating Detective McGonagle?

A: Yes.

Q: Is there anything else about this case that you want to say that we haven't covered?

A: No.

[End of statement.]

After his confession, Kelly's life was again absorbed by the system. They kept him at Kings County Hospital for medical care until his bones had mended from his fall from the church steeple. Then he was sent to Rikers Island to await trial.

In preparation for filing the writ, Kelly and I had a series of meetings, during which he gave me a long account of his life. Personal history, as related by a patient, is considered a great tool in the psychiatric industry for evaluation and diagnosis. Whether believed (and verified) or not, it says a great deal about the nature of that person's thinking to a psychiatrist. Even if it is garbled, confused, or incoherent, it nonetheless sheds a certain light.

A lawyer's perspective in regard to history is not that different from a psychiatrist's, but his or her purpose may be. Aside from educating myself and filling in blanks, my objective was twofold: (1) to see if Kelly was coherent, capable of linear speech, and free from psychotic symptoms; and (2) to see if he had confronted his history and understood its relationship to where he was now. It would all come out in court, and I needed to see what kind of witness Kelly would make. Eventually I might suggest changes in the narrative for tactical reasons, but for the present, I was just there to listen and observe.

As Kelly spoke to me, it was clear he was not hallucinating, nor was he having dangerous fantasies. He was remarkably coherent about his early history. He had been born in 1950 at Bellevue Hospital in New York City; his mother had a five-year-old daughter from a prior marriage. His parents had met at Bellevue, where his mother was a nurse's aide and his father sold candy. They never married. In Kelly's own words:

"A couple of years after I was born, my parents brought home a little sister. Now I was the middle child, between two girls. My mom's mother, we called her Nanna, she moved into our little apartment to help out with us kids. It was a crowded house.

"My dad was not good at making money. He was superintendent of our building and that paid peanuts, but it gave us an apartment. He was not even good at drinking and got an ulcer that helped cause his death in 1957; but in the meantime, he drank and hollered at my mom and she hollered back, and he beat me. Like that was what I was there for.

"Nanna was also not the kindly, loving type. She was a screamer and tough with me and my sisters, but not as free with the strap as she might have liked, because my dad scared her. As drunk as he was, he was the man of the house and was ready to prove it physically. That held her back. After my parents separated, Nanna took charge and openly ran the household. She said Dad had convinced her of the worthlessness of men, and his visits only led to fights.

"Nanna gave us kids chores around the building, and my special position as the only son was over. One of my new jobs was to mop the halls while my younger sister supervised, and even at six years old that girl was very particular about my work, calling on Nanna if I didn't do everything her way. I hated that.

"It was around this period that I thought I saw my father commit suicide. Some drunk had fallen from the roof, like a blur that I saw out of the corner of my eye. I thought it was my dad, driven to suicide by my mom. In fact, my dad died in a hospital not much later, and I never saw him again.

"I was a real unhappy, fat, angry kid. After Uncle Marty—a neighbor and not my real uncle—after he sexually molested me, I lost control. I started biting the teachers at school and attacking other kids in the schoolyard, and by the age of nine I was sent to live at Rockland State Psychiatric Hospital. I lived as a ward of the state until I was over twelve years old. Then they sent me to my mom, but two years later I was back, unable or unwilling to live with her.

"Most of this stuff is a blur. I was in and out of psychiatric facilities—on-again, off-again—well into my teens. When I was seventeen I fell in love with another patient; her name was Christine. She had family problems more than a mental illness.

"In 1968, while Christine was pregnant with my child, I was locked up for nine months on a burglary conviction. I was released from Rikers Island Correctional Facility in December 1968 and went back into a psychiatric hospital soon after. But they let me go. By January I was living on the streets and in cheap hotels. I got really sick, and I killed a woman in March.

"I should have been executed for what I did. They should bring back capital punishment. I am totally in favor of the death penalty. I believe in revenge. I feel that way now, and I felt that way then.

"But that's the only way I haven't changed—in every other respect, I'm not the same person I was twenty years ago. Literally not the same person. That person deserved to die and that's why, in 1969, I tried to kill myself. Two days after the murder, I jumped from the top of a burning steeple, hoping to fall to my death. I set the fire myself just to make sure I wouldn't lose courage and change my mind. That stuff in the paper about robbery is bullshit. I broke into Lutheran [Hospital] because I couldn't get directly into the church next door. The church had this great iron fence with spikes, so I went in through the hospital and pretty much slipped upstairs. If I had wanted to rob the place, I could have gotten away with no problem. Nobody would ever know it was me. But that wasn't my purpose.

"When I got into Lutheran I went up, like I said, to the top floor and made my way over to the windows by the church. It had to be a church, for some reason, through which I would meet my maker. I was drunk, and psychotic, too. I wasn't hearing no voices, but I had no sense of time or reality. My mind was all confused. For example, before I crawled out of the hospital window onto the roof of the church, I tried to light a cigarette. When the whole book of matches went up I just tossed it over my shoulder, on fire, and didn't worry no more about it. Out of sight, out of mind. A little fire started behind me, but I was somewhere else in my head. I don't know how long I stood there. It must have been a while because next thing I know I'm there, still inside the building, and it starts to rain. Inside the building. It doesn't occur to me that a hospital would have a sprinkler system. I climbed out of the window onto the roof of the church to get out of the rain."

The image of indoor rain underscored the dreamlike nature of his psychosis. Kelly believed himself powerless to control the circumstances of his life. But for that sprinkler system, he might have killed countless others, yet he was not even aware he was risking lives. Such things didn't occur to his psychotic mind; to him, there was no cause and effect. He thought it was raining inside, so outside he went.

"It's a clear cold night, but I'm too drunk to really feel the chill. I climb up the steeple, up as high as I could go, thinking about fire, how beautiful the flames are, and feeling bad about what I done to that lady. With some lighter fluid and another book of matches, I set the steeple ablaze. I know what I come for, but I'm still terrified when the fire surrounds me and I begin to burn. I jump.

"The next thing I know I'm filled with tubes, tubes up my nose, tubes in my veins, and strapped in and tied up, with my leg suspended from the ceiling in a cast up to my hip, and all other kinds of shit, all wrapped up like a gift, in a hospital bed. Then the cops came. The rest is history."

At Rikers, Kelly swallowed bedsprings, razors, anything that he thought could really hurt, but they wouldn't let him commit suicide. When he swallowed something really dangerous, the system's doctors would open him up, so he tried other means. The psychiatrists at Rikers considered Kelly's suicidal behavior to be indicative of mental illness. Kelly, however, didn't think his attempts at suicide were anything other than a realistic reaction to his circumstances.

As a tall teen-age white boy, not yet hardened by Rikers standards, Kelly must have appeared girlish to the other inmates. Other inmates wanted him for sex. Through a messenger, he was offered protection. Everybody knew that white boys couldn't make it at Rikers without protection: they'd get cut, or worse. "I killed a black woman and I cut out her heart and ate it," Kelly whispered to the messenger. "Would he trust his cock in a mouth like that?"

By the time Kelly was back in his cell the word had spread, and he was marked. Kelly remembers "White boy gonna die" as a chant taken up by the inmates, a Rikers game to amuse the mugs. He had his own cell but, like everybody else, at lockout he lived in the prison's communal areas.

"I relaxed in my cell. I could hear the murmurs and they gave me an excited feeling, like I was alive. I got off my cot and screamed through the bars, 'I cut that nigger's heart right out of her chest, right the fuck out of her chest, and I fried it up with garlic in olive oil. Best fucking meal I ever ate!'

" 'You gonna die at lockout, white boy. Billy gonna shove a piece of steel up into your ribs right through your liver,' said the man next cell over. 'Don't you wonder how that gonna feel?'

" 'Is that true, Billy?' I shouted through the bars. 'You gonna kill me? Or you just wanna suck me off?'

" 'You already dead,' growled Boom-Boom Billy. 'At lockout I got a shiv your belly gonna taste. Say your prayers, cracker-boy, you gonna meet Jesus.'

" 'I hope you're not just bluffing. I'm so tired of niggers bluffing. Gonna do this, gonna do that. Nothing ever happens. Please, save me the trouble. I want to die, today, if you got the balls. Do you? You got the heart to take me out? Let's see. Do me the favor!' I was practically begging the guy.

"They stayed away from me during lockout. Billy and the rest just stayed away. But my mind had already drifted. I had gone back to my own world in hell, and I forgot about them others."

In December 1969 Kelly was transferred from Rikers to Matteawan State Hospital for the Criminally Insane as unfit to stand trial. Psychiatrists had found that he either did not understand the charges or was unable to work with his attorney, or both. In any case, Kelly was sent upstate to Matteawan with the other unfit patients. The only way out was to stand trial, or get carried out in a box.

Matteawan was an impressive facility—like a red brick castle—with big barred windows and plenty of light. Kelly says he got the usual treatment when he arrived; he was stripped, and a black rubber tube was shoved up his rear end. This was a cavity search conducted on each new patient in turn, with the same tube for each patient, rinsed off between each use. It was inserted by the experienced hand of a big white fellow with a gimp the patients called Lurch.

Lurch announced the rules to the new patients: "I know some of you can understand me, and some of you can't. It doesn't matter. The rules is the same. If you don't do what you are told, you get a beating. If you talk back to the staff, you get a beating. If you won't get out of bed when it's time, you get a beating. If you mess your bed, you get a beating. If I think you should or any of my people think you should for any reason, you get a beating. It's just that simple.

"Now, some of you won't understand what I am saying, and some of you would like to pretend that you don't. It doesn't matter. Not everybody understands language, but everybody understands beatings. I use a black rubber hose just like this one, that's what I like, but I'd rather not have to use it. I don't like to give beatings. It makes my arm tired. And you don't have to get beatings; we have to give them, but not necessarily to you. You don't have to be the one. Let the others find out if I'm kidding. It doesn't have to be you."

In 1971 Kelly was found fit to stand trial and was sent to the Men's House of Detention in Manhattan—also known as The Tombs—but it didn't work out. His lawyer did all the talking and none of the listening, and Kelly lost his temper. He knocked down his lawyer in court and was sent back to Matteawan as still unfit. Now he was as content as anybody who wanted to kill himself could be. The doctors left him more or less alone.

The members of the staff who spend real time with the patients are today called therapy aides, but back then they were called guards. Nurses also spent more time with patients than did the doctors, who, as always, were too busy with administrative duties. Kelly had a good relationship with the staff. By now considered a lifer, he rarely had a problem.

In 1974, however, something changed. According to Kelly, three guards were beating a patient until Nurse O'Reilly interrupted them. The guards warned her not to interfere, but, Kelly says, she told them off.

"A few days later this big monster guy named Pim, a big, stupid guy who believes anything, he corners her in the corridor. These guards, who had been whispering in his ear just before, they all go on break and disappear. This Pim, they must have told him something about Nurse O'Reilly and sex, because this huge guy begins to slobber and he's grabbing his dick.

"Nurse O'Reilly sees what's going on and tries to talk him down, but Pim can't concentrate on her words. He wants to fuck her. He reaches for her.

" 'Pim! Pim! It's Kelly. Let me help you,' I call from behind him. 'Listen to me.'

"I run up alongside him.

" 'That's O'Reilly, the nurse. She helps us. If those guys told you something, think about who is going to pay for it. They'll tie you up and beat you with hoses. Pim!'

"He pushed me away, but I had distracted him. In that moment Nurse O'Reilly slipped away. He lumbered off, trying to remember what was so important. He had already forgot.

"If the guards had it in for Nurse O'Reilly, I didn't want to be caught in that mess. During six years at Matteawan I had seen fifteen patients die from abuse."

I had no way of knowing how accurate he was, either about the deaths he witnessed or about the matter concerning Pim and Nurse O'Reilly. Any records that existed were not available to me.

"I requested to be found fit," Kelly continued, "and didn't have much trouble convincing the doctor that I was ready to stand trial for murder. I'd decided I wanted to live. I was sent back to the Men's House of Detention in Manhattan. And a good thing for me. There was a big scandal at Matteawan, followed by an investigation, and Matteawan Hospital for the Criminally Insane was closed in 1975 while I was still being held in the Men's House of Detention."

Kelly was assigned a lawyer, and the district attorney's office made him an offer: ten years for a plea of guilty to manslaughter, with the understanding that because he had already spent five years as an unfit criminal patient he could get out on parole after only another year and eight months. His lawyer didn't think that was too bad, but Kelly wasn't sure. His lawyer suggested that they might want to ask the court to send a psychiatrist to see him, which they did.

Dr. Carp, appointed by the court to evaluate Kelly's mental condition, told him to fight the conviction and cop an insanity plea. Kelly remembers hearing Dr. Carp saying these words: "No question at the time of the crime you were not responsible for your acts. Your brain wasn't there, it's that simple. A conviction would mean you did it with purpose. We know that's not true. An insanity ruling is a not guilty determination; you'd go to a hospital. When the doctors there see what I see, and I'm sure they will, they will let you go a lot sooner than a year and two-thirds. You'll spend 90 days for observation, that'll be it. Don't take the D.A.'s offer."

The Manhattan district attorney would not accept Kelly's insanity plea, and the trial lasted five days, during which, Kelly claimed, Dr. Carp testified that Kelly had been one of the sickest people that he'd ever met.

"That motherfucker," said Kelly, "was the first of a series of psychiatrists to sell me out. I'm not angry anymore," he said, not very believably, "but if you're not crazy, these doctors will make sure you become crazy." Kelly was found not guilty by reason of insanity and sent to Mid-Hudson Psychiatric Center. According to Kelly, with him went a written recommendation from Dr. Carp that Kelly be kept forever; he said Kelly had the potential to be a serial killer.

The psychiatrists at Mid-Hudson Psychiatric Center gave Kelly psychotropic medication to control his hallucinations and delusions, and talk therapy to explore his thinking. Kelly began to get better, slowly stumbling along toward remission, and as his mental state improved, he began to create a new kind (for him) of institutional life. He discovered work and the personal satisfaction of a job well done when he began training as a reupholsterer at Mid-Hudson's rehabilitation workshop. Eventually he became a patient-instructor, a kind of a tutor, and this was how he met Chakka

Bokuu. He talked of her as the sweetest thing on earth, as the only woman who could understand what he'd been through—because she, too, had killed another person during an acute psychosis. He admired her classic Ethiopian beauty, her heart-shaped oval face, her medium-brown skin, her radiant white teeth, and her thin, straight nose that looked in profile like one on an ancient Greek bust. He said she had the appearance of a woman for whom things happen (and *to* whom things happen) because men want to make them happen.

Chakka Bokuu had been charged with murder and spent nine months in the Women's House of Detention before she was sent to Mid-Hudson Psychiatric Center. In 1984, just as her relationship with Hugh Kelly was beginning to flower, he was offered a transfer to South Beach Psychiatric Center, a non-secure hospital on Staten Island. He refused, both because he had already had a bad experience at South Beach and because he didn't want to abandon Chakka. Chakka was transferred to Kirby by administrative order when it opened in 1985, however, and Kelly was left behind. (Coincidentally, I became her lawyer at Kirby, years before Kelly and I met.)

With Chakka gone, Kelly was finally motivated to want to leave the safety of a secure hospital, and he began to work closely and seriously with his therapist. Eventually he concluded that in his psychosis he had symbolically killed his own mother for hounding his father into desertion, for allowing him to be sexually abused, and for failing him in a hundred other ways. He saw this as a breakthrough, as did his therapist.

"It's true. The only way my mother could show a man affection was sexually; I see the parallel with Lola Freeman. Killing her was a catharsis. I released my hate on this poor woman. I should have killed myself instead."

A lot of Kelly's account was self-serving, but a lawyer's job is to represent his client. To be effective it helps to believe, but almost every case can be looked at in different ways, and a lawyer can choose the way that best supports his client's position. His or her job is to win if at all possible.

Maintaining one's balance is not easy. Emotionally and ethically, I sometimes feel a tug between my personal fears and my professional duties. In this case, though, my client's position was supported by his treatment history. Despite all that Drs. Bayberry and Blau had to say, twenty years of hospital records showed that Kelly's dangerous mental condition had gradually improved. By 1986 he was no longer hallucinating or exhibiting other symptoms of psychosis. Based on psychiatric testimony, a judge found him to be no longer dangerous and ordered his transfer from Mid-Hudson to Manhattan Psychiatric Center. And since his transfer, Kelly continued to show no signs of psychosis. In fact, he had not needed antipsychotic medication for almost ten years.

In June 1986 three doctors of the MPC hospital forensic committee had examined him and found him to be in good contact with reality, without psychotic features. They approved his treating doctor's recommendation that Kelly be able to walk the hospital grounds with a staff escort—what is called "escorted privileges." However, the application for these privileges was disapproved by the Office of Mental Health in Albany, which had final say over hospital policy, and Kelly continued to remain confined to the ward. In December the application for escorted privileges was renewed; the forensic committee made particular note of his withstanding an attack without losing self-control—another patient had tried to puncture Kelly's eyeball with a radio antenna, but Kelly did nothing to retaliate. Instead he began wearing heavy-framed glasses, even to bed. "That guy needs help. He's just sick," Kelly remarked about his assailant. His behavior during the whole incident was evidence of Kelly being in good control under bad conditions. Escorted privileges were granted.

He did so well that by March 1987 an application, again noting his lack of psychosis, was made to grant him unescorted privileges—provided he was willing to consent to be retained by the hospital for an additional two years. By July Kelly was enjoying private walks around the grounds. He hadn't realized how much he'd missed the public solitude of a stroll without chaperon. It was such a little thing, but it led to a problem: the ready availability of street

drugs on hospital grounds, which soon led to Kelly's abuse of cocaine. When this was discovered, all his privileges were revoked.

In January 1988 Kelly, still showing no signs of psychosis, was again
considered for escorted privileges—but it would be a long time before the hospital would approve his doctor's application for unescorted privileges again. Kelly realized he'd made a terrible mistake,
took responsibility for it, and focused on working toward regaining
unescorted privileges. In June of that year his doctor's application
for Kelly's unescorted privileges was disapproved by the hospital
forensic committee. It was at this point, feeling anger and frustration, that Kelly called upon me to file the writ.

By August 4, 1988, I had completed my initial investigation. I realized that I could not conduct Kelly's case in standard fashion: A
writ of habeas corpus application is typically heard by the court almost immediately, and I would need at least several months before
we were truly ready for court. But because Kelly had agreed to a two-
year retention order in March 1987, only a legal application before
the court would help get him the kind of psychiatric attention I
knew he'd need. With a pending writ, I could prevent the doctors
and the hospital from procrastinating to the degree that they might
with no court involvement. So I filed a writ of habeas corpus for
Kelly even while I worked on my theory of the case.

Clearly, when Kelly was psychotic he had committed a horrible
act. Once his illness went into remission, however, he was more
comfortable playing tough guy than sick guy. He drew personal
strength from taking a stand against the world; it helped keep his
ego intact. I'd known guys like that my whole life, from the old
neighborhood in Brooklyn. They were considered normal.

Kelly believed that he'd been getting better through his own efforts and his own resolve. He had stopped taking medication in
1982 because it made him feel physically ill. That he had continued
to improve without medication only reinforced his growing belief in
himself. He decided that no one was going to push him around, including doctors—that he was going to get better because it was
within his own power. This independence helped him survive his

many years of institutionalization, but now it was hurting his chances of getting out because it was perceived by the authorities as evidence of an attitude problem.

Kelly's personality was problematic, but you don't get a new personality just because you're on your way to court. He wanted respect for who he was now, not who he had been twenty years ago. He felt he was being punished for getting better, for standing up for himself the way any normal person would. The positive side of his personality—his willingness to stick to his position despite the trouble it would surely lead to—bespoke an integrity and an ego strength that had both been necessary for Kelly's remarkable recovery. In fact, most doctors will admit that when the prognosis is bad (and after a lifetime of institutionalization, Kelly's certainly was) demanding "bad" patients do better than compliant "good" patients. In short, fighters have a better chance of recovery. What I needed was an expert witness to introduce that idea to the court, and I needed him (or her) to look better and more convincing than the testifying hospital psychiatrist. This, in turn, meant I needed to make the hospital psychiatrist look bad.

I combed the hospital record and selected dozens of obscure, detailed entries with which I thought I could trip up a testifying psychiatrist after he'd just told the judge that, yes, it was important for a treating psychiatrist to be familiar with the hospital records of the patient. Making a psychiatrist look unprepared rarely changes the outcome of a case on its own, but it can influence a close decision. Moreover, the embarrassment of looking foolish on the witness stand so unnerves some psychiatrists that they may lose their composure. If they lose the luster of professionalism, then their entire testimony may become useless.

Once again I spoke to everybody involved in Kelly's treatment, hoping to find somebody who would testify in his behalf. Again I examined all the evidence. Although Kelly's record had some positive points, no hospital doctors had allowed these points to sway them. But each argument they made against him seemed founded in the past; they all refused to address my client's current mental state. Given these circumstances, I felt we had nothing to lose by asking the court to appoint an independent psychiatrist. It turned out to be the crucial first step in a long process.

Independent psychiatrists are doctors not affiliated with the institution in question who are paid by the court to make a psychiatric determination and report their findings. (And because they are paid by the court, they are not beholden to any of the advocates.) A negative report essentially destroys any chance of winning; a positive report can make a formerly bad case look good.

The degree to which doctors' opinions will vary given identical data can be amazing. Some doctors are known to be liberal, and others conservative. There is also a small group that is somewhat unpredictable. Dr. Bauer, the independent psychiatrist in this case, was one of those. After examining Kelly and his voluminous file, he issued a report to the court that described Kelly's clinical history and hideous crime in light of his attitude toward women—and then moved on to focus on the change in Kelly's attitudes in recent years.

His report noted that Hugh had been the only male in a house of females; that he "blamed his mother for 'driving [his father] to drink' "; and that he had been ridiculed by his grandmother when he complained of having been sexually abused by a neighbor. "At age seven he was subjected to fellatio by an adult male in his apartment house: his resultant revulsion and fear were such that he defecated in his underdrawers, but when he went to his grandmother and reported the incident her response was to make him sit in the foyer of the building with his dirty underdrawers on his head, like a crown of some sort. . . . While he sat there, the man who had abused him passed by and winked at him. Hugh has said he 'put up a wall and never took it down again.' "

This "wall" stayed up, though Kelly was able to form a relationship with a young woman and to father a child. Still, Bauer notes, Kelly "felt 'numb' " inside, and, before the event in which he killed the prostitute, had reported "drinking heavily . . . in an attempt 'to be able to feel.' " The crime may have started when the prostitute "taunted him, proposing that he was 'afraid.' "

After describing the gruesome attack on Lola Freeman, Bauer also described Kelly's attitude toward the event: "He later reported that he felt no emotion during the homicide and mutilation and that it was as though he were observing the behavior of another person. He noted that when he cut open her abdomen her intestines looked like his father's penis, and he attempted to climb inside her stomach and back up into his father's penis so he wouldn't be born anymore, as though it were possible to reverse the process of his existence."

Bauer's report mentions Kelly's original diagnosis of "chronic undifferentiated schizophrenia," his attitude of deep resentment toward women, and the assessment of his being "rated as potentially dangerous because he was 'compulsively motivated to seek sexualized maternal omnipotent protection from a woman.' " However, he also noted that in the years that followed, Kelly "gradually acquired insight into his problems and his attitude towards women" during psychotherapy, eventually establishing "a good, warm relationship to his mother."

As to Kelly's continued combativeness and contentions that he was being persecuted by hospital staff, Bauer found that, given that the problem dissolved after departure of staff involved in these alleged incidents, "[one] wonders, accordingly, whether he can in fact correctly be termed 'paranoid.' " In spite of his misadventures with cocaine, he did not become assaultive; in the face of an attack by a fellow patient, Bauer noted, Kelly had not become violent or expressed a desire to retaliate, but rather "speaks of the attack and his subsequent circumspection with laudable, wry humor."

Where Kirby's doctors saw a patient who was a real troublemaker with a bad attitude, Dr. Bauer saw a very different person:

Mr. Kelly presents as an animated, communicative, pleasant, direct individual. He strikes me at once as energetic, and philosophical. He tells me that he believes it important to express and discuss feelings, and that it is hazardous routinely to obscure, hide, or deny one's feelings. He is aware that he might do better in certain respects to be "docile," but he knows that feigned civility can lead to explosion as well as frustration. I find him frank, and salty, not overbearing or cocky. He was courteous and cooperative throughout the session, and all his responses and spontaneous statements were relevant and coherent.

I see no evidence of psychosis. The picture, in my opinion, is one of character disorder undergoing further amelioration. I am satisfied, as before, that he was affected at the time of the homicide by a paranoid disorder, now in remission.

Interestingly, he has established intimate liaisons with a series of female patients over the years. He assures me both that these patients are aware of his history and that he has never menaced or injured any of them. This report certainly seems to bode well for the future.

He has acquired important insight and matured socially. He relates the homicide to incestual pull, in effect, and attendant rage: the woman he killed and mutilated "was a carbon-copy of his mother, who could only express her love for a man by going to bed with him." Now he sees his mother every other week, and he describes a good relationship between them.

Mr. Kelly seeks conditional release from Manhattan Psychiatric Center. He "wants to live in a Group Home." He feels that after having been institutionalized for so many years he is dependent upon some direction, although he wishes now to move towards autonomy and privacy. He speaks also of a strong desire to be employed and he believes he could obtain employment as an upholsterer. He is not only agreeable to regular psychotherapy, but asks for such psychotherapy. He asks also to be placed in a Group Home which is "drug-oriented," although he doubts that he would again use cocaine or other illicit drugs.

What is the likelihood he would abscond from or discontinue outpatient treatment? "If I escape, what the hell would I do?" He indicates that his life is now centered about self-renewal and social function. He seeks acceptance.

In summary, Mr. Kelly is a man given over essentially to self-control 20 years after he killed and mutilated a woman in a state of psychotic rage. He is viewed by some persons as paranoid and hostile because of his complaints that he is singled out for harassment, but he reports credibly being maligned by individuals morbidly preoccupied with the homicide he committed. He asks to be approached and treated not as "an odd-ball" but as "the person he is today." His manner strikes me as frank rather than hostile, his stance as dignified rather than paranoid.

I find no further need for in-patient psychiatric treatment. The conditions of his discharge should include residence within a supervised Group Home and attendance at a psychiatric clinic for regular psychotherapy and such other professional treatment as seems appropriate.

From Kelly's point of view, this report was extreme good fortune—particularly because, given the same facts, the hospital doctors had reached a very different conclusion. But in some ways, getting this report only turned up the heat. The district attorney's office, no longer looking at an easy victory, began its campaign in earnest, presenting Kelly's purported cannibalism as a fact, knowing it would disgust and outrage people. And this tactic had an effect. My lawyer colleagues, who had no interest in Kelly's current mental condition, expressed dismay that I would pursue a writ in such a case; in fact, one senior lawyer suggested I might want to give the case less effort. I understood this "suggestion" to imply that a successful writ in Kelly's behalf would have a negative public impact on our efforts as attorneys for *all* mental patients.

Nevertheless, I worked hard, particularly outside the courtroom. In view of Dr. Bauer's positive report, I asked the hospital's chief psychiatrist, Dr. Zebulon Taintor, to review the clinical evidence and reconsider its determination that Kelly was still dangerous. Then we had another stroke of luck. Dr. Bayberry transferred to another ward, and, because there was no immediate replacement, Dr. Taintor took over his duties. He had the opportunity to observe Kelly daily, and they met regularly in therapy.

By November 1988 Dr. Taintor agreed to request an independent consultation on Kelly's state. Under his direction and using various techniques, from intimidation interviews to co-conspirator posturing, doctors from Albany, from Bronx Psychiatric, from Brooklyn, called on Kelly to explain his view of the world. Nothing fazed him.

What came next were a series of compromises. Rather than resolving the issue of release, the hospital proposed that Kelly get unescorted privileges on hospital grounds, with the written understanding that a graduated, step-wise approach to release, with increasing freedom, was the recommended course. Shortly thereafter Dr. Taintor recommended that Kelly be allowed to take trips, first accom-

panied and then alone, into the city in order to prepare himself for
the real world. Coupled with Dr. Taintor's request, although not
officially a part of the hospital's application, was a request for
conditional discharge. Dr. Ford, the executive director of Manhattan
Psychiatric Center, signed his name to Dr. Taintor's application,
adding the remarks, "Prepare for conditional release before Feb-
ruary 1989." The hospital was moving quickly now. But court, by
its nature, is a slow and careful process.

Of course Kelly and I accepted these terms as they were presented; each was a step that brought us closer to our goal. But we
steadfastly refused to withdraw Kelly's application for a writ from
the court calendar, because it was the pressure of the writ that was
making so much happen. Instead we allowed these other applications to supersede the writ, which was often adjourned as we continued to press for increasing freedoms.

In many cases delays in commencing court proceedings appear to
be deliberate tactical moves intended to frustrate the presumably
unstable patient. The pressures of court, and court adjournments,
can cause some clients to decompensate; the patients scream,
shout, threaten, or insult. This often results in a win for the assistant
attorney general or assistant district attorney handling the case.

But Kelly handled each delay as an opportunity to prove himself,
and with each passing month his case only got stronger. Even the
district attorney's doctor was unable to find significant evidence of
current dangerousness. By March 1989 all parties had consented to
the hospital's application for Kelly's escorted privileges into the city,
and the judge on the case signed an order making it official. Discharge planning had already begun, and the hospital began to seek a
residence for Kelly for after his discharge. He was sent on interviews.
Related papers were sent to every city outpatient residence that
might even consider accepting a forensic patient. And the wheels
slowly turned.

The hospital proposed a number of conditions for Kelly's release.
For example, he was required to report for outpatient follow-up as a
part of a legal "order of conditions" that, subject to renewal, would
remain in effect for five years after Kelly's release.

In the summer of 1989, almost a year to the day after the writ was filed, Hugh Kelly and I appeared before a judge for the very last time. On the basis of the accumulated evidence, including psychiatric testimony by the chief psychiatrist of the hospital, Dr. Zebulon Taintor, the independent psychiatrist appointed by the court, Dr. Robert J. Bauer, and the patient himself, we had won our case with very little opposition. And I'm proud that we won; I have no regrets. I followed the law.

But although I have real confidence in Kelly, I cannot say I've never had a doubt.

There is a Willie Horton in every prison, every mental hospital, just waiting to get out. Unfortunately, we don't know who he is. Until it is too late, we don't know which individuals will turn again to acts of violence. For all its sophistication and advanced theories, the field of psychiatry has no reliable way to predict future dangerousness. Any doctor who says otherwise is lying.

As a lawyer, I do not suffer from a guilty conscience. But lately I've been having nightmares. Last night I dreamed I was traveling cross-country with a friend, no one I recognized but in context clearly a good buddy, and slowly it began to dawn on me that he was doing horrible, unspecified things and drawing me in as his unknowing accomplice. We were sought by law enforcement officials and eventually brought in for questioning. I was grateful to awaken before I learned any more details. Although I try to concentrate on the positive progress of increasing human dignity, my waking hours can be nightmarish enough.

Maybe what led me to such a dream was a newspaper report I read in a recent *New York Times,* headlined: HOMELESS MAN CONVICTED OF MURDER IS TO BE FREED. A murder conviction was overturned on appeal because the cardboard box in which the defendant slept was searched without a warrant. In the box the police had found blood and belongings that tied this man to the strangulation death of Theodore Genovese, a supervisor in the radiology department at Yale–New Haven Hospital.

Whoa! Let's face it: the guy did it. He killed Theodore Genovese, and he was found guilty beyond a reasonable doubt. But his lawyer argued on appeal that the warrantless search violated the Fourth Amendment, which guarantees the rights of individuals "to be secure in their persons, houses, papers, and effects, against unreasonable searches and seizures." I appreciate that the principle here is to curtail police power and protect all of us from unwarranted intrusions that could easily lead to even greater abuses. But this guy killed someone, and now he'll be back on the street.

Of course, what I do for my clients might in some cases be even worse. What would I have done for the killer of Theodore Genovese if I were his lawyer? Maybe exactly the same thing. Maybe that's why I have bad dreams.

The problem is that as an attorney for criminal mental patients, I never meet the victims. I never know their histories, their faces, or their anguish; only that of my clients—histories of their abused and battered childhoods fill the hospital records, as doctors try to figure out what made these people lose their minds. The hospital is there to help, and so am I. The assumption is that with proper care and treatment, lives can be saved—the lives of mental patients. Some will recover (go into remission) and lose their demons, learning to live as members of society. Others will spend their lives within the hospital. But everybody gets a chance.

And the victims become only a part of the history of someone's psychosis.

Hugh Kelly was released to a group home, but his problems weren't over. The group home chosen for him by the state was located just over the bridge in Harlem, and Kelly was the only white resident. Accompanying him to his new home was a written psychiatric history meant to aid his subsequent treating psychiatrists. It was replete with references to his girlfriend's "similarities" to his victim, and to racial antagonisms of the past. Shortly thereafter, he felt he was being singled out by staff: They knew who he was and what he'd done, and all the problems he'd experienced with staff at MPC were back. But Kelly was lucky. Despite weekly notations of the group home's clinician that Kelly was becoming paranoid, Dr. Taintor, who was now unofficially supervising Kelly's release, did not readily accept this as true. By now, he knew Kelly too well. Instead he supported Kelly's effort to get his own apartment, and his support helped Kelly hang on.

Within ninety days Kelly found a small basement kitchenette in Queens. He prepared a homey set-up in anticipation of Chakka Bokuu's imminent release.

Since his release I've seen a great deal more of Hugh Kelly than I expected to. Usually I hope never to see clients again because seeing them again usually means that somehow they've decompensated, failed in the world, and returned to the hospital. But Dr. Taintor, who had become something of a friend to me, kept me abreast of Kelly's trials at the outpatient clinic in Harlem and his move to Queens. Our conversation was business in that should a problem develop, I would need to go to court on Kelly's behalf, but it was also more. We had both stuck our necks out, and we both had a personal interest in this case.

I began seeing Kelly again sometime the following spring. After discovering how difficult it was to get employment when one is over age forty and has no real history of work, Kelly found a job at the patient rehabilitation center on MPC hospital grounds. It was unsatisfying to him—he wanted to be clear of hospital associations—but he needed to make a living and they were willing to pay him. He was hoping to get a "real" job, buy a van, move furniture, reupholster couches and chairs, and ultimately own a small business—the American dream. Instead he was pushing a broom, or taking names of patients and giving out athletic equipment at the rehab gym. The gym is in the building just across from Kirby, and often I see him when I come to work in the morning. We talk quite often. He seems happy, but not satisfied; he is too ambitious to be satisfied.

He married Chakka Bokuu, now Chakka Kelly, just after her release. Some people say she resembles his victim, but how could they know? True, she's African; ethnically she has that much in common with the victim, but nothing more. She works at the hospital, too, for similar reasons. In this economy it's very hard to get a job in the private sector when you have a psychiatric history. She also talks with me, but not as often as Kelly does. Sometimes the three of us meet for coffee. She's not the great talker that he is. In fact, she's rather quiet—secretive, even. But now that she's been released (also with an accompanying order of conditions), she talks a great deal more about her life.

Men have always been interested in beauties, but Chakka had more than men on her mind when she came of age. She wanted an education and maybe to travel. She was born in Ethiopia, during what she calls the Thirty Year War, and parts of her family were politically involved with the successful insurgents. She found it necessary at one point to escape (although why is not exactly clear) and, at nineteen years of age, she took off across the desert on camel, traveling only at night with an older woman and her two children. After ten days they arrived in Sudan, where Chakka was offered a position as a governess by a wealthy Saudi family. (Members of her father's family worked at a military hospital in Riyadh, and apparently her Saudi employer had some connection to or knowledge of them.)

Chakka became responsible for looking after five children in a somewhat communal setting, where several families shared daily life. She was surrounded by chatter and bustle and a sense of being a part of something greater—a family. Some of the women tried to make a match for her with one young man or another, but Chakka was still full of ideas about adventure and education. Eventually the family by whom she was employed came to America, landing at Kennedy Airport in New York City and leaving immediately for a home they maintained in Syracuse, New York. Chakka felt much more isolated in Syracuse than she had in Sudan. The sense of being part of a larger community was gone; now she felt like she was merely a household servant. She loved the children, but after several months in Syracuse she left for New York City with two Ethiopian men who were friends of her family. One of them, a man of about fifty named Takelyymont Monghstab, was in charge of an Ethiopian relief organization. Shortly after arriving in New York City, she checked into the psychiatric wing at St. Luke's Hospital because she was hearing voices, but she was released when the voices stopped.

Chakka had come to New York City with the desire and expectation of going to school. She lived in Manhattan near 96th Street with the two men who were friends of her family. She found work as a cleaning woman, but problems developed. Her money, which she put into her purse after each payday, would somehow disappear. She also had problems getting around. She wanted to go to church, and to school, but she was confused by big-city transportation and she was not encouraged to be independent by her mentor, Mr. Monghstab. She didn't want to depend on him. Finally, after much insistence on her part, he took her to apply for a green card so that she could legally reside in the United States. He told her he would take care of everything, but after he had her sign numerous papers, that was the last she heard of it.

Again she started hearing voices. She began blaming Takelyymont Monghstab for her frustrations. She wanted to get married, go to school, and see her family. She felt that he was keeping her prisoner, isolating her so that the people she saw on soap operas were her only companions. She began to believe that Erica from the soap opera "All My Children" was communicating with her directly. She thought Erica told her to pour a soup pot full of hot tap water onto Mr. Monghstab while he slept. She did, he was scalded, and he died in the hospital four days later of a heart attack.

Chakka Bokuu was found fit to stand trial and acquitted of the charge of murder by reason of mental disease or defect. She spent a year and a half at Mid-Hudson, where she met Hugh Kelly. When Kirby was opened as a new facility, Chakka was transferred down as a dangerously mentally ill patient, a lateral transfer with no change in her legal status. For a short time I was her attorney, and her case looked decent almost from the start because she seemed to understand far better than Kelly what was required of her. She took the position that the doctors knew best; the doctors, impressed with her good judgment, saw signs of continuing improvement. Her eventual transfer to MPC was rather uneventful—she was so demure, in stark contrast to the kind of patient that Kelly was. She followed her doctor's orders, kept to herself, presented herself in court as a frail, sweet thing, and gave very little evidence that anyone could use against her.

But although she admits to me that she doused her victim with hot water, she still doesn't believe that hot water alone could have induced his heart attack. She believes it was the incompetence of the hospital where he was brought, combined with a deliberate effort on somebody's part to do away with him, that caused his death. Still, she seems so unthreatening.

At MPC Hugh Kelly and Chakka Bokuu renewed their ties. Together, they had goals: release, then marriage.

Hugh Kelly still likes to talk, particularly about social policy matters with which he feels familiar. Only last fall, on another bright day, we were having coffee at one of the picnic tables at MPC, and he was again working through some of his thoughts about retribution and death.

"Sure, I believe in capital punishment, because I believe in revenge," he volunteered. "I believe society should make people pay for their crimes. You know, eye for an eye, tooth for a tooth, that kind of thing, because criminals understand what that means. Locking some guy up for a number of years whether he set a fire, killed somebody, raped a child, or embezzled money from a bank—the same punishment, more or less, for very different crimes—doesn't make as much sense, because the connection requires too much thinking. Most criminals aren't that smart. That's why you need the death penalty. But my sense of revenge is more personal than leaving it to society to punish evildoers."

Later he would elaborate on this point, explaining that he would apply capital punishment selectively. He believes, for example, that "Son of Sam" killer David Berkowitz should have been executed; that Manson should have been executed; that he himself should have been executed. He told me that both Ted Bundy and Gary Gilmore were appropriately executed and that he would have felt frustrated personally if either of their death sentences had been commuted. He does not excuse anybody for actions taken, knowingly or not; unlike the Penal Code of New York State, he does not take the mental outlook of the perpetrator into account.

And yet there are homicides he would have excused.

For example, in Kelly's mind, Dr. Herman Tarnower's murder was justified, and Jean Harris got a sentence that was far too harsh. He feels that the doctor tortured this woman and deserved what he got (in Kelly's words, "The guy's a scumbag!"). Thus he doesn't look to the mental culpability of the actor but to the innocence of the victim: if the victim was innocent, the killer should die.

He argues for victims' rights—including those of his own victim, whom he sees now as blameless, a poor woman doing her best to make her way in a difficult world. Today Kelly says he would excuse his mother if she had in fact actively killed his father, an idea that haunted him for years after he saw the drunk fall from a roof. This leads me to speculate that perhaps he holds women to a separate standard, believing that they are less responsible for their acts or that men are less innocent. And how convenient to support the death penalty for others, and even for oneself, if that self no longer exists.

And Kelly himself is not a thrilled supporter of the insanity plea, either—at least not for some former mental patients:

"Take the case of my man Harmon Brown. It took many years and more than just not taking his happy pills for him to arrive at a point where he took a machete onto the D train at West 4th Street and hacked six people to pieces. Do I believe the fruitcakes who declared him to be sane *when he is on medication?* No way! What a joke! Do I believe him to be crazy? Without a doubt.

"The doctors are hypocrites. If they weren't, they would have told the courts that Brown would need years of one-on-one therapy before they could even consider him for release. But most of the time real therapy isn't provided, because it costs too much money. It's a lot cheaper to treat the symptom by giving someone a pill than actually attacking the cause through therapy.

"Just think about what will happen if Brown breaks his promise, stops taking his medication, and starts to hear God's little whispers in his head again. When that happens, I guess he'll be fired from his job as cashier in the lunchroom of Bronx Psychiatric Center." Kelly said this with a cynical laugh, as though he were remembering only now that he was employed at Manhattan Psychiatric Center. He lit up a Camel nonfilter and spit.

He believes he has insight, a result he attributes to therapy only reluctantly, because he would like to claim he was "cured" entirely through his own efforts. He believes that Harmon Brown does not have insight and must rely on medication for a kind of "synthetic" sanity. "I wish I could tell the world what really goes on in the state mental hospital system. Why don't you write a book about me? Like you say, Denis, 'Just tell the truth.' " Kelly is sure he will never again become psychotically violent, but—still the tough guy—he doesn't rule out violence entirely. He took another drag on his cigarette.

"A long time ago I knew I'd have to stop taking medication or I'd never really get better, because my improvement would have been artificial, not something that I was responsible for. I'll never lose it again, because I don't depend on medication. I depend on myself. The only reason I'd ever kill again is if someone hurt my wife. Pure vengeance. Let me show you what I mean: Let's say some guy rapes and kills my wife. He's convicted and goes to jail. I'm gonna have to commit a crime to get into prison, so I can get next to him and kill him myself. It's better if the state does it. Electrocute the motherfucker, and even that's too good for him.

"Now, I know what you're thinking, me being the guy that killed a woman and cut her up pretty bad, even cooked a piece of her flesh. And I know it's in the record, but I did not eat her. I did not eat her heart; I just told the doctors I did to make myself interesting. The autopsy report will show you that it never happened. It's just something I said at the time to get attention, and for over twenty years now I've been getting it. I actually got the idea from two books I read, *Bury My Heart At Wounded Knee*—where when a brave kills a worthy enemy he eats the heart, partly out of respect and partly to take into himself the courage and character of his conquered foe—and *The Boston Strangler*. But that poor dead lady wasn't my enemy. She was just a woman who was unlucky enough to meet a sick young man. She didn't deserve to die. I did."

He still hasn't gotten over his remorse. I guess I'll be seeing something of Kelly as long as we're both still working at the hospital. I continue to believe, though, that both Kelly and his wife have been rehabilitated. Through the "wonders of psychiatry" or otherwise, Hugh Kelly is a man back from hell.

Now Hugh and Chakka Kelly have put their crimes behind them. They want to be "normal." They live moderately ordinary lives in a residential community in town. They are trying to have a baby. They plan to find a bigger apartment.

The Exorcists

The refusal of modern "enlightenment" to treat "possession" as a hypothesis to be spoken of as even possible, in spite of the massive human tradition based on concrete experience in its favor, has always seemed to me a curious example of the power of fashion in things scientific. That the demon theory will have its innings again is to my mind absolutely certain. —William James

The telephone rang in my Manhattan State office one Tuesday in October.

"Hello?"

"Is this lawyer Woodchuck?"

"Close enough."

"Is that an Indian name?"

"No. Who is this?"

"I was told you could help me," said a low female voice. "I want to explain what is really happening. They are killing the women here. And they call it medicine. What this so-called doctor calls mental illness is really evil spirits. Spirits will not stay in a dying host. His drugs only work by making the body sick, bringing it closer to death. So the spirits leave. But when the drugs are stopped, they return. Only Jesus keeps evil away! Only Jesus lets you live! I will not die, not even a little, for this drug-dealing witch doctor!"

"Who's calling, please?"

"My name is Sants. Mary Sants."

"Where are you?"

"Kirby, Ward 3 West. But let me explain. . . . Demons are like disease. When they are driven out, they need a new home. And revenge. I know I was at risk. . . . they must be driven out! But not with drugs. I won't take them! No! Get me a priest!"

"You have a legal right to refuse medication."

"I refuse! I want a priest! They want to keep me here! For experiments! Torture me! This is worse than prison! And I didn't do it!"

"Why don't I come to see you this afternoon? Are you busy?" I asked, partly to be polite—often a client isn't up to a meeting right away—and partly because of the reality of hospital programming. As it was, she wasn't scheduled for therapy or other rehabilitative treatment, and we made an appointment for later that day.

From the outside the three white hospital buildings on Wards Island appear almost identical—except that Kirby, the most southerly, is surrounded by razor wire and double cyclone fences. On the inside Kirby is very different from the other two, at least in part because patients committed for criminal reasons get a lot more attention from the state than do more run-of-the-mill mental patients. Therefore it is cleaner and fresher, with refurbished floors and freshly painted walls—and surveillance at every turn, courtesy of security equipment ranging from monitoring cameras to motion sensors. Anyone wishing to get in, from the professional staff on down, has to go through a magnetically controlled steel door and into a small observation chamber, pass through a metal detector under the watchful eyes of security personnel, and finally wait as electronically regulated steel gates rumble open. There are no exceptions.

The corridors leading to my Kirby office are scrubbed and white, and that day, as always, I passed one administrative department after another before coming to those offices set aside for lawyers, way at the end of the west wing. Cases come to me at Kirby in much the same way as at Manhattan State. An application by the hospital—perhaps to medicate, perhaps to retain—including the essentials of the hospital's evaluation (such as a patient's history, diagnosis, prognosis, and legal status) is forwarded to my desk. I was not surprised to find legal papers already on my desk naming Mary Sants as the respondent. Her underlying commitment order had expired, but her psychiatrist had found she was not yet mentally fit to stand trial on the criminal charges facing her, so Kirby needed a new judicial order to continue to hold her.

According to the file, Mary Sants, twenty-four years old, believed herself to be an exorcist. Along with her mother, Tasha Sants, Mary had been charged with nineteen criminal counts of fraud and larceny. The pair were accused of defrauding sixteen people of more than $350,000—in most cases, their life savings. The district attorney's office brought charges based on complaints made by the adult children of several alleged victims, as opposed to the alleged victims themselves. That the complainants were not the parties actually injured was extremely unusual.

To establish fraud, the district attorney must convince a jury beyond a reasonable doubt that the perpetrator made representations she *knew* to be false and that the victims not only believed such representations to be true but relied on their truth. Without actual victims coming forward, this is next to impossible to establish. Several of the alleged victims in this case were quite elderly, however, and an adult child of one victim was a newspaper reporter. From the district attorney's point of view the potential for bad press apparently outweighed the difficulty of making the case, and charges were filed.

When Mary and her mother were picked up by the police at their storefront location on lower Second Avenue, neon lights still flashed "Psychic Reading, Spiritual Advise" [sic] behind the plate glass window. (A small legal disclaimer, painted in the window's lower left corner, indicated that all activities were for entertainment purposes, fortune-telling being a misdemeanor in New York.) Mother and daughter were given a proper *Miranda* warning; they waived their right to have a lawyer present. At the police station they made a statement that they had not defrauded anybody. Their customers, they claimed, had gotten what they paid for. They were indignant at their arrest and demanded release. But once the wheels of prosecutorial justice began turning, several of the alleged victims came forward to offer evidence.

Apparently the Santses had gained the confidence of a number of senior citizens who were tormented by thoughts of death, by dreams of deceased husbands and forgotten lovers, lost children, and abandoned wives. Although most of their clients were elderly women, their renowned success up and down Second Avenue was a fifty-nine-year-old man known as Hector, a former professional dancer and entertainer who had been crippled in an accident. After meeting the Santses he was able to throw away his crutches and he opened a dance studio where he gave lessons to women in dance forms that nobody had taught for years. He claimed the Santses had made a new man of him and had banished the ghosts of his three ex-wives. In whispers he told his students (none of whom actually did much dancing) that the Santses had made predictions that were better than luck, that they knew how to interpret signs. He said he was winning at the track, at the numbers, and on the stock market, and it was the most incredible experience of his life.

Several of his students, followed by their friends, and then friends of friends, cousins, and even the merely curious, visited the Santses for readings and predictions. Although none of them came into a great deal of cash, quite a few were suddenly and unexpectedly lucky in love, at least for a little while. A few with severe problems or depression required more than just a few quick sessions. The Santses suspected that their souls had been sullied by demonic spirits, and that was delicate, expensive work. But nobody complained. Most of their clients initially claimed to be satisfied with the results. Nobody was physically forced to pay, and the Santses had never claimed the improvements would be permanent.

It was that delicate, expensive work that was at the root of the Santses' legal difficulties. Some of the complainants swore the

Santses had coerced the money out of them, even threatened them through a kind of psychic terrorism. All kinds of charges were levelled, growing in severity and number, and the Santses ended up at the Women's House of Detention to await trial after bail was denied and the evidence continued to mount. (Although Hector was not formally charged with anything, he disappeared suddenly. No criminal complaints had been made against him, and the official word was that he was merely wanted for questioning as a potential witness. The word on the street, though, was that he was likely to be indicted as a co-conspirator. He never surfaced again.)

The Santses decided they didn't need a lawyer and would represent themselves (a sign of poor mental functioning), but after several weeks in jail they engaged a private attorney, Ellen Lorraine MacIntyre-Cohen, whom I knew from law school.

Two psychiatrists at the Women's House of Detention found both Mary and Tasha to be delusional and "not fit to stand trial"; without any objection from Ms. MacIntyre-Cohen, the criminal proceedings were put on hold. Although neither of the Santses had ever been violent, they had been charged with felonies and so were sent to Kirby for a ninety-day period. The idea was that the doctors there, through a regime of medication and other therapies, could restore the women to a fit mental condition, whereupon the criminal trial could proceed.

Once at Kirby, however, the Santses refused to take medication, an action that was looked upon as further proof of both their illness and their continued lack of fitness for trial. Therefore Kirby, in the application on my desk before me, asked the court to allow them to hold Mary (and Tasha as well, I would soon discover) for an additional six months for further treatment.

The hospital record indicated that Mary Sants had been raised near Seattle, the daughter of a musician-turned-fisherman father and a housewife mother. Upon the death of her father when Mary was eleven, her mother took her out of school and they began to travel extensively. During this period they pursued their interest in the occult.

Mary was noted to be attractive and attentive to her appearance, as well as possibly hypersexual. These traits led their psychiatrist, Dr. Eugene Dirk, to suspect childhood sexual abuse and to postulate that she might have been prostituted prior to the age of ten. Eventually he dropped that idea for want of confirmation, although he maintained an informal interest in this theory. Officially he diagnosed Mary Sants as suffering from, among other things, a *folie à deux*—a delusional disorder shared with her mother, who was also his patient. Theoretically, if the two were separated, the delusion would disappear, as it required both parties to flower. But because the Office of Mental Health had sent both women to the Kirby facility, which had only one woman's ward, they were in constant contact. I'm sure that Dr. Dirk realized this problem, but he didn't protest, possibly because if mother and daughter were separated he would not have been able to observe the course of this "disease," which he found fascinating. I didn't fault him for allowing them to stay together—or bring this "contraindicated circumstance" to anyone's attention—because it comported with my client's wishes. Either no one else in authority was paying attention, or the other options were impracticable (the Santses were charged in Manhattan, and there were no other forensic facilities nearby).

Generally, the population of the women's ward at Kirby tended to be more diverse than that of any of the men's wards. Whereas the existence of five wards for male patients at Kirby allowed for some grouping of patients according to level of violence and type of illness, all the women patients at Kirby shared a single ward. This meant that although they had no documented history of violence, Mary and Tasha Sants were living with women who had been acquitted by reason of mental disease of killing their husbands, children, neighbors, or friends. They also lived with women who had never actually killed anybody but couldn't resist attacking passersby. Some of the women would never be fit to stand trial but needed to stay in a maximum-security facility because of their propensity for dangerous acts. Others were quiet, fearful women who huddled in corners, careful of what they said and what they did—and who, when they got frightened enough, would explode in self-protective rage.

Mary's diagnosis also included erotomania, a manic sexual desire of which Dr. Dirk believed himself to be the subject. Dr. Dirk noted Mary's low frustration threshold, her inability to tolerate even mild criticism, and her highly manipulative personality, but he especially noted that she "appeared preoccupied with a romantic fantasy involving a male psychiatrist who has been on the ward since her arrival (the undersigned)." This was evidenced in part by her asking him questions about his personal life.

Psychiatrists often believe themselves to be the subject of a patient's sexual fantasies, but only sometimes are they correct.* For tactical reasons I took the position that this sexual preoccupation was a figment of *his* mind, not hers. I knew he was recently divorced and lonely, but I chose my position because I thought it might serve my client, not because it was necessarily founded in fact. Lawyers strive to make the facts fit their theory of the case, not the other way around. I'd worry about the truth later—right now it seemed strategically sound to question his medical judgment.

Dr. Dirk's notes indicated that Mary refused to discuss the details of her case or respond to his questions, and he recommended "that she be retained at Kirby for an additional six months or until she has a better grasp on reality and can assist in her own defense." He also recommended medication on a voluntary basis, it being a mental health axiom that medication is far more effective when taken electively.

I made a call to Ellen Lorraine MacIntyre-Cohen—Elly Cohen, when I first knew her. Although I don't usually contact the criminal attorney of my unfit clients, the fact that Elly was an old friend of mine gave me an excuse to say hello and glean what I could about the nature of the criminal case. Then I went to meet with my clients.

I met Mary Sants that afternoon on the ward. Despite her description as attractive and what I had decided were Dr. Dirk's fantasies about her, I was stunned by her appearance. Tall and slender, with long ebony hair framing her pale features, she might have been a model instead of a mental patient. She did not have that puffy,

---

* Sometimes in civil practice a therapist figures out a way to "help" such a patient, which can lead to a malpractice lawsuit. Interestingly, it is always only the attractive patients that such therapists feel can benefit most from this unorthodox form of treatment.

bloated appearance that comes so often with psychotropic medication and hospital food. I decided not to question her about erotomania; experience had taught me that conversations about sex are better left until after several meetings. Right now we needed to talk about the law.

"Good morning, Ms. Sants," I said. "My name is Denis Woychuk. I'm your lawyer. We spoke on the telephone earlier today. I've come to talk to you about your legal situation. But first, let's find an office."

One of the therapy aides let us into an unoccupied office, and we began our interview.

"Please sit down," I said. "Before we really begin, there are a few things I'd like to say regarding my role here. I am a psychiatric lawyer, a mental health lawyer, and my job is to give you legal assistance and represent you in court as long as you're in the hospital. I do not work for the hospital. I am paid by the court to represent you, and to try to get for you what you want for yourself. I work for you: what you want, I want.

"I am not a criminal lawyer, and I will not be handling your criminal case. I have spoken to Ms. MacIntyre-Cohen, your criminal lawyer, and she informs me that the D.A. will not drop the charges or offer a reasonable plea bargain. Too much publicity."

Mary's intense blue eyes caught mine and did not waver. She seemed defiant. I continued.

"Your doctor feels you are not mentally ready to go to criminal court, and a request has been filed with the New York Supreme Court to keep you here for another six months. He says you have delusions that you are an exorcist. What do you say?"

She looked at me coldly and said nothing.

"You've been charged with a number of serious felonies. The district attorney wants to put you in jail. If you feel that you are ready to face the criminal charges, that you are competent to stand trial, we can go to court and oppose the hospital's application to keep you here. However, if you don't feel ready to go to trial and want to stay here, you can. Any time you decide you want to leave this hospital to go to trial, I can ask the court to send you back. Those are your choices."

Still no response.

"Dr. Dirk doesn't think you're ready, and there is no hurry as far as I'm concerned, but this is your life. You decide. Just tell me what you want."

"I want a brown piece of paper and either a pen or pencil," she said, "it doesn't matter. Give me a piece of that bag. No, not the pad, the bag. It must be brown. Yes, that's good."

She ripped off a small piece of the bag in which I carried my lunch and flattened it out on the table before us. Then carefully, she wrote on it, covering her writing with her left arm, which circled over the top, as though she didn't want me to see her paper. Then she gave it, and my pen, back to me.

On one side she had written: "Doctor Eugene Dirk, Kirby Forensic Psychiatric Center, 600 East 125th Street, Ward's Island, New York. Date of Birth: September 17, 1955."

On the other she'd written: "Leave Me Alone!"

"Now take this," she said, "and put it in your freezer. He did not give me his real address. He is very parsimonious with anything important, especially information. But I have his date of birth, and that will be enough. Put this paper in your freezer. Put it there, and don't ask questions. That is what I want. Now go away."

I am often told to go away. I am used to it, and I don't take it personally. I speculated that Dr. Dirk *had* taken personally the questions that Mary had asked him about himself, although her desire for this information was for very different purposes than he had envisioned. By putting personal information* about him into a freezer, she was casting a spell intended to make him "chill out" and stop pushing medication at her.

I believed her intended magic was not so much a sign of mental illness as an indication that she held a different set of beliefs. (I can't even call them an unconventional set of beliefs, since many more people the world over believe in demons and magic spells than in psychiatry.) Of course, cynics might say that she was deliberately posing as mentally debilitated in order to postpone going to trial,

---

* In accordance with hospital policy, he'd told her very little—only his date of birth.

but I didn't think so. The hospital was already so much like jail that she wasn't getting away with anything; the best exit for her was criminal court.

On my next visit she brought her mother to meet with me.

"We want you to represent us both," she said. "Our criminal lawyer does, and we also want you to. We waive any conflict of interest you might have. It's better for us. We want the same result."

Mary's mother, Tasha, was forty-four years old. She had the same haunting blue eyes as her daughter, but a battered, withered expression obscured what once must have been great beauty. When she opened her mouth to speak, I could see her teeth were filed to nubs, small and flat-topped and brown with stains. I found this so disconcerting that I made a point not to say anything about her appearance. Patients often get upset if they believe you are critical of their looks, and I didn't want to upset her. "These women are not sick," Tasha Sants told me in a rapid whisper. "Evil spirits infect this place, and they are infested. We can help them. We are not witches, we are healers. We must minister to our sisters. They need us.

"Eugene Dirk is not a real doctor," she continued. "He lives in Satan's shadow, and like Satan, he is an accuser, an adversary. In ancient Hebrew, the language of the Old Testament, the word *Satan* means adversary. He tries to fool us to confess to a crime. We did no crime.

"As you know from the book of Job, piety is seen as self-interest by perverted eyes. Dr. Dirk is suspicious, and he lives for entrapment. He wants to poison us, kill us. He is persecutor, prosecutor, and executor, but we are not guilty. Maybe we are crazy?" she asked, raising her left eyebrow.

Like much of the public, many of my clients are fooled by myths that surround the insanity plea—misinformation that is presented as accepted fact but is just plain wrong. Part of my job is exposing these myths so that my clients can make the right decisions regarding their cases. Both Mary and Tasha, for example, seemed delighted to have learned from their criminal defense attorney that the insanity defense was not limited to murder cases. They came to Kirby with the full expectation that a successful insanity defense would mean that they'd be released in a few short months, after the psychiatrists had concluded that they were not (or were no longer) crazy. But that was fantasy. It was my duty to inform them of reality.

"Ms. Sants. . . ."

"*Mrs*. Sants," she corrected me.

"Mrs. Sants," I began again, "you may not understand everything I am about to say, and that is okay. I will say it again. I just want you to think about my words.

"If you think the insanity plea is just an easy scam," I explained, "then you need to get educated. As you were told by your criminal lawyer, when you go back to criminal court, you will have three choices: you can plead not guilty, not guilty by reason of insanity, or guilty.

"If you raise the insanity plea at your criminal trial and you are unsuccessful and get convicted, statistics indicate you will get a longer sentence than if you do not. But if you are successful, it may be even worse. Rarely does a successful insanity defense lead to a quick release.

"I'm not saying that I know what will happen exactly. And you have some advantages. In my experience, judges are less frightened by women. But, statistically speaking, perhaps with the exception of murder, people who are acquitted by reason of insanity spend almost twice as much time locked up as defendants found guilty of similar charges. And then, when they're finally released, they are subject to years of follow-up supervision by the hospital, the courts, and the district attorney, and they cannot leave the state.

"Regardless of whether or not you raise the insanity plea, if you are convicted, you will get the time spent at the hospital as time served—and it will be set off against your sentences.

"Think about it."

They both looked at me suspiciously. The mother made the sign of the cross. "We were only trying to help," she said. "We didn't know it was wrong."

Everybody who gets caught says that: they didn't know it was wrong. That simple concept—lack of mental intent—forms the basis of most defenses to criminal charges that require a knowing wrongfulness. To an even greater degree, that concept also forms the backbone of the insanity defense: in order to be eligible for a plea of insanity, a perpetrator cannot know or appreciate the nature of his act or know that his act was wrong.

"Your belief in spirits is your own affair as far as I'm concerned, but your belief will not be accepted by Dr. Dirk, who thinks you both are delusional and psychotic. He also thinks that Mary is sexually obsessed with him. If either or both of you come back to this hospital as insanity acquittees, he will be your doctor because this is the only women's ward, and he is the only doctor for it. He will feel the need to change you. That is his job.

"Here at Kirby they have to change your mind before they let you go. If you want psychiatric help, I'd recommend voluntary treatment outside the forensic hospital setting."

"I will not take his drugs!" Mary cried. "They make you ugly. They make you shudder and shake, and your tongue comes twisting out. They make you fat and old. I will not take any drugs. I'd rather hear voices than dope my soul and spirit with that poison. Those other women, they pollute their spirits with what Dr. Dirk calls medicine and walk like zombies in a fog. He tells me, 'Look how much better Sheila is doing'—the same Sheila who likes to sleep on the bathroom floor." She whined this part, exaggeratedly imitating Dr. Dirk's gentle coaxing. "It's disgusting!" she cried. "But what he wants to do to me and my mother is worse than disgusting. It's tragic! It is nothing but a witch hunt, and I want to see a priest. Not that old fool chaplain, but a *real* Catholic priest. An exorcist!"

She was really working herself into a frenzy. She seemed much more fragile than her mother, much less calculating and practical. It wasn't what she said as much as it was her whole persona. Pain and confusion played across her face. Suddenly I had the feeling she wanted me to go.

As I got up to leave, Tasha said to me coolly, "You've been looking at my teeth. Don't deny it. I saw you!" I could see anger flash into her eyes and her brow furrow—and then I saw her force herself to relax. "You know," she said, almost in a whisper, "a short time ago I had beautiful teeth, the best money could buy. While I was in prison my caps fell off. When we get out of here, I want you to sue my dentist. I can pay."

Once upon a time, all mentally ill people were considered to be possessed by demonic spirits. However, with the advent of modern medicine and particularly psychiatry over the last fifty years or so, the witch hunts of earlier ages became discredited. Psychiatrists displaced priests in many circles as the custodians of inner peace, and the belief that science would someday answer all questions had its passing moment.

In recent years, people have lost their faith in the miracles of science as well, and from New York to Rome, from Switzerland to Siberia, from China to Brazil, a belief in spiritual possession has been rising worldwide. America's leading Catholic prelate, John Cardinal O'Connor, has authorized a growing number of exorcisms in the New York archdiocese, and Pope John Paul II has expanded the number of priests performing exorcisms in Turin and Rome.

Despite the continuing struggle between religion and psychiatry, I did not believe that the Santses' faith in the existence of evil spirits and practice of exorcism necessarily meant they were mentally ill. I considered this their religious conviction, and I supported their right to refuse medication in part because I didn't really believe they needed treatment. They didn't believe in psychiatry. I didn't think any doctor had the right to attack their spiritual beliefs.

On behalf of Mary and Tasha Sants I sought advice from a psychiatrist with whom I had worked in the past. Dr. Bauer, looking as always a little like Santa Claus, leaned back in his leather chair and put his feet up on the desk when I dropped by his office. "Have a seat," he said. "What's on your mind?" As I told him the story he nodded sympathetically, noting that exorcists have been in business for more than fifty centuries. "Today's times are more tolerant of all beliefs. Exorcism has helped some people recover sanity when other means alone have not been successful. In these rare cases, exorcism has been of significant value when used in a conscientiously applied program of mental hygiene and regular professional psychiatric care," he told me, sounding disconcertingly like a toothpaste commercial.

"An exorcist's approach can be useful in the modern age," he continued, "particularly if your clients came from a sociocultural setting that subscribes to the idea of demonic possession. Working closely with an exorcist, priest or otherwise, might be helpful because the ritualistic setting, the incantations, and the authority of a religious faith can soothe a troubled psyche." He was pragmatic: if something works, use it.

"Dr. Bauer," I asked, thinking that he might be useful to the Santses in criminal court, "would you be willing to testify to the clinical legitimacy of exorcism at a criminal trial? I'm not their criminal attorney, you understand, but I was just wondering."

He abruptly declined, suddenly remembered another appointment, and ushered me out. But he did refer me to Martin Molina, a psychiatrist at Bellevue Hospital who had made a study of this area.

Dr. Molina, regarded as the reigning expert in folk belief systems in the New York area, was more than willing to meet with me once I told him I had been referred by Dr. Bauer. On the telephone I pictured myself speaking to a distinguished gentleman in a lab coat, his gray hair in a clipped military crewcut. When we met I was surprised. Despite his lab coat—I was right about that—he was the youngest-looking psychiatrist I'd ever met. And although he did wear his hair clipped short, it had the unexpected effect of making him look like a punk rocker. He spoke with a great air of dignity and reserve, as though to compensate for his youthful appearance.

According to his research, community spiritualists (whether you call them exorcists, *santeras,* priests, or witches) functioned as local religious leaders for those groups of people who recognized them as such. Mentally ill individuals within these groups were not ostracized but instead legitimized by their respective community spiritualists. Because people hearing voices or having other manifestations of psychosis were embraced by these spiritualists, they were more likely to be accepted by other members of their community. Thus the social network of mentally ill persons was essentially extended by community spiritualists, whose ministrations further reinforced feelings of self-worth and helped such persons cope with their problems.

He noted that on staff at Lincoln Hospital in the Bronx there was a *santera* from whom patients on the psychiatric ward could get "treatment" that was culturally congruent with their beliefs that an external force, such as a bad spirit or a curse, was causing the symptoms. The psychiatric approach of Western medicine, by contrast, confronts patients with their internal selves as the source of their mental problem, a practice that tends to be misunderstood as blaming the patient. Dr. Molina had found that the spiritualist's recommendations to patients and their families were more readily embraced than the psychiatrist's, often with positive results—and a recommendation by a *santera* working with a psychiatrist that a particular patient take prescribed medication could give that patient both the blessings of modern medicine and the comforts of traditional spiritual healing.

But when I asked Dr. Molina if he could help my clients either with an exorcism or with testimony, he laughed. "I don't know a thing about actual technique. Call Father Robert Mahoney, over at Kings Park Psychiatric Center. He's one of the leading exorcists for the Catholic archdiocese of New York. And as far as testimony is concerned, I won't be an effective court witness until I lose this face," he said with his right index finger on his cheek. "It's a child's face. Who would believe a child?"

Speaking to me from his office by telephone, Father Mahoney also espoused a practical approach. More than Drs. Bauer and Molina had, however, he distinguished clearly between spiritual infestation and mental illness. According to him, the church's position was quite strict, recognizing mental illness as a medical disorder and requiring that it be eliminated as a cause of the symptoms of a potential "possession" before an exorcism could be sanctioned. He made it clear that mental illness did not necessarily rule out demonic possession, but only after psychiatric testing had been exhausted and science had no more answers could exorcism be considered as a remedy. Particularly where mental illness was suspected, Father Mahoney insisted on psychiatric input. He suggested a trial of medication for the Santses.

"Don't you think you ought to see them before you conclude that they should take medication?" I asked.

"No," he replied. "That won't be necessary. I'm really very busy and cannot drive two hours to Manhattan merely because some mental patients claim they're possessed. You have no idea how many calls like this I get. Just send me the psychiatric reports. You have my address."

I had discussed with the Santses my intention to seek outside experts before I contacted anyone, and they accepted what I told them about my interviews with Drs. Bauer and Molina without comment. But when I told them what Father Mahoney had said, they looked as though they were going to be physically ill. They had vested a lot of their faith in the priesthood, knew of Father Mahoney as the most prominent exorcist in this geographic area, and had come to believe he would be their salvation. Now that bubble had burst. His legitimization of Dr. Dirk's recommendation for medication appalled them.

"He feels threatened!" cried Tasha. "The ruling patriarchy wishes to reduce the competition—yes, that's it, those bastards want to preserve the sexist monopoly they never had!" cried Tasha, her eyes rolling. She seemed quite mad, but a moment later she looked cool and rational, even pensive. She and Mary dropped their demand for an exorcist and decided they were ready to go to trial. My recent efforts must have persuaded them that I could be trusted, because for the first time they were garrulous.

It was then that I began to see the basis for each of them having her own lawyer and to question my decision to represent them both. They were such different people, despite their "shared delusions" (as Dr. Dirk would have it), that their cases could require very different approaches—although the importance of separate attorneys was likely to matter less at the hospital than it would in criminal court.

Mary was drifting in her speech, clearly confused, in her own world. Although she was talking almost incessantly, her voice had dropped so low that I got the impression she was talking to herself. Tasha, in contrast, rose like a phoenix. Her words were measured and logical, and although it was a logic to which I did not subscribe, there was no hint of madness to it.

"As long as we're here we will be treated as though we are crazy. I am an educated woman," Tasha stated in a voice filled with measured pride. "I am a disciple of Jesus. Like Jesus, I too am an exorcist. My belief in the spirit world is founded on ancient principles. I was ordained according to the Fourth Council of Carthage, Seven, and the Tenth Canon of the Council of Antioch. I have been in serious study for twenty-five years and have trained with *Santeria* and *Espiritsmo* spiritualists from Rhode Island to Vancouver. I am familiar with Freud, Jung, and a whole bunch of other phonies. The primary distinction between psychoanalysis and *espirista*, other than semantics, is that *espirista* works."

She explained the hierarchy of the spirit world to be a pyramid, with God at the pinnacle, followed by the pure spirits (the angels), then the saints, and then the heroes and leaders, with the spirits of ordinary people forming a broad base beneath all of those above. Finally, still part of the spiritual pyramid but spilling into the world of incarnate spirits, were the intranquil spirits, those spirits that do not know they are dead. They wander among us—the living, incarnate spirits—and sometimes attempt to take over our bodies, which results in a great struggle. As exorcists, Tasha said, their job was to assist the living in their fight against the dead.

"This place should be run by priests, not doctors. The women here are troubled, not sick. I am skeptical of 'scientific progress'—science will not create heaven on earth. Mary and I could do more good in a month than ten Dr. Dirks in a year. We had clients on a waiting list. We were successful entrepreneurs. We didn't need guaranteed clientele provided by a state institution. Our clients came to us by word of mouth.

"We advertised only a little, fliers, that sort of thing, but there were so many gypsies out there"—she spat the word *gypsies* as though it were a curse—"that the fliers, they brought in only people who were out for amusement, not very serious, not much money. Young men and their lady friends, that sort of thing. Some will be back for afflictions, this I know, but not for many years. Our real clients, the ones who need us, they are in pain, seething pain. They are seekers who find us because of someone we brought peace. Someone who loves them told them about us. We interview them before any money changes hands to decide if we can help. Some we have to turn away. But spiritual infestations, that is our specialty. We doctor their souls.

"In a series of sessions—treatments, if you will—over a course of weeks or even months, we use our powers to call the bad spirits away from the host. We use ritual, incantation, and a secret religious magic. Mary is a born healer and has a special gift. We work together to draw out the evil, at great risk to ourselves, and we charge accordingly. We are not venal. Often we do not charge enough. We take what our clients can afford. What they have. And if we are not successful, we do not keep the money. How many doctors can say that? Sixteen thousand dollars for a three-hour operation, and my husband still died. And whoever heard of a psychiatrist returning a fee?"

We talked about their clients, maybe two dozen, but the Santses wouldn't tell me their names. Reasons of confidentiality, they said, private business. Mary couldn't believe the people they saved would turn on them. It had to be the evil spirits' revenge; that was the only explanation.

"We did good for them, all of them," said Mary in a whisper. "One old lady came to us when she could barely talk. She was weak and could not fight the spirits. Her sister who brought her to us, she told us she sat on a hard wooden bench howling day and night. Like living death. She had very bad spirits, smart but ignorant. When they finally quit her, they would not recognize they were dead; they sought new bodies. They wanted revenge. Mother and I had put ourselves in peril. I thought we were ready."

She looked sad, fooled, baffled.

Tasha smiled ruefully. "We were so sure that we could do the job," she said, "so cocky of our ability to exorcise Satan's miserable agents. We were guilty of the sin of pride. We were not humble, and our pride made us weak. We made ourselves vulnerable. And now we pay the price. The 'doctors,' my daughter and myself, have caught the disease. We need a real priest. Not that Mahoney, he is an agent of darkness. I know a good priest we'll go see when we get out, and we will get out because we are not guilty. That much of the future I can foretell. Who's to say we aren't true believers?"

"That's an issue for the jury," I said.

Mary, too, was sure they'd be acquitted. "We performed a valuable service. How much we charge for our services is nobody's business. We got results!"

They were both willing to plead guilty to practicing exorcism without a license, or even to engaging in the unlicensed practice of medicine (certainly psychiatrists practice a form of exorcism), if only to be rid of the criminal charges. But fraud? That, Tasha noted, required criminal intent. And their intent was benevolent, like a doctor's. And if they charged like doctors, well, they had trained like doctors.

"We can't be convicted of fraud because of a number of reasons," Tasha told me, counting off on her fingers. "One, evil spirits do exist. Two, we believe they exist. Three, even if they didn't exist, our belief that they do is enough to negate any intent to defraud. The state will have to prove that evil spirits don't exist and that we don't believe in them, and that is impossible. We will be acquitted. I don't need my crystal ball to tell me that."

I felt compelled to point out, however, that if the jury found beyond a reasonable doubt that they had deliberately and systematically bilked innocent people of money through intentional trickery with the aim of self-enrichment, then they probably would be convicted. "That's a matter you should fully discuss with your criminal attorney."

They looked at each other and then at me.

"Our clients would never betray us," said Mary.

"In all honesty," I replied, "they already have. There's a nineteen-count indictment, most of it based on the accusations of people you say are loyal clients. Their testimony will be the district attorney's primary evidence."

"No, no," said Tasha. "I think they know better than to tempt the devil. Lying is a sin. They will not betray us."

I paused for a moment and said, "Maybe you should think again."

I always give my clients at least the benefit of the doubt, but Tasha was straining my credulity. Her easy discussion of the elements of fraud led me to believe she'd had more experience with the criminal justice system than she let on. When I questioned her about this, she claimed that her defense attorney had explained it all to her, but Elly had told me that Tasha was practically raving when they tried to discuss the criminal case. Tasha was convinced she could control the situation, when in fact she was too clever for her own good.

The next morning the Santses and I spoke again. "We want to leave," Mary said. "We are ready to go to trial."

If they wanted to be found fit, it was my duty to do my best to see that they were. I had no doubt that Tasha had the nature of criminal court within her mental grasp, but I was not sure about Mary. I expressed my view that perhaps they shouldn't be treated as a unit but as two individuals. They were obstinate, though, insisting that it was their decision, not mine. They wanted to go back to criminal court *together*. And while it was true it was not my decision, it was not entirely theirs either. They had to convince the psychiatric staff (or, failing that, a judge) that they were able to stand trial. "You must show an understanding of the criminal court system, including the roles of the prosecutor, the judge, and the jury," I said. "You also must be able to cooperate with your attorney."

"Yes, we can do that," Tasha said. Mary nodded her head in agreement, so later that day I stopped in at the office of Dr. Dirk. He had a few moments to discuss this case, so I put on my most affable personality and made my pitch. As lawyers do, I exaggerated for effect.

"You know, Doctor," I said, "there's really no risk to anybody in sending the Santses back to criminal court, even if you are not entirely convinced that they are fit. If psychiatrists at the Women's House of Detention feel they are unable to go to trial because of their mental condition, they will be sent back to Kirby, that's all, and no harm done. And certainly the district attorney will not object to their being found fit; now he will have his opportunity to go for a conviction." All of this was true enough, although if the Santses revolved between Kirby and the Department of Corrections, it would be systemically inefficient. "Furthermore, if they actually are fit, however borderline, and they aren't returned for trial, their criminal lawyer will have a basis to move to dismiss the charges because of the state's failure to afford her clients a speedy trial." While theoretically correct, this was a real long shot. The Santses were being held on a judge's order, so any challenge to that order would likely fail. But I said it because I thought it would help them get what they wanted. It was a bluff posing as a subtle threat.

"Let's set up a meeting," Dr. Dirk replied, smiling. He really was a decent guy, trying to do the right thing. "If they seem fit," he continued, "we can send them back without a judge. If I don't think they're fit, you can bring a writ of habeas corpus, as you're always threatening to do, and we can have a judge decide."

So we arranged to meet the following morning, just the four of us, in the Ward 3 West conference room. Dr. Dirk was a trifle late. Just as our meeting was scheduled to begin, a great commotion had come from the patients' dayroom, and he had been called away to sedate a patient who'd embarked on a slugfest. When he joined us, he was slightly short of breath, and his brow was covered with beads of perspiration. He wore a cotton plaid shirt, mostly red, with a white plastic pocket protector advertising the Merck pharmaceutical company; he had paired it with striped blue pants and white high-top basketball sneakers. He was short and balding with tufts of wiry blonde hair sticking out at either side of his head. In short, he looked as strange as some of his patients. Since his divorce, it seemed to me, he'd been making it a point to dress this way in defiance of his stylish ex-wife's influence. I tried to discuss his anti-fashion statement as a means of breaking the ice and introducing a note of informality to our meeting, but he waved me off, clearly annoyed. He suggested we get right down to confirming the Santses' fitness for trial: What does a judge do? What does a district attorney do? What does the jury do? What does the defense attorney do? What is a plea bargain?

He fired these and other questions at Mary and Tasha in rapid succession. The Santses responded so knowledgeably that it was clear they'd had experience with the criminal justice system in the past, confirming my earlier suspicions. They correctly answered all of Dr. Dirk's questions, even fairly sophisticated questions that neophytes to criminal trials often get wrong. Occasionally I'd lean over and whisper to one or the other to demonstrate that they indeed could cooperate with their attorney. Finally, Dr. Dirk said they might be "borderline fit" despite their delusions, and he agreed to send them back to trial without a judicial order. Six weeks later, the typical time frame, they were picked up by the Department of Corrections.

Usually I lose track of former clients who have been returned to the criminal system, and unless they return to the mental hospital I expect not to see them again. But because I knew Elly MacIntyre-Cohen, I felt I had an excuse to stay in touch. I cautioned her against raising the insanity plea. I told her what I could about legitimizing exorcism through psychiatric testimony; it was a tough theory to sell but still viable if she could get it into evidence. I gave her the names of the two doctors I'd interviewed, explaining that although neither had expressed interest in testifying, one or both might be persuaded to appear if approached just right. "I don't know," Elly said. "The whereabouts of the money are still unknown to me, and I can't get a thing out of the girls. They ponied up my retainer pretty quick, but they really don't like psychiatrists. I'll speak to a few doctors as long as they don't have their meters running, see if I can get a handle, but my guess is the trial isn't going to go in that direction. It looks like the most damning evidence is pure gypsy scam. Come on down when the trial gets going; we can have lunch."

"I don't think I can get away, Elly. Things have been pretty crazy here at the mental hospital."

"Well, see what you can do. And thanks for your suggestions."

Five weeks later I was downtown in criminal court on another matter (in rare cases, a criminal court judge will maintain jurisdiction of an insanity acquittee), and I happened by the courtroom where the Santses' case was being tried. My own case had been adjourned temporarily because a witness had gotten stranded out in Brooklyn, and I had a few hours to kill.

The witness testifying as I quietly entered the courtroom was a white-haired old woman named Dorrie Little. She was explaining why it was that she gave every penny she had to two women who claimed to be exorcists. I could barely see the Santses, but in a glimpse from my vantage point I did notice that Tasha's teeth had been recapped.

In painful, stumbling testimony, Mrs. Little told her story, coaxed by a young assistant district attorney. The difficulty she had expressing herself only made her words more believable. I looked over at Elly at the defense table. I felt sure she was considering what a sympathetic witness Mrs. Little was to the jury and how badly it would go for her clients if she were to attack too forcefully on cross-examination.

Mrs. Little explained that her dreams had begun turning to nightmares several months before she'd met the Santses. Her deceased husband came to her in those horrible dreams, berating her, screaming in words she couldn't understand. She had become so preoccupied that she stopped eating and sleeping properly, and she lost her ability to talk in full sentences. She could only mutter a word or two at a time, and only then with the greatest effort. Her sister, concerned, pushed her to seek spiritual counseling; she gave her a leaflet that promised results. The address was on lower Second Avenue. Immediately upon meeting the Santses, Mrs. Little felt she'd come to the right place. These women seemed to know all about her, what her problems were. More importantly, they described solutions, and Mrs. Little was desperate for solutions. Over the next several weeks Tasha and Mary convinced her to part with twenty-two thousand dollars.

"It was so much money," Mrs. Little said. She looked very tiny and old up there on the witness stand, dwarfed by everything and everyone around her. "It was all I had, but I was frightened. I didn't want to give them everything. I tried to make a deal. I had already given Madame Tasha five thousand dollars after the first treatment, and now she wanted more. She scared me.

"We met in the same dark room as the first time, a storefront with the curtains drawn, but she was burning something that made a different smell than before. I sat there for a long time before Madame Tasha would look at me. I was squeezing my hands together, she made me so nervous, and then suddenly she turned to me and looked right through me; then she reached across the table that was between us, grabbed my hand and put a warm egg in my palm. 'Just hold it,' she said, so I did. We sat there for a long time and then, like she was in a trance, she said, real spooky-like, 'The seeds of the spirits inside you are inside the egg I take from you,' and she took back the egg she had given to me. 'Now relax. Be strong. Put your faith in Christ. Don't scream.'

"Well, when she said, 'Don't scream,' I got really scared and thought something terrible was about to happen. Madame Tasha held the egg up in front of my eyes. I was wheezing pretty good because of that stuff she was burning, and looking behind her at a wooden crucifix with a silver Jesus the size of a child. It was lit up real nice, it gave me comfort, and everything else was so dark. I couldn't look at that egg, it scared me, but she kept shoving it at me.

"Then she said, 'There is no other light but Jesus,' over and over, like a chant, and she held the egg above her head. 'Believers will be saved, and the wicked spirits driven from them. Scoffers will be consumed by serpents, eaten from the inside by evil spirits.'

"Then she paused and looked through me again. Suddenly she smashed the egg into a small silver bowl on the table." Her face curled in a disgusted grimace. "Worms! Hundreds of them, pulsing and waving! Like maggots! Like sickly white snakes! They were writhing, reaching for me from the broken shell. I was scared. Sick to my stomach. 'God help me!' I screamed, throwing myself onto the floor.

" 'God helps those who help themselves,' said Madame Tasha calmly, and she turned away. " 'Mary!' she called loudly. 'Mary! We need some help!'

"Then Mary entered the room. She was dressed in white taffeta and she carried a candle. She knelt beside me. 'Maybe we can save Dorrie Little,' she said to her mother. 'Maybe not. It will be painful. It will be expensive. Dorrie Little has to really want it. I don't think she does. The spirits will have to go back inside her,' and she shoved that sickening silver bowl toward my mouth.

" 'Please help me, Mary.' I pleaded. 'I'm so afraid.'

" 'I think the serpent spirits have Dorrie Little's soul,' said Mary, talking about me like I wasn't there. 'Look at them writhe. But they are still small, and I can save her. Yes, if she believes in me, and in Jesus, I can save her now. Soon it will be too late.'

" 'Oh, save me!' I cried. 'Thank you, thank you!'

"I would have thanked her for throwing me out a window. Just to get me away from those worms.

"Then I threw up."

I stayed abreast of the rest of the trial by telephone consultation with Elly, but I was unable to be present.

"How's it going?"

"Not so great," she replied. "You saw that little old lady? Well, there're ten more who'll be just as bad for the Santses as she was. And the judge is an idiot. Over my strenuous objection he qualifies as an "expert" some oily old man who testifies that a hypodermic needle can be used to inject a kind of roundworm into a hen's egg, and he demonstrates the result. It was disgusting. There's a long-shot basis for appeal, but writing briefs has never been my favorite, and the Santses are tight, extremely tight, with the cash. I mean, if it comes to dental work, well, that's another story—you check out the caps on old Mama Sants? Then she goes for the big bucks. But for an appeal, with no guarantees? She looked at me like I was a thief, and I was only making a passing reference."

"If you're talking appeal, I guess it looks pretty bad."

"It does look bad, all right. And the funny thing is, they really seem to believe both in spirits and in themselves as exorcists. So they really shouldn't be convicted, but they used so many tricks and illusions to convince their clients they had unworldly powers they have probably conned themselves right into the big house."

The "big house"—leave it to Elly to make light when things were so grim. She loved those old movie clichés. But I understood her sentiment. When law is your profession, you are aware that "truth" is a subjective choice. Elly could not actually know what was in the Santses' heads, and in terms of her obligation it did not actually matter what she thought; nevertheless, she chose to believe they did not have the requisite mental intent to be guilty of fraud. Her job was to take their position, to make their defensive case. She chose to believe them innocent.

"My defense starts tomorrow. I don't want to call Tasha to the

stand because you can see her brain ticking just watching her.
I know she's just trying to figure a way out. She really believes
that what they did was a bargain and sale and that no fraud was
involved—but she's got that way about her, she just reeks of
scam. Sure, we can put in a good direct case, and she can tell the
jury about her fine education in matters of occult and of her
eminent qualifications to perform delicate exorcisms, but on cross-
examination the D.A. will kill her. If she were still acting crazy, then
maybe I could use her for some sympathy, but how is she going
to explain those worms, for one?

"I told her I wasn't calling her as a witness this morning. So we
had a big fight, and she threatened to fire me. And I wish she had,
because I hate to lose in court. I'd much rather get canned.

"I do intend to call Mary to the stand because she's so guileless,
so vulnerable. And I think she'll do a pretty good job, but I'm not
too optimistic. It wouldn't be too hard to make her nonstandard beliefs look like delusions—or vice versa, depending on your point of
view—but the jury's not buying that Mary and her mother were in-
nocently telling fortunes and driving away evil spirits for over a third
of a million dollars.

"If we raised the insanity plea, I think it would be a new ball-
game. I know what you said before about the insanity plea, and
you're right, of course, but things are looking pretty grim right now.
Have you got any good advice?"

"I guess it's too late to call those doctors we spoke about earlier?"
I ventured. "I know you're tight for time, but maybe you could make
it a battle of experts, with your experts being doctors—scientists—
against the prosecution's gypsy trickster. After letting that guy qualify, I can't imagine the judge could keep a real doctor's testimony
out of evidence. If these doctors tell the jury what they told me, I
think the jury might view exorcism in a different light." Even I knew
it wasn't a great idea, but one must try to keep hope alive.

"Thanks for the suggestion, but it's way too late." Apparently Elly
had already spoken with both Dr. Bauer and Dr. Molina, but to no
avail. I wished her luck and hung up.

Her position regarding the Santses was not so different from what my own had been. When I represented them it did not matter whether I thought they were malingering (faking a mental disorder), psychotically delusional, or neither. Whether they were scam artists who sold snake oil without belief in its medicinal properties or true believers with a different doctrine than that of the dominant culture, I was their lawyer, not their doctor. I was concerned about their legal condition. But I too chose to believe that their belief in the infestation of evil spirits was real, along with their belief in their own special powers. Because of the risks they believed they took and the expertise they brought to the enterprise of exorcism, I believed they felt entitled to the thousands of dollars they were paid. They claimed to operate much like therapists do, relieving distress through a technique that is as successful, and as legitimate, as many therapeutic "treatments."

In a free society one should be able to trade one's expertise to a willing buyer for an agreed-upon price. The fact that the Santses "enhanced" their exorcisms with theatrics did not necessarily negate their underlying belief in evil spirits. In their own minds it may have been part of the rite, and, psychiatrically speaking, it would have reinforced the effectiveness of their roles as exorcists. As Dr. Bauer would agree, the subject of exorcism who fully believes in the capabilities of the exorcist experiences a greater sense of recovery than one who does not; it is akin to the psychiatric position that only those who believe in voodoo can be affected by voodoo. The Santses had had a history of success. They had succeeded, for example, with Dorrie Little. When she came to them she was so frightened she could barely speak; now she was capable of speaking up for herself in a crowded courtroom.

Could I believe the Santses were successful charlatans who sold their technique in exorcism as a form of religious fraud? Well, that was one way to construe the evidence, particularly in light of the sums involved. Certainly Dorrie Little was a sympathetic witness. But truth is elusive and subject to interpretation—that much is clear when law is your profession—and one's view of the truth is often subject to a conscious choice. I chose to find them innocent. The jury had other ideas.

At the conclusion of the trial, in spite of Elly's putting a sympathetic Mary on the stand, twelve jurors found beyond a reasonable doubt that Mary and Tasha Sants had induced others to believe in powers they themselves *knew* they did not possess. I do not believe the jury was correct, but I can understand how such a verdict was reached. It was the worms—and the money. The jury no doubt concluded that so much money was clearly a motive for fraud. Tasha Sants was sentenced to ten years in the state correctional facility for women, and Mary to five years.

Maybe they would have been better off at a mental hospital than prison, but I don't think so. Certainly not Mary. After she had worked her way through the Kirby system, she would have been transferred to the civil system and gone through the whole psychiatric process once again. To escape both hospital systems as quickly as she completed her sentence for fraud would have required a level of cooperation—a willingness to trust the psychiatrist's judgment over her own—that few patients can muster. Mary wasn't the type. If she'd pleaded insanity, been acquitted on that basis, and sent to Kirby, she would have spent many unhappy years as doctors poked at her mind. They'd have wanted her to take drugs, and her refusal would have worked against her. The doctors would have forced her to become someone else; despite all that prying and prodding, state-administered psychiatry rarely evokes a happy cure. Mary would get out of prison in substantially less time than she would have the mental hospital, in all likelihood with less stress.

Timewise, Tasha Sants might have broken even. Still, if Tasha behaves herself in prison, I expect she'll be out shortly. And Mary, who was released after three years, will be waiting. That's how prison goes; you serve a portion of your sentence, and they let you out.

I understand that Mary set up shop again as a spiritual advisor in another state. What other business does she know? It's better than prostitution. And if she stays small-time, offering spiritual comfort to believers without getting greedy, she can avoid a repeat performance in jail or the mental hospital.

I never did find out what happened to the money.

Today I believe the Santses should not have been mental patients at all, although certainly their temporary detour into the mental health system was not a miscarriage of justice. Mary was flustered, but her confusion did not rise anywhere near the level of true mental illness. Anyone in a tough situation like Mary's is bound to be somewhat unsure, although Tasha seemed to believe she could control both systems through scheming and the strength of her will. Maybe that was her real delusion—the delusion of hustlers everywhere until they are caught.

Razor Fruitcake

I was once asked by somebody, I don't remember who, if there was any way sex offenders could be stopped. I said no. I was wrong. I was wrong when I said there was no hope, no peace. There is hope. There is peace. I found both in the Lord, Jesus Christ. Look to the Lord and you will find peace. —Last words of Westley Allan Dodd, hanged on January 5, 1993, in Walla Walla, Washington, for the sex slayings of three boys

I was still a young lawyer, and still new to the mental health business, when I first came to represent Derek Diesel. He was still a young man in his twenties, muscular and barrel-chested. His naturally white hair was cut somewhere between a Mohawk and a military crew, with a bristling ridge rising from his skull like a center crest. His skin was so pale that at first I took him for an albino. He'd contacted me on his doctor's advice, and I sat with him on the plastic furniture in the patient visitors' room, holding his hospital chart on my lap. We didn't speak much; mostly I read from the chart.

173

Diesel had been arrested by the police shortly after he cornered his landlord's adolescent son by the comic-book section of the neighborhood candy store and insisted that the boy accompany him to his room "to talk." The boy refused, Diesel's voice rose, and the shopkeeper called 911. No charges were filed, but the police brought Diesel to Bellevue, and from there he was transferred to Manhattan Psychiatric Center (MPC). He told the doctor that a computer at FBI headquarters in Washington, D.C.—what he called "Radio Free Washington"—was directing him with radio waves to sexually assault this particular child. Despite clear symptoms of a psychosis exacerbated by street drugs*—(including acid, pot, angel dust, uppers, downers, cocaine, and alcohol) he was well educated and held a good position as a copy editor for a slickly published pop science magazine. Initially he had agreed to treatment, but after several days on a locked unit without being "cured," he decided he'd had enough, saying that if he wasn't released, he'd lose his job. That someone with a mental illness has a job is a great inducement for the hospital to release him—a job offers structure, income, and concentrated activity, things that help a fragile mind find balance and health—but in this case the chart indicated that Dr. Bellows, his treating psychiatrist, didn't agree that Diesel was ready to leave.

I was sitting there looking at the chart, with Diesel looking at me, when suddenly there was a knock on the door. It was Dr. Bellows. We'd never met in person, only over the phone. She was a new doctor at MPC. I opened the door and she stepped inside.

She was young, fresh, dark, and tall; quite lovely, really. Her attitude was all business, but I could sense a probing intelligence underlying her polite inquiry—and quite possibly a lively sense of humor, so rare among the doctors here. This last point was pure

---

* A high proportion of young mentally ill patients, whether or not they are officially classified as dangerously mentally ill, have what are called in psychiatric parlance "dual disorders"—in other words, addiction to a controlled substance in addition to some underlying psychiatric disorder. Some clinicians speculate that users of street drugs are seeking as much to medicate themselves for an unrecognized mental illness as to experience the recreational pleasures of getting high. The advent of crack cocaine, with its psychosis-inducing qualities, has led to an upswing in the number of drug-addicted dangerously mentally ill patients.

guesswork. She didn't say anything funny, but there was something about her facial expression, something about her eyes.

"I don't mean to interrupt any confidential discussion you might be having," she said, as she stepped in briskly, "but I thought this might be a chance for the three of us to discuss Mr. Diesel's case face-to-face, to confront the real problems. Would this be a good time? I can come back later if that would be more convenient."

"No, no, Doctor," said Diesel. "You just come right in. That's okay with you, Lawyer, isn't it?"

I had no objection. Sometimes, when a patient and a doctor are in conflict about treatment, a meeting with both doctor and patient can save all of us a lot of time and stress; it's not unusual for everyone to work out an understanding right then and there. After a few niceties, Dr. Bellows came straight to the point.

"Derek, I know why you really want to leave the hospital: you want to get high. But getting high will not help you. You need more treatment," she told him. "You've been medicating yourself with street drugs for so long that you've lost the ability to distinguish between internal and external stimuli. You think that because you have a good job, those drugs are not affecting you, but they are. Pills, marijuana, cocaine, LSD, and all that drinking. Why do you think you do so much of it? You're running away from something. Your imagination has become more real to you than what is actually happening.

"We can beat this problem, but it will take time and work. I'm going to suggest you try some medication for a month or so. You'll find my drugs are much better for you than anything you can get on the street. And that is why I have converted your status to that of an involuntary patient. As I told you when I suggested that you call your lawyer, you have a right to contest this by putting in a seventy-two-hour sign-out letter. You'll be in court within three days. . . . I'm not recommending that you go to court, you understand. I'd rather you didn't. But it is your right. Why don't you talk it over with Mr. Woychuk after I've gone."

"That won't be necessary, Dr. Bellows," he said. "I've already made up my mind. I look forward to seeing you in court. Good day."

He was usually very polite, and this had been noted as evidence of a "manipulative personality" in the hospital chart.

As a court date approaches I like to discuss intended testimony with the treating doctor, who is almost sure to be called as a witness. Dr. Bellows was more forthright than most. She told me that she recognized that lots of delusional people manage quite successfully outside a hospital setting, that Diesel's need for further inpatient treatment was not a simple question of his being ill or not ill, but rather a combination of symptoms and conditions the totality of which were open to subjective interpretation—more like fruit salad than merely distinguishing apples from oranges. She acknowledged she could be wrong; like human lives, mental illness can be complicated. Nevertheless, she felt that releasing Diesel would be premature. She intended to testify that although he was improving, his psychosis was still apparent, and that if he were released prematurely he'd be back through the revolving door soon. She was going to request six months' further retention for fuller treatment, with the expectation that they'd be able to release him considerably sooner.

The vast majority of mental health cases that actually come before the court are losers. For every patient granted a judicial release, there are dozens or perhaps hundreds who are not. This is because the outcome of a prospective case is rarely in doubt. Most court-bound patients have a mental condition about which a lawyer can do nothing. If a patient's case looks good, on the other hand, the hospital is usually willing to negotiate a release with conditions or some other result acceptable to the patient in order to avoid litigation. So almost all the winners settle out of court.

Without expert testimony to the effect that Diesel was ready to go, it would be difficult to overcome Dr. Bellows's intended testimony and win a release in court. And I had no such expert. But my responsibility was to give my client the best odds he could get, and I planned to do this by emphasizing Diesel's condition today, in the hospital. He'd been drug-free since his admission, and I would stress to the court that he held a responsible job, which he was in jeopardy of losing—and that this job was the glue that kept his life together. Denying him his freedom would actually jeopardize his mental health by potentially pulling away his livelihood, making him a ward of the state on a potentially long-term basis.

Both Dr. Bellows and I realized that our espoused views were based on our perspectives as doctor and lawyer, respectively, and we both were grateful that the ultimate responsibility lay with a judge. But particularly because Diesel's delusion involved a child, neither of us had any doubt that he would be retained. Courts are loathe to release patients who are a potential threat to children.

As our court day approached—and it was closer to two weeks than three days because the court calendar was overcrowded—Diesel wavered in his resolve. He became ambivalent about release, and Dr. Bellows managed to convince him that until his psychosis was brought under control he was a danger to that young boy. Diesel agreed to stay and to take the medication she was prescribing.

"He'll get better," Dr. Bellows told me a few days later.

My impression of Dr. Bellows at this early point in our acquaintance was that she was exceptional, and this had nothing to do with gender or looks. Women psychiatrists at MPC are hardly a rarity; maybe 40 percent of the doctors I deal with are women. She had been educated at Johns Hopkins and Georgetown, and she was clearly excited by theories of treatment. I sensed she was a good psychiatrist, that she knew about and was comfortable using both drugs and talk therapy. And unlike many psychiatrists, she was still willing to discuss her theories with attorneys, or at least with me.

Now we were having coffee in my MPC office. She was relieved at not having to testify, and I was trying to decide if I were relieved at not having to grill her on the stand. I often make friends with psychiatrists only to have some of them later claim I've "turned" on them in court, even though I am just doing my job.

"Diesel will get better—and the fact that he will is partly my concern," she said as she scrunched her nose in recognition of how bad my coffee was. "We won't hold him for long, because we won't be able to. He wasn't charged with anything criminal. The police brought him to Bellevue, dropped him into the system, and forgot about him. Now, while he's here, he'll be in forced remission from his street drug problem, medication will straighten out his mind, probably get rid of the psychosis, and in a few months he'll be released to the life he had before—only now it will be worse. The system is set up as if time will stop during a patient's hospitalization, but real life rolls along. When we do let him go, he may or may not have a job, but he certainly can't go back to his old apartment—not when his landlord is the victim's father. And the outpatient system is not properly geared to deal with him.

"At the state level, drug treatment and mental health care are divided into different bureaucracies, but patients' problems are not compartmentalized the way agencies are, certainly not Diesel's. The proportion of discharged mentally ill patients who are also dependent on drugs or alcohol more than doubled in the last year, going from 20 to more than 40 percent, but the bureaucrats haven't made any adjustments. They're all worried about their turf and about having in their programs only those outpatients with a high likelihood of success. No one wants clients like Diesel—he's too high-risk. So he'll be sent to a mental health clinic and they'll say, 'Your problem is drugs, not mental illness; we don't treat addicts here,' and send him to a drug clinic. The drug clinic counselor, similarly, will tell him his problem is primarily mental illness and send him back."

She was right, of course. I'd seen that happen before. Clinics compete to keep the lowest-risk patients because impressive-looking statistical results can be used to show that a clinic's program is successful and worthy of continued or even increased funding. As a result, the sickest people and the highest-risk patients usually don't get the best care. As a pedophilic drug user, Diesel was hard to treat and at high risk for relapse.

Dr. Bellows continued: "Derek will bounce between the drug clinic and the mental health clinic, and eventually they'll lose track of him. He'll stop taking the medication. But that's not the scariest part.

"Look at his profile. When Derek was born, his young mother was still in mourning for his father, who had died in a hunting accident when she was halfway through term. From the ages of one though five he was raised by his grandparents while his mother went away to business college on the life insurance money. When she came back, she had a new husband—a blue-collar gambler whom she met at the dog track. She said he made her laugh, but after they were married he turned out to be a tyrant who consigned her to the kitchen despite her business degree. From what I understand, he was a brutal disciplinarian with young Derek. Probably beat him quite severely. And did you notice the burn marks on the back of his hands?"

"No," I said. "I didn't notice."

"They're old, probably from childhood. I suspect his stepfather had something to do with them, but Derek won't talk about them. . . . I even suspect sexual abuse, but Derek denies it. He didn't get his break until his stepfather went to prison for passing bad checks. Derek talks about it like it's no big deal—prison, that is, which only reinforces the picture.

"I would never say this in court—I wouldn't use it to assess future dangerousness—but that kind of profile is very typical of a serial murderer."

"You're crazy!" I blurted out. She'd caught me off guard. I'd been thinking of her as a doctor who was willing to admit that doctors didn't know everything, one who didn't pretend that the hospital's judgment was infallible. She'd been candid and willing to attack the system for which she worked. I thought she might be a potential activist, ready to fight for a better system. But this last remark was completely unexpected, and it seemed so unfounded, that it struck me as dangerous. Doctors like her were exactly why patients like Diesel needed attorneys like me, I found myself thinking. "What kind of doctor are you, anyway?" I asked.

"Don't get yourself into an uproar," she said. "It's just a hunch. He's still a little young, but he could grow into it. I've studied the materials from the FBI Behavioral Sciences Training Center at Quantico, Virginia, and his profile is shaping up nicely." She said *nicely* with such a sneer that I knew she didn't mean it that way at all. "Now all we need is an escalating event to confirm my fears. I'm just guessing, of course. This is certainly not to 'a reasonable degree of scientific certainty.' But this kind of thing is my real area of interest—I don't understand why; I had a perfectly normal childhood—and I'm leaving MPC. I'm going over to Kirby, where I can pursue my interest in the truly twisted," she said with a laugh. Such humor was indeed rare among psychiatrists at both Kirby and MPC.

There is no question Dr. Bellows was right in the short run. The medication worked exceptionally well, and, although Diesel had lost two months of his life to inpatient care, it seemed a happy ending for all parties. The hospital was willing to release him as an outpatient without a court order, and Diesel went back to his Greenwich Village life as a copy editor for a scientific publisher by day, weightlifter by night.

And Dr. Bellows was right in the medium term as well. After three months of excellent voluntary attendance at the 17th Street Clinic, Diesel began to miss appointments. And when he began missing appointments, he wasn't able to get his medication. With an overloaded staff and insufficient manpower to pursue "no-shows," the clinic could do nothing about those outpatients who stopped attending. And a private citizen can miss appointments with his psychiatrist without legal censure.

So it wasn't hard to guess that Diesel would decompensate. And, unfortunately, he wouldn't necessarily know it when it happened. Unlike diabetes, the reappearance of the symptoms of mental illness is generally not coupled with unpleasant physical consequences. When Diesel stopped taking his medication, Dr. Bellows was not there to convince him of his own best interest.

Several months went by without incident, but then Diesel sent a letter to his ex-landlord's son expressing his desire to "touch him where he'd never been touched before." The boy was frightened and told his parents. The boy's father confronted Diesel and Diesel disappeared, supposedly to Texas, where his aunt lived. Nevertheless the boy's parents were cautious, even vigilant, in their concern. The boy, now fourteen, was sent to a boarding school. But he was unhappy there, and when it seemed that all this fuss was much ado about nothing, the boy came back home to his family and friends.

Just before the Easter holidays, a delivery man found the boy unconscious in the vestibule of his parents' brownstone. He was beaten and bloody. His flesh was torn around his neck and shoulders; so was his rectum. When at last he was able to talk, he said that Diesel had bitten through his flesh and had raped him twice, once with a Coca-Cola bottle. Within three or four hours the police found a nearly unconscious Diesel in a local park with an empty bottle of bourbon between his knees. He had pills and pot in his pockets. He was so high he didn't even know he was being arrested.

Derek Diesel was found unfit to stand trial and was sent to Kirby, where he again became my client. Because he'd been criminally charged, his defense counsel was far more important to him legally than I was. Any significant change in his legal circumstance would likely take place at the criminal court level, and my expectation was that he, like most patients initially found unfit, would be found fit within a matter of months. With psychoactive medication as treatment and without the availability of street drugs, Diesel's acute psychosis was expected to lift—at least to the point where he could stand trial. Although I expected to have little to do with him while he was at Kirby, as his in-hospital counsel I still followed the case, obligated to guard his rights as a patient.

Diesel was assigned to Kirby 4 East, which predominantly housed patients also considered unfit. Dr. Bellows, who now worked on a ward for patients acquitted by reason of mental disease or defect, was off the case, and Dr. Sedetto was assigned to be Diesel's psychiatrist. Having worked 4 East for several years, Dr. Sedetto was considered something of an expert in helping unfit patients regain their competence to stand trial.

Any assumption that the mentally unfit defendant is in fact the criminal perpetrator conflicts with the legal presumption of innocence. Dr. Sedetto made it plain to Diesel, however, that only by full acknowledgement of both the crime and the illness could a patient make "true progress." When he was told about the importance of showing insight, Diesel concluded that Dr. Sedetto couldn't be trusted. Diesel said it seemed like a trick to get him to admit his guilt. He told me that Dr. Sedetto was not bound by patient-client confidentiality and would testify to anything that reflected on his condition. "I plead the Fifth," he said.

In a matter of months, Dr. Sedetto tried to send him out as fit, back to criminal court, despite Diesel's insistence that he wasn't ready to go to trial. He said that Diesel was malingering, faking illness, in order to delay his trial.

While Kirby doctors attempt to show that their treatment works by moving patients back to criminal court, the psychiatrists at the Department of Corrections bounce back to Kirby any patient who doesn't appear to understand the charges against him or the nature of court proceedings, as well as any patient who does not appear to have the ability to cooperate with an attorney in his own defense. It can be a matter of a legitimate difference of psychiatric opinion, or of a patient's decompensation once out of the hospital. Sometimes a patient will cycle between Kirby and Corrections for months or even years.

This is the busiest revolving door in the system: Kirby sends them out as fit, Corrections sends them back as unfit. If there is a legitimate question of fitness, even if the patient himself is raising it, a patient should not be forced to go to trial—because in the United States the conviction of a recognized mental incompetent who is unfit to stand trial is unconstitutional. So the determination of the mental condition of the accused at this stage gets lots of latitude. And the general attitude is "no harm done" because, after all, the patient is already locked up, albeit in a hospital; it isn't as if he is out on bail and a threat to the community at large.

While the issue of fitness is being addressed, time stops, at least as far as the criminal case is concerned. But in this case, Dr. Sedetto felt he had an ethical obligation to send Diesel back as fit to face his criminal charges. The doctor believed Diesel was manipulating the system, but the doctor was aware of the difficulties of making a fitness finding stick; he wanted my cooperation. This was a clear conflict of interest for me: I thought that Diesel very likely was fit, but I couldn't take that position publicly. Without promising Dr. Sedetto anything, I agreed to meet with Diesel's treatment team. I was surprised to see Dr. Bellows sitting in as the hospital's consultant. In the course of our meeting we reviewed the facts, and I explained to them that regardless of my personal views I was professionally bound not to betray my client's wishes. Thus there was nothing I could do to help them make a fitness finding stick. Although I might have liked to, I realized that ethically there was nothing I could do.

"There's that escalating event we spoke about back in the old days," Dr. Bellows said as we emerged from the meeting, referring to the rape. I was impressed with her ability to recall our past conversation. "I'm glad I'm not his doctor," she continued. "It's so draining to treat the untreatable. Which isn't to say that he's untreatable—I would never say that about a patient; it'd be bad for my career. And also not to say that I don't have my share of very difficult cases of very ill individuals over on the women's ward. But I'm still in touch with my FBI friends at Quantico. From what I can see, any effective treatment for a guy like Diesel is only temporary. . . . This is pretty sad stuff we've got over here at Kirby. I guess I asked for it."

"You're doing a good job, Doctor," I said. "Hang in."

"I'm even more glad I'm not his lawyer. Want to hear my next prediction?"

"Sure, Doctor B. How about over a cup of coffee?"

"Excellent! How's tomorrow?"

"Fine."

But we didn't get to it. Something came up, some emergency or other, and after a few attempts, it became something of a joke. "I'll have my girl call your girl," she'd say to me as she was rushing past me down the hall, although neither of us had a "girl" who would do that sort of thing.

Diesel was again sent out as fit, but, as I expected, he was bounced back as unfit by the psychiatrists at the Department of Corrections. Three months later he was again sent back to Corrections, where again he was examined by their doctors. He may have left Kirby truly fit and then relapsed while at the Department of Corrections; Corrections may have applied the standard more stringently; or Diesel may have deliberately acted the part of an unfit defendant.

Over the next year and a half he was twice more sent back to Corrections and twice more returned to Kirby as unfit. Finally the hospital decided to respect Diesel's wishes and stopped sending him. Between Corrections and Kirby, Diesel spent almost three years unfit for trial.

During the first of those three years, the boy's parents sold their brownstone in an attempt to help their child forget, and they moved to an apartment uptown, on East 57th Street. The boy didn't want to leave the old neighborhood; he didn't even want to leave the house. He entered a therapy program, but it was apparently a failure, because at seventeen years of age he committed suicide. It was all over the newspapers. The prosecution lost its witness, the criminal case against Diesel fell apart, and Diesel declared himself ready to go to trial.

But by now the district attorney had no case. Without the kid to testify, there was no positive identification, no collaborating evidence, just a bunch of papers that were mostly inadmissible as evidence. There wasn't even a trial: The charges were dropped, and Diesel was released.

After his release, Diesel began to attend the 17th Street clinic again voluntarily. Somehow he knew that without medication he would never get another job. He wanted to overcome his paranoia and stop living in a men's homeless shelter, to get into an apartment of his own. He'd been smart enough to have won a scholarship to a good school when he was a youth. He was still smart. He had a chance.

The medication gave him some mood stability and eliminated his perception that "Radio Free Washington" was still broadcasting sexual commands. But it also made him nauseated. According to the notes in his chart at 17th Street, he felt lethargic, and at times he had the sensation that worms were crawling up under his skin and trying to make their way into his heart. He realized that without the medication his delusions—and he referred to them specifically as "delusions"—would only get worse. He complied with the doctor's directions, and eventually he was able to find work in a downtown bookstore. Certainly it was not the career track that he'd had before, but it was related and he felt he could overcome his past and move back up within a year or two. He took a studio apartment in Chelsea and slowly began to rebuild his life.

During the snowstorms of the next winter, however, he slipped and tore ligaments in his knee. Again he began to miss clinic appointments, and he started getting high to kill the pain. "Radio Free Washington" returned, and one night he raped and killed a young Chinese immigrant, a sixteen-year-old delivery boy who had the misfortune to bring him an order of chicken chow mein. He bit deeply into the boy's neck and shoulders. According to neighbors who called the police, the boy's high screams were followed by hooting laughter. Though the screaming stopped abruptly, the hooting continued.

When the police arrived, Diesel was gone, but the boy's mutilated body was not. Diesel had cut off the boy's penis with a fishing knife; whether the boy was dead at the time was unclear from the record.

Diesel was picked up by the police later that night, wandering aimlessly around Times Square. He was disoriented and didn't recognize the police officers as lawful authorities, but they took him in without a struggle.

Because Diesel was a "fruitcake with a razor," an ex-patient with a history of probable violence, the Department of Corrections sent him back to Kirby as unfit almost by presumption. He was still there when his criminal lawyer told him that a forensic lab had made a perfect match of the bite marks and Diesel's teeth. Then Diesel conceded that he had raped both of his victims (he now admitted to the first crime). He said he hadn't intended to kill or even rape anybody; he claimed he was an innocent agent of sinister forces in Washington, D.C., who had set him up. He was merely their puppet, controlled by a radio device.

He seemed rational, even thoughtful, weighing the risks and benefits of the various options open to him. But my experience had taught me that juries find for insanity if the crime is impulsive, if it is not motivated by personal gain, and if there is strong evidence of psychosis. The criminal case against Diesel would have to be proved beyond a reasonable doubt, and if he raised the insanity defense, the prosecutor would have the burden of showing that Diesel wasn't insane. Whether Diesel would technically qualify depended on his understanding of the nature of his act and whether he knew it was wrong.*

He told me he was going to plead insane; did I think he had a chance? Yes, I told him, a very good chance.

---

* Serial killers rarely get acquitted on the basis of insanity because they usually have learned to cover their tracks, and this is taken as evidence of knowledge of wrongfulness. There was none of that here.

By this time, though, I'd had enough. I felt like I'd been mugged. I'd done my job, fulfilled my role in the system, and done the "right" thing. And he'd gotten out. But he didn't comply with the treatment plan, and I became an instrument in another senseless death.

Everybody may be entitled to a lawyer, but I'm not necessarily that lawyer. Whatever had happened to them to make them the way they are—and Dr. Bellows was convinced that Diesel had been brutally abused as a child—I didn't want to represent the killer-rapists of children. I had recently refused the case of Jonas Brand, who was acquitted because "God told him to kill those little girls" and carve into their lifeless bodies the cross of Jesus. I didn't feel I could give Brand the best representation of which I was capable, even if he were "no longer dangerous." In fact, I hated him.

In the mental health industry this is called "countertransference," and clinicians are warned against the dangers of "personal bias and exaggerated response to human behavior that is totally unacceptable to society's moral standards." But I am not a clinician. I knew my clients as a whole were despised by society, and I had accepted that long ago; but every lawyer has to draw his or her own line about what he or she is willing to do. And I decided I didn't want to represent guys like Brand and Diesel anymore, even though I was willing to represent the woman who pushed a child from a roof in an act of revenge against the child's grandmother. By now I had enough clout to refuse certain cases as long as I did my share, and I was willing to represent parricides, cannibals, killers, and dismemberers. But the sexual abuse and murder of children filled me with a revulsion that I could not overcome. The image of these children and their mutilated bodies filled my nightmares.

A year and a half later, when Diesel was returned to Kirby after being acquitted of murder and rape by reason of insanity, we were short of staff. I asked that he be reassigned so that I could be taken off the case. When I was asked to reconsider, I agreed to think about it. And while I was in the process, I ran into Dr. Bellows at a conference at Regent's Hospital in Manhattan.

"Hello, how are you, Doctor?"

"How about that cup of coffee, Lawyer?" she asked. "You look like you could use it. I know I could."

We had coffee. It turned into dinner. The talk turned to Diesel, who had been assigned to her new Kirby ward.

"You know," she said, "representing him shouldn't be so bad now, so don't worry about it. He's put away. What's the big deal? He can't be a serial killer now. We've got him for life. If the powers that be want you to keep the case, keep it. He's beyond your help."

"Great," I replied sarcastically. "You really know how to make a lawyer feel good. That's just the kind of encouragement I need."

"Oh, I didn't mean it like that. Don't be offended."

"I'm not."

"We get so very few serial killers. And Diesel had such potential that way. . . . You know, the first murder is generally an aberration from what later turns out to be a repetitive pattern. Usually the first murder is, if not an accident, not exactly planned, or at least not planned in intricate detail. Often that first killing is in the course of another crime—incidental, say, to robbing a convenience store.

"In Diesel's case, I'd say he kills to relieve tension. Of course, that's not really a guess. Not anymore. Did you see the autopsy report? He's clearly a sexual sadist. And a guy like that, he'd get out of prison eventually; convicted murderers don't do life anymore. But thanks to Kirby Forensic and the maximum-security hospital system, he'll be frustrated in his career as a serialist.

"I know what I'm talking about. Most serial killers are white men, in their thirties to early forties. They are usually intelligent and attractive, or at least not unattractive," she said, smiling, as she took a sip of wine. "Which reminds me of President Clinton. I read something about this. I'm not making this up; I took notes. Clinton fits the profile almost perfectly." She fumbled with the clasp on her purse and pulled out a folded sheet of letterhead, which she unfolded and held under the light. Her mood had lightened considerably. "You'd never be able to read my writing," she said, "so I'll read you the pertinent parts. Here, listen to this:

" 'President Clinton's mother was still in mourning at the time Bill was born, his father having died in a car accident four months before his birth. For two of his first four years he was raised by his grandparents while his mother was away getting nursing training. When she did come back she had a new hubby, who turned out to be abusive.' A depressed unavailable mother; an abusive stepfather. A very typical starting point for a serial killer."

"I guess that's the point. Half the men in this country fit the profile," I said, perhaps exaggerating. "But very few become serial killers."

"Oh, c'mon. Don't stop me now. I'm on a roll," she continued, flushed and excited. "Listen to this: typically mom starts as homemaker while blue-collar dad goes out and works some shitty job, but he's usually mixed up with alcohol and some kind of get-rich-quick criminal activity, which ends up destabilizing the family. If he goes to jail, it's treated as part of a normal course of events, and no stigma attaches. The dad beats the wife, the wife beats the kids, you know, sung to the tune of 'The Farmer in the Dell.' . . ."

Now she was singing. What a mood swing!

"You know you're getting very sick yourself, Dr. B.," I interjected.

". . . yes, I know. They say mental illness is highly contagious. But listen. I found out some more stuff, and according to records we just received at the hospital, when Diesel won a scholarship to Texas A & M, his father beat him in a drunken rage. Diesel hit him back. The autopsy report shows that his father *officially* died from a heart attack, but apparently there were recent lacerations and bruises that could lead one to suspect that the heart attack was *induced* by Diesel's violent acts. Causality. That would make Diesel's subsequent acts against children less arbitrary and more part of an emerging pattern.

"All the components are there: aggression in family, family sexual problems, father figure degrading toward son, cold mother, sexual trauma. If you look at his early history, you'll find Diesel was isolated from his peers, probably from the humiliation of the physical abuse at home, at least in part—but even then, Diesel clearly thought he was something special. Clearly he had his own fantasies about who he was and what he could become. My own guess is that that science scholarship to Texas A & M grew out of animal experiments. I'm sure they involved torture. I don't have any evidence, but I'm sure. Absolutely sure."

At Kirby, Diesel lived quietly for months without improvement or incident. This time the medication seemed to have no effect, and he began to get very tense. He spent most of his afternoons pumping iron in the weight room on the eleventh floor "to relieve tension," according to a note in his hospital record. He developed a mutual antagonism toward another of my clients, a Jewish ex-biker who filled a similar ecological niche, so to speak; both of these guys were barrel-chested strongmen. The biker, Avi Goldman, had killed a man who he said (self-righteously) tried to sell him kiddie porn in Times Square. According to the hospital record, though, the battle was actually about who in fact was the real incarnation of the Incredible Hulk, Goldman or this other guy. Goldman was acquitted by reason of insanity, and now he shared a ward with Diesel.

Apparently there also developed between them some ethnic or religious animosity. Diesel, who had been quiet on this issue for the years that I knew him, suddenly started spouting anti-Semitic remarks. Goldman seemed to take it as playful camaraderie, the banter before battle in which icons of the screen and page seem always to engage. Errol Flynn, Spider Man, James Bond—each one laughs at insults and danger. So too did Goldman, which only seemed to enrage Diesel. "I will crush that Jew," the hospital chart quoted him as saying to no one in particular.

Several weeks later, that remark was repeated in a new incarnation: "I will crush the Jews." Drs. Kaplowitz, Greenstein, and Rosenbaum met with Diesel during a forensic committee review called specifically to address this new symptomatic development, and they asked him to explain what he meant. I didn't mean doctors, he explained, I meant patients. This was obviously not exactly a sign of improved mental health, and he was counseled on developing insight. He responded quickly: that was just talk, he said, I didn't mean anything by it. But then another patient, Barry Silverberg, was found comatose in his bed. He died several days later from complications relating to brain damage caused by suffocation and an injured trachea. Diesel was the prime suspect.

"He's trying to send me a message," confided Goldman, "or he's trying to make me angry. Which do you think?" he asked me.

There had been two Jews on the ward, and now there was one. Young Barry Silverberg, who had burned his family home to the ground with everyone in it, was dead. The hospital was embarrassed; it was the first on-site murder there since Kirby had opened. Kirby had so much security that things like that weren't supposed to be able to happen. Three patients came forward to say that they had heard Diesel make threats to kill Goldman and Silverberg, and Diesel was indicted.

"They're setting me up, man," Diesel told anyone who would listen. "I think Goldman did it." Then they took him away. He was assigned a criminal defense attorney named O'Brien. I was surprised that Kunstler didn't somehow get the case, but I suppose he was busy. I spoke to O'Brien once or twice, and he seemed to know what he was doing.

Because of Diesel's questionable mental health, matters proceeded slowly, and with caution. During the pendency of Diesel's trial, Kirby didn't want him back. To the other patients who knew Silverberg, Diesel's reappearance as unfit would be tantamount to his getting away with murder, at least temporarily. That was not the kind of signal that Kirby wanted its patients to get. So Diesel continued to be held by the Department of Corrections at Rikers Island, in a very limited facility for mentally ill accused persons awaiting trial who cannot otherwise be sent to a facility under the auspices of the State Office of Mental Health, and there he spent the better part of three years.

When he was finally found fit to stand trial, the district attorney somehow lost track of Diesel. And when Diesel's criminal attorney made a motion to have the case dismissed for failure to prosecute, no one from the district attorney's office showed up. Perhaps they assumed that Diesel would be returned to the hospital for the criminally insane. If so, they were mistaken.

Judge Kaplan dismissed the criminal case against Derek Diesel.

There was nothing in the court papers that remanded him to the custody of the Commissioner of Mental Health, and once the criminal matter was dismissed, the Department of Corrections had no basis to hold him.

"Does that mean I can go, Your Honor?"

"I have nothing in the file to indicate anything else. No outstanding warrants. Yes, Mr. Diesel. You are a free man."

So to everyone's surprise except his own, Diesel was free. He immediately caught a bus to Dallas, where his aunt lived in a retirement community.

Of course, the story doesn't end there. The New York district attorney's office, realizing they had let this one slip away, sent out an order for extradition from the governor's office to the state of Texas; it charged Diesel with second-degree escape from the custody of the Office of Mental Health. To the amazement of his aunt's elderly neighbors, a troop of Dallas police surrounded her apartment and seized Diesel for extradition, and they did it rather peacefully. He was returned to New York but never prosecuted for escape; instead he was sent to Mid-Hudson, the maximum-security hospital.

Something interesting happened there. As it had within the period of our acquaintance, Diesel's condition continued in flux. Even during his initial psychiatric examination he showed signs of improvement. His symptoms of paranoia and delusion had abated; he cooperated with treatment, and he heard no more "broadcasts" from Radio Free Washington. And because the charges regarding Silverberg's death had been dismissed and had therefore somehow not made it into the hospital record, there was no evidence of any recent violence. Within just over a year the doctors at Mid-Hudson found that Diesel had improved to the point where he could be transferred to Manhattan Psychiatric Center, and he consented to an application for continued retention in exchange for a transfer. MPC was not a happy place for him, however, and when he tried to hang himself from the shower with a torn bedsheet, he was recommitted to Kirby as dangerously mentally ill.

Diesel was aggrieved by this turn of events. He was angry at the poor quality of his legal representation during the recommitment hearing (because I was on leave at this time, I did not observe the court proceedings), and he felt a terrible injustice had been done him. Finally, acting as his own attorney, he filed a writ of habeas corpus against Kirby, claiming to have no dangerous mental illness or other infirmity by which he could be held over his own objection. He was incensed that after his release by Judge Kaplan, he'd been extradited from Texas—kidnapped, was how he saw it—and returned to New York without having done anything wrong. In his opinion, Judge Kaplan had let him go because he deserved to be free.

His papers were based on boilerplate and didn't properly express the basis for his position, and after he made a brief *pro se* appearance before Judge Chambers, I was directed by the judge to represent him. Judge Chambers was not interested in my personal feelings. He made it clear that in his view it was my obligation, and not a matter for discussion. Reluctantly, I took the case.

Nine years had passed since I first met Diesel, and I wasn't a young lawyer anymore. But what I'd lost in enthusiasm I made up for in expertise. I recharacterized the basis for the writ as a failure to extradite properly—a technical ground that involved fraudulent intent on the part of the district attorney to bring Diesel into New York jurisdiction using improper means. The case proceeded on purely technical grounds, and at the conclusion of our oral presentation, the judge, weighing the pounds of paper each of the litigants had submitted in written support of his position, asked the assistant district attorney, the assistant attorney general, and me to step up for a bench conference. Diesel stayed seated out of earshot at the table we shared during the proceeding.

"How can I let this guy go? Not in my neighborhood. Look at his record of violence," the judge whispered from the bench. "Maybe he can go and live near you," he said to me, attempting to be funny, and reinforcing my belief that Diesel had no chance before this judge.

"That's the beauty of the remedy that I'm requesting, Your Honor," I replied, attempting to respond with the same kind of humor. "I'm asking the court to see that he's returned to the position he was in before the district attorney's fraudulent misrepresentation in its extradition request." I felt it was my ethical obligation to make one last plea, but I also was relieved to know that it would never be realized. Judge Chambers would never send another jurisdiction what he saw as a problem of this magnitude. Nevertheless, I continued to state my case. "Put him on a bus to Texas. Let him live with his aunt, and let Texas take its chances. If he comes back to New York, then the district attorney can have him arrested. He won't be back. Let's make it legal."

The assistant district attorney twisted his hands into fists, and the assistant attorney general snorted in contempt, but Judge Chambers raised his right hand, indicating that they should settle down.

"On the record," stated the Judge in a loud, clear voice, signaling the court reporter, and the other lawyers and I returned to our respective places in the courtroom. Diesel looked at me, and I averted my gaze.

"Decision reserved!" announced the Judge.

"What does that mean?" asked Diesel.

"It means he's not going to tell us now. He has to think about it, review the law, and I expect he'll write a decision. We'll know in a couple of weeks."

In his decision, when it finally came, Judge Chambers noted that mentally ill patients, dangerous or otherwise, are excluded from the jurisdiction of the Interstate Agreement on Detainers Act,* which, as he put it, "allows dangerous mental patients to remain at large once they leave the state of their retention until they do harm to either society or themselves." He suggested that the legislature correct this "procedural gap in the extradition process." But because Diesel had been judicially found dangerously mentally ill when he was first sent to Mid-Hudson and again at the recommitment hearing that brought him back to Kirby, Judge Chambers concluded that these findings had superseded the basis for the writ and that Diesel had waived his right to challenge his extradition by waiting so long. So, on the basis of timing, the writ was denied.

Would Diesel have won if he challenged the extradition before

---

* Art. VI, 18 U.S.C.S. app. at 122.

further findings of dangerous mental disorder? I strongly believe Judge Chambers had already decided on the result he wanted, and his decision was merely the means to that end. If Diesel's challenge had been more timely, Judge Chambers would have reached the same result by a different avenue.

Dr. Bellows, whom by now I called Adrienne, came to my Kirby office several days later. She looked wonderful in her professional dark blue suit, which she wore with a white, high-collared ruffled blouse and two-inch heels. She still looked like a doctor, but a smart and sexy doctor, like one on TV. She sat down on the edge of my desk.

"How would you have felt if you won that case?"

She didn't have to be more specific. We both knew which case she was talking about.

"Good," I lied. "I would have felt good. Wouldn't you be more comfortable in a chair?"

"I'll pretend you're not lying to me. . . . But I came to admit to you that I feel pretty bad about it. When we first met, close to ten years ago, and you were young and I was younger. . . ."

"Adrienne. . . ."

"Don't interrupt. So, ten years ago, approximately, we shared a common professional interest named Derek Diesel, a patient who had never killed anybody, never raped anybody, never did much but show some potential inclinations towards violence which I could see clearly, and which you could probably see, too, though I expect you to deny it. We let him slip through our grasp—I don't mean you and me specifically, I mean the entire system—and as a result a young boy committed suicide after being raped by the man we let go.

"And I took that pretty hard. I thought I was pretty worthless, that I could have done more. That we could have intervened in some way. I carried that thought for years, and I suffered over it. And then he was out again. And I thought, uh-oh, here it comes, and I was powerless to stop what I felt was going to happen because I didn't know how, or when. But I had a bad feeling, not a very scientific feeling, but an intuitive feeling that Diesel would not stay on the path, that he would stray. And sure enough, he was back again. And more blood was on my hands.

"Do you know that psychiatrists see psychiatrists? I struggled with this. I know the limits of science will not let us predict human behavior, and certainly the limits of the mental hygiene system will not allow us to act on a hunch. But when that hunch is right, we suffer more for it. My own psychiatrist helped me through it, but I am still suffering. And I can see that you are suffering. But don't worry, it doesn't really show, not unless you know what to look for. And again, I'm speaking on a hunch, I'm just guessing because you look like you're going to cry whenever those poor boys get mentioned.

"But I just wanted to say that science, and the system, and even the law—they all have limits. There was nothing we could have done. We mustn't keep blaming ourselves.

"Sometimes I need to remind myself of my successes. There aren't that many with this patient population, but there are some, some who get better and never come back. But we judge ourselves by our failures, we tabulate where we met with less than we hoped, and we blame ourselves when we fall short. We take our successes for granted, as though they weren't worthy of note, as though we had it coming. But we suffer over our failures. We suffer. It makes us human.

"But it's not we who have failed. We did our jobs as best we could. It was the system. I keep telling myself that if Diesel had had proper follow-up, he could have been just another one of a hundred men whose propensity for violence was averted by proper care and treatment. It wasn't your fault, and it wasn't my fault. I keep telling myself. . . ."

Her face had grown red, and she was losing her composure. She took a deep breath.

"I can see you're not very chatty today. And I have to go. Why don't you call me sometime, and we'll have lunch."

"I'd like that, Adrienne," I said. "I will."

A Suitable Punishment: The Future of the Insanity Defense

To find the suitable punishment for a crime is to find the
disadvantage whose idea is such that it robs forever the idea of a
crime of any attraction.—Michel Foucault

The lawyer's profession is based on appearances. You don't have to believe in your case, but you have to appear to believe in it. Emotional honesty is difficult for all but the very luckiest—those who believe in their clients wholeheartedly, those who have no doubts. I myself have always had doubts. And not just about my insanity clients, but about all my legal endeavors.

I have always been able to see the other person's point of view. Sometimes that's a problem. Years ago, when I was still in law school, I interviewed for a position with the New York district attorney's office because I have always been interested in human drama, in human lives—and because I wanted to go to court. On my third callback I was interviewed by two senior assistant district attorneys, a man and a woman. The woman asked me if I could prosecute hookers, pot smokers—low-level perpetrators of "crimes without a victim," as she called them. And I said, "Yes." Then she asked if I'd have any doubts. And again I said, "Yes." She jumped on that. The color flushed into her face, and she leaned forward, stared at me intently, and said, "You'd go easy on them, wouldn't you? You don't have the stomach for getting tough, isn't that so?"

So I leaned forward as well, until our faces were about eighteen inches apart, and I looked into her eyes and quietly asked her, "Haven't you ever had any doubts?"

And she said, "No."

"No?" I asked.

"I haven't had a moment's doubt since I joined the office," she declared, her back stiffening.

"I can't believe that," I said. "Anybody who never had a doubt about anything isn't thinking broadly. Or perhaps not thinking at all."

As soon as the words were out of my mouth I realized I had made a mistake; I was being confrontational. That quality works in court, but not when you're applying for a new position. But she had made me angry by suggesting that I wasn't up to the job. And I felt sure that self-righteousness and the inability to recognize another construction of the facts were ultimately liabilities. Although it is bad form to display doubts of your client's case in court, it is thoughtless and unprofessional not to consider the case from different points of view.

Shortly thereafter I received a job offer from the litigation department of a corporate firm, and I decided that I would go for the money, accept that job, and turn down the district attorney's office if they also made me an offer. As it happens, they never did. My friend Dr. Bellows, with whom I've shared this story, now jokingly whispers to me, "Revenge is sweet," whenever she hears that I've whipped the D.A. in court. She suggests, jokingly again, that it's the vindication of the jilted suitor, a kind of Napoleonic complex for tall men. She tells me that since I lost my taste for "the pure cause of freedom" for my clients regardless of their dangerousness, I fill the emptiness with vengeance on my adversaries. She says, "I'm a psychiatrist. I know about these things."

But the fact of the matter is I've always had doubts. Causes are for true believers.

It's easier to believe in a cause when you have no experience. Putting bad guys away, letting good guys out; these are not difficult concepts. And you can choose to believe, to some degree, in whatever cause suits you. In that sense, it is the operation of free will. But sooner or later you have to confront your own reality.

My education in this respect began relatively early. It became clear to me during MacKnight's jury trial how far from perfect our legal system is. Although the moral complexities of the MacKnight case were merely a foreboding of more difficult things to come and resolved themselves without tragedy, I thought seriously of quitting at that time. Already it had become clear to me that I could not stay in this business and come away emotionally unscathed. I knew I would eventually win a case I should have lost and feel responsible for a tragedy with which I would otherwise have had no connection—and which might not have taken place without my participation.

But feelings are not part of my job, unless I can exploit them for my client's benefit. That was the case with Mtumbo Balinka. Maybe he actually did assault two police officers, but in my heart I saw him as an innocent, caught up in a web of circumstance he didn't understand. Helping him get free so that he could live a life, get a job, and get off the public dole gave me terrific satisfaction.

The Hugh Kelly case was more fraught with moral ambiguity. If the system functions as it is supposed to, then patients who are no longer sick are supposed to be released, whatever their crimes. Because Kelly had served twenty years in various psychiatric facilities, my helping him win his release was not as hard to justify as it might otherwise have been. After all, he did not beat the system; he did twenty years.

But Diesel was my great disaster. My association with him will haunt me perhaps forever. If I had not asked Dr. Bellows to let him out—oh so many years ago—well, he would have gotten out anyway; after all, making suggestive remarks to a minor is regarded neither as a serious crime nor as evidence of a serious mental disorder. But I can't help thinking I share some responsibility for the rape of that first unfortunate boy and his subsequent suicide. And if we could have stopped Diesel then, he would not have gone on to rape again, and that time to kill. But the district attorney didn't have the evidence he needed, even though we all knew Diesel was a time bomb.

I live with the painful knowledge that I am somehow complicit in the horrible acts some of my clients commit after I ease their legal constraints and help them get released or transferred to a setting that gives them the opportunity to do the wrong thing. Has this knowledge made me jaded and cynical? Well, I like to think I've gotten smarter over the years, but in some ways I retain a somewhat stupid innocence. The trouble is that after so many years working in a maximum-security hospital, when I meet someone who hasn't killed and eaten parts of his mother, I tend to think, "This guy isn't so bad." I know New York City has at least its share of hustlers and con artists, as well as people who appear ordinary enough but who will take anything that is not nailed down and not consider it stealing, but I remain largely unwary. In retrospect I can see that they are fishy characters, even thieves, but my tendency is to give everyone the benefit of the doubt.

I trust people. And after all these years of looking for the good in my clients, finding the best in them that I can whether it's really there or not, I tend to see the good in all people. It's just the opposite for prosecutors and cops, who tend to become increasingly distrustful over the years, to find a suspicious motive in every soul. It seems to come with the territory.

Which brings us to the insanity defense. The insanity defense has many detractors, and perhaps rightfully so. The actual verdict, as currently worded in New York law, is "not responsible by reason of mental disease or defect." As we collectively and individually consider the issues of crime, rehabilitation, and punishment, everybody gets hung up on the words *not responsible*. And well we should.* Under the current strictures of the insanity defense, the perpetrator escapes blame—and the public hates that.

The general public think the insanity defense is a means of allowing the guilty to "get away with murder," figuratively and often literally. Instead, the public want convictions. They want punishment. They believe the insanity plea is "an easy out," one that encourages perpetrators to give in to their wildest impulses. It is seen as a way for a violent individual with a hard-luck story—and who hasn't suffered some trauma in his lifetime?—to avoid jail time and find his way back to the freedom of the streets relatively quickly. The public see lawyers as being in cahoots with criminals, twisting the facts about a perpetrator's mental state to abrogate his criminal responsibility for an admitted act of deadly violence. Psychiatric defense witnesses are viewed as another weapon in the criminal's arsenal.

And the public have evidence that they believe supports this view. The battered-wife syndrome, post-traumatic stress disorder, brain cysts, the "Twinkie" defense (based upon high levels of blood sugar), and defenses based on the use of prescription medications such as Halcion† and Prozac have been used successfully to defend against charges ranging from assault all the way up to murder.‡ Only a few years ago these defendants would have been convicted as charged, and the fact that they've been acquitted doesn't change the public's opinion that they are criminals.

Expert testimony is now central to every criminal case in which the prosecution can show the defendant did commit the act and the defense lawyer's only choice is to question the mental component of the crime, the criminal intent. The case then becomes a battle of ex-

* Even in the forensic hospital, where doctors are specially trained in legal language and court-related matters, these words create special problems.
† In fact, a Utah woman acquitted of shooting her mother subsequently won a civil settlement worth several million dollars against the manufacturing pharmaceutical company when she claimed Halcion had made her do it.
‡ Middle-class people in the web of the criminal justice system can raise these defenses, and all it takes is the money to pay their lawyers.

perts, with each purporting to know the true mental state of the defendant at the time of the crime, construing the "facts" in the best light for his or her purposes. So the psychiatric tail wags the legal dog. The public sees this as a scam, a view supported by important public officials. Former Chief Judge Sol Wachtler of the New York Court of Appeals, the highest court in the state, went on record as saying, "An insanity defense can be concocted with relative ease."*

It's gotten to the point where an awful lot of people believe that knowing the difference between right and wrong is a legal liability, and that criminals act out in the most vile, violent ways in order to be able to fall back on the insanity defense if they get caught. So the lawyer of a black man who kills six people on the Long Island Railroad claims his client's anger at white people is of such a proportion as to constitute a mental state for which he is not responsible (the "black rage insanity defense"). The lawyer of an Arab immigrant who shoots up a vanload of Hasidic Jewish students claims that the man's hatred rises to the level of insanity because of the trauma he experienced growing up in Beirut (the "Arab trauma insanity defense").† The lawyer of two young men from a wealthy family who killed their unsuspecting parents by shotgun claims her clients' actions were psychological self-defense against sexual abuses committed by their father when they were children. And the lawyer of the young woman who purposefully drove her car into a lake to drown her two children who were strapped into their car seats offered a theory about depression and abuse as well. Psychiatrists and psychologists were hired to support each of these claims with expert testimony.

Despite the general public's fascination with these cases, how-

---

* And although the former chief judge ultimately did not employ this defense in his own criminal trial, he considered it.

† The jury convicted the defendant of one count of murder, fourteen of attempted murder, and one count of criminal use of a firearm, rejecting his insanity defense—despite the testimony of two experts who claimed his violence was the result of a flashback and not under his control.

ever, juries are rarely convinced by such defense counsel arguments; in every case of the aforementioned but one, the jury voted to convict. In the one exception, the jury was split, and the case is being retried.*

Although the insanity defense in fact leads to very few acquittals, the general public find it an affront. They believe that it lets guilty people off the hook and makes the others jealous. Fed up with the idea of "coddling offenders," the public have an expressed preference for punishing perpetrators, as opposed to treating them. Society is disillusioned, even disgusted, with the view that sick persons need help, not castigation, because people don't believe such help works. They want convictions. They want punishment. Nobody likes to feel like a chump.

The fact is, legitimizing a criminal's sense of his own lack of responsibility for his actions does break down his inhibitions against acting violently or impulsively—and not his alone. When one person gets away with an antisocial act, the public know, others who also would like to be able to claim a lack of responsibility for impulsive acts become envious. So, to protect the fabric of society and to discourage a potential epidemic of violence, the general public do not want to see anyone get away with anything. They'd prefer to abolish the insanity defense.

Even the felonious public believe that the insanity defense offers an opportunity to beat the rap. And the insanity acquittees themselves, if they've thought about it at all, often don't believe they really are sick. They come into the hospital thinking they will beat the system by spending a few months in comfortable idleness before the doctors confirm there is nothing wrong with them and they can return to the life they left behind. It is this "temporary insanity" that has greatest appeal of all to this constituency and is most repugnant to the general public. Theoretically it allows the perpetrator, now

* The Menendez brothers' first murder trial resulted in a hung jury. As of this writing there is no verdict on the retrial.

"recovered," to avoid hospitalization as well as criminal incarceration. In fact, however, this almost never happens.*

Regardless of the fact that they are based on inaccurate information, these various perceptions are firmly and generally held, and they should be recognized and confronted.

I don't think it ultimately matters whether we characterize incarceration with mandatory psychiatric therapy as punishment or treatment. The fact is, saying someone is "not responsible" for his acts, for whatever reason, raises the public's collective hackles. I propose that we change the terms and call psychiatric incarceration punishment. Let's eliminate the insanity defense—not because it doesn't work, but because the public think it's a scam. That's really the only good reason, but it is good enough. Any system of criminal justice in a democracy must have public support on a grassroots political level, because ultimately it is the public who foot the bill. So let's satisfy the public. Let's eliminate the insanity defense—but first, let's understand the context in which it functions.

The vast majority of mental patients are hospitalized solely through civil rather than criminal proceedings. In New York State they number about eight thousand today, down from a high of more than ninety-three thousand in the 1950s, before the policy of deinstitutionalization emptied so many mental hospitals. Back then, mental patients were locked up in such great numbers because we, as a society, didn't know what to do with them. What made possible such vast

---

* The insanity defense is invoked in less than 1 percent of felony cases, and is successful only 25 percent of the time it is invoked. Thus any kind of insanity plea is rare. There is no "temporary insanity" plea as such, but theoretically one could "recover" and therefore not be in need of further hospitalization, or even any hospitalization at all, because of an absence of dangerousness. Lorena Bobbitt was found insane at the time of her act—cutting off her husband's penis—according to North Carolina law, and she spent a few months in a psychiatric hospital before being released. As a result, millions of Americans believe she got away with it.

Actually, her assault on her husband was in response to her husband's repeated assaults against her, a tortured but arguable case of self-defense. The insanity plea should not have been invoked. Cases like this give the insanity plea a bad name.

deinstitutionalization were advances in the field of psychiatry, most notably psychopharmacology.* The advent of new kinds of medical compounds that corrected deficits in brain chemistry allowed thousands of patients to return to community living and reclaim their lives, and psychiatric treatment was hailed as a wonder cure.

The very small percentage of hospitalized mental patients who engaged in activities that were dangerous and violent were also treated—by trial and error—in an attempt to find a cure for the mental defects that had caused their unacceptable behavior. These patients were unusual in a number of respects. Unlike other mental patients, their acts were criminal; unlike other defendants, however, they were confined in hospitals. To understand why these people had been sent to mental hospitals instead of prison, we must look at the very foundation of criminal law: the intentional misdeed.

For a crime to occur, a perpetrator must act *deliberately* in some manner. Thus the purely accidental act, without recklessness or intent, cannot properly be judged to be criminal. For example, if X shoots at a tree and Y, hidden in the woods, suddenly steps out and is killed by bullets from X's gun, almost anyone would agree that X should not be convicted of murder. (Whether X was negligent is another issue.) It is X's state of mind, more than anything else, that distinguishes murder from accidental death. Yet the results, at least as far as Y is concerned, are identical.

So, too, the insanity plea rests upon the state of mind of the perpetrator. If X, in his psychotic delusion, really believes that Y *is* a tree and shoots, again he is not criminally responsible for his act. He did not intend to kill Y; he intended to shoot a tree. And although he can be locked up as a danger to others, he should be incarcerated not as a criminal but as a mental patient suffering from psychotic delusions.

---

* Electroconvulsive therapy (ECT) and brain surgery (prefrontal lobotomy) were also, for a time, hailed as miracle cures, but perhaps they were overenthusiastically embraced by the medical establishment, resulting in public distaste and a fall from favor. Interestingly, ECT is currently making a comeback as a treatment for forms of depression for which medication has been found ineffective.

The idea that an individual with impaired mental functioning should be held to a lower standard of legal accountability goes back at least to the tenth century A.D. laws of England's King Aethelred, which distinguished between the unintentional misdeed and an act of free will with criminal intent. However, the rule of law on this issue, still followed in some form by almost every American jurisdiction,* was espoused much later, in the 1843 English case of Daniel Mnaghten. The Mnaghten rule states as follows:

> To establish a defense on the grounds of insanity it must be clearly proven that, at the time of committing the act, the party accused was laboring under such a defect of reason, from disease of the mind, as not to know the nature and quality of the act he was doing, or, did he know it, that he did not know he was doing what was wrong.

There is no real agreement about what this actually means, least of all among psychiatrists; lawyers and doctors have been arguing about all this for years. What *is* clear is that some individuals are deeply disturbed and unaware of the nature of their acts. When charged with a crime, some of these people are held responsible and end up in prison. Others, based on the legal advice they get, how they plead, and how their case goes, are held not to be responsible for their acts and end up in forensic psychiatric hospitals.† The latter generally occurs to the rage of the public, who believe that the

---

* Although the insanity defense has been eliminated in Utah, Idaho, and Montana, there are forty-seven other state jurisdictions, a federal jurisdiction, a jurisdiction for the District of Columbia, and a military jurisdiction, each of which may have a slightly different standard. Some, for example, have an "irresistible impulse" component such as was applied in the Lorena Bobbitt case.

† For low-profile cases, an insanity defense is usually an acceptable plea bargain to the prosecutor, and approximately 90 percent of insanity acquittees had their pleas accepted without going to trial. The district attorney knows that insanity acquittees will usually be locked up for a long time. And although "convicted" has a better ring to his ear than "acquitted," the results of an insanity acquittal might, for his purposes, be preferable—particularly since the D.A. can oppose release of the insanity acquittee at a court hearing, in contradistinction to his or her noninvolvement in parole hearings for convicts.

In high-profile cases, the D.A. can no doubt find his or her own doctors to refute any insanity claims, and the juries will believe whom they choose to believe, for better or worse.

perpetrators in mental hospitals have gotten away with something and are likely to be released, unrepentant and still dangerous, back into society.

The general public is unhappy with the insanity defense because they feel it encourages violent crime. But where does violence begin? Almost to the last individual, my clients at Kirby were abused, often sexually, as children. They were victims of a cycle of abuse beyond their ability to cope, a cycle that must be broken if we are to begin to control violence. As my friend Dr. Bellows would point out, given the proliferation of drugs, the widespread abuse of children, and the rampant poverty and bleak prospects that shadow great numbers of people living in the United States, the question is not why there are so many psychotic killers in our country, but why there are there so few. *If violence arises because of abuse and neglect, why aren't there more people who are dangerously mentally ill?*

Well, there are.

There are a lot of people who are "dangerously mentally ill," but most of them aren't classified that way, and they are incarcerated in prisons rather than held as patients in forensic mental hospitals. The fact is that most defense attorneys know better than to raise the insanity defense—even when their clients are psychotic and raving—because insanity patients generally spend so much more time locked up than convicts for a similar offense. With prison overcrowding and plea-bargaining options, even a homicide with overwhelming evidence can often be pleaded out to only a few years of prison time. Once the convict's "debt to society" has been paid, he *knows* that the prison will have to release him. Practically speaking, the result is that convicts are generally incarcerated for shorter periods and get out more easily than insanity acquittees.

The typical convicted killer, for example, is found guilty of manslaughter, not murder. This is because manslaughter is so much easier to establish, whether by plea or by trial. For this crime in New York State he will receive a maximum definite sentence on the order of five to fifteen years—and is likely to serve five years or less before he is released on parole. That same individual, if acquitted of the same homicide charge by reason of mental disease or defect, initially would be committed to a mental hospital for only a six-month period . . . *but* that period could be stretched indefinitely into the future by requests from state hospital authorities at regular intervals. As long as a mental patient is found to be dangerous, he can be held in a mental hospital against his will, and there is no guarantee that he will ever get out. So most perpetrators who might otherwise qualify as not guilty by reason of insanity choose prison on advice of defense counsel.* They generally raise the insanity defense only as a last resort.†

Does that mean that imprisoned convicts necessarily are more "responsible" for their crimes, that they had a greater modicum of free will in the commission of the criminal act than the typical Kirby patient? Not at all. Are they less crazy? Not necessarily.‡ With (or without) advice of counsel, they have decided to take their chances in prison. As a result, more dangerously crazy people are in prison than in forensic hospitals.

And thus we have overlapping sets of perpetrators, both crazy, but with one set found legally incapable of exercising free will and sent to hospitals for treatment. The other set is considered

---

* And if they do not seek acquittal on that basis, neither may the prosecution, at least not in New York.

† If the death penalty becomes functionally reestablished in New York, the insanity defense suddenly will become very viable from a defense lawyer's view, and you can look for a big rise in the frequency with which this plea is raised in capital cases. I myself would not support the elimination of the insanity defense in capital cases because I am against having a state with the authority to kill.

‡ Which is not to say that all convicts, or even most, are mentally ill. As a practical matter, I accept the widely held assumption that many convicts are career criminals who believe that crime does pay, like any other job, only better. To them the risks don't outweigh the benefits—at least until they get caught, and often not even then. And although many psychiatrists contend that all convicts are mentally ill with some form of an antisocial personality disorder, there are other psychiatrists who claim there is no such thing as mental illness, period. The leading proponent of the latter theory, Dr. Thomas Szasz, states flatly that a finding of mental illness is a psychiatric abuse of power. According to Dr. Szasz, "Psychiatrists have always had the right to declare innocent persons guilty (of mental disease) and guilty persons innocent (because of mental disease)—and thus place both classes under coercive psychiatric control. . . ." And he would eliminate not only the insanity plea but also the classification of mental illness. He says mental illness doesn't exist; I know better.

legally sane and is therefore sent to prison for punishment. It's society's crapshoot—a form of insanity roulette. Aside from their legal definition as being in different classes, in most other respects these perpetrators are exactly the same. What is generally not recognized by the public nor acknowledged by the pundits is that the forensic psychiatric hospital system, despite its inarguable shortcomings, actually does a better job of protecting society from the dangerous than do prisons, if only because prisons do such a horrible job.*

The prospect of prison is hardly a deterrent to most would-be felons.† For great masses of poor Americans, there is no stigma attached to going to jail.‡ It is instead viewed nearly as an opportunity. After all, life's tough on the street; prison offers a chance to dry out, clean up, kick deadly habits, perhaps even get your teeth fixed.

---

* Statistically, the mental hospital release system works better than its prison counterpart in terms of results. According to the New York State Office of Mental Health (OMH) in its publication, *Striking a Balance: An Assessment of the Conditional Release Program in New York State*, the percentage of clients rearrested (22 percent) is dramatically better than rearrest rates associated with prison populations (63 percent). However, rearrest rates alone do not give a fair picture, so OMH includes data in its report showing that the percentage of clients either rearrested *or* rehospitalized is closer to 40 percent.

Naturally, bureaucratic self-perpetuation results from bureaucratic self-justification, and a bureaucracy's first goal is to survive. However, a follow-up after release of insanity acquittees published in the *Bulletin of the American Academy of Psychiatry* found a recidivism rate of 54 percent within five years of release—still lower than the rate for released convicts. Clearly, conditional release is a better system than prison parole as presently devised.

The only clear success of the prison industry has been to provide jobs across the socioeconomic spectrum. And now this is true not only for corrections officers, lawyers, and judges but for architects, construction contractors, medical doctors, psychiatrists, psychologists, nurses, sociologists, manufacturers of riot shields (and handcuffs, restraining gear, and other devices for use by prison guards), and support personnel for each of the above, all laboring in service of an increasingly robust correctional-industrial complex. The prison industry has been so successful in creating jobs and an economic base (albeit on a foundation of taxes) that, despite the same failing results for almost two hundred years, the prison industry continues not only to exist but to flourish.

† Crime statistics show that violent crime is up 355 percent between 1960 and 1990, with rape leading the growth charts.

‡ For rich and powerful felons, prison doesn't seem to be much of a deterrent, either. They take their chances on making illegal millions—via insider trading, bank bleeding, investor fraud, mob business, whatever—and end up in a country-club setting with time to write their memoirs, if they aren't too busy still running their operations from the inside.

You have a roof over your head and "three hots and a cot." You might even be able to go to school. To many, prison life offers structure for the first time—a not unattractive prospect, albeit one often unacknowledged.*

Furthermore, prison is a temporary measure at best, removing the perpetrator from the street and sending him to criminal "college," where he will probably learn better ways to get the job done. He will come out tougher, meaner, and more prepared to confront society. Thus even punishment, the last great stronghold of prison philosophy, has lost its grip.

Yet the public see imprisonment as being tough on crime while viewing incarceration in the forensic mental hospital as a soft-on-crime idea that plays everyone for suckers. And they have enlisted their political representatives into the fray. Today even liberal politicians call for "three strikes and you're in," or "life without parole."† Not one dares mention mental hospitals.

To date, the "tough on crime" advocates have had their way, and the prison industry is booming.‡ The U.S. prison population is at an all-time high. More than 1 million convicts are incarcerated in

---

* And prison systems have found that they must provide recreational facilities and other outlets for prisoners, or the prisoners will become restless to the point of being uncontrollable. So every prison system has some kind of program. For example, a fellow who is serious about becoming dangerous can sign up for regular workouts, learn the self-discipline of a weightlifting regime, and emerge as an intimidating mass of well-toned muscle when his sentence is over.

† And, of course, tough-talking conservatives call for death.

‡ But all this political tough talk not only fails to address the proven inadequacy of the prison system as presently instituted, it completely avoids addressing the tax consequences. Prisons cost big money. Nationwide, estimates range from $30 billion to more than $74 billion to be spent on crime this year, up from $4 billion in 1975. Financed by taxes, prisons are America's boom industry—a guaranteed economic titan at least through the millennium.

But if you think this means we really *are* getting tough on crime, you aren't familiar with the important numbers.

There are 35 million crimes committed each year in the United States—and 25 million are serious, but only 15 million of those are reported to the police, who arrest 3.2 million suspects. Of the 3.2 million arrested, 1.9 million are convicted. Then come sentencing laws, which vary from state to state. Ultimately 500,000 or so persons are sent to jail. That's a tiny percentage of 35 million. So, despite all the billions in taxes, the stream of crime is almost unperturbed.

American prisons*—but only 4,000 patients are hospitalized in psychiatric facilities for the criminally insane. In New York State alone, there are over 65,000 incarcerated convicts but fewer than 600 involuntarily hospitalized insanity acquittees.†

But we are fooling ourselves if we think prisons are serving society well. Once upon a time we could feed ourselves a fourfold theory that prison's purpose was to (1) *punish* the criminal for his antisocial act, (2) *deter* him and others like him from similar acts in the future, (3) *incarcerate* him, thereby removing him from the community for a definite period of time, and (4) *rehabilitate* him to be a functioning member of society. But we can't fool ourselves any longer. Prison doesn't rehabilitate, nor does it deter. The level of recidivism among released convicts makes that clear. All prison does is incarcerate and punish, and these are not enough. Prison has failed to accomplish its essential aim, which is to teach the lesson that "crime does not pay." Its philosophical foundation has crumbled, and all prisons produce are better criminals—at a phenomenal cost.

It is the failure of the punishment to fit the crime that is often blamed for the failure of prison overall, and not just in America. In France, Chabroud said in *Archives parlementaires, XXVI,* "So that if I have betrayed my country I go to prison; if I have killed my father, I go to prison; every imaginable offense is punished in the same uni-

---

* The United States of America is the most violent civilized country in the world. Here, homicide is the eleventh-leading cause of death. Moreover, we have 74 percent of the world's known serial killers (despite having only 5 percent of the world's population; all of Europe reportedly has 19 percent). Very little violence in America is considered to result from the mental disorders of the perpetrators.

† Almost 800 patients have been found not responsible by reason of mental disease or defect in New York State. Nearly two thirds were acquitted of violent felonies—a third being charged with murder, attempted murder, or manslaughter. Approximately 250 of them have worked their way through the system and have been released subject to an Order of Conditions imposed by the court, the first of which lasts for five years. Most such orders (91.4 percent) require compliance with a treatment program; some (69 percent) specify an address where the client/former patient is to reside. The majority of active clients receive individual therapy (79 percent), usually twice a month. Nearly half (46 percent) have medication monitoring once a month. Smaller percentages received psychiatric assessment services (39 percent), case management (21 percent), or other continuing treatment (20 percent).

form way. One might as well see a physician who has the same remedy for all ills."

But it was not always so. Two hundred years ago, prisons were not supposed to constitute the punishment itself but existed solely to hold people *awaiting* either trial or punishment. Prisoners had to pay for their food, or they had to beg, and often they starved to death before their punishment (which was often some form of torture) took place. But since that time the convict's cost of crime has moved further away from eye-for-eye, tooth-for-tooth retribution and toward a sacrifice of time and time alone. The correlation between the crime and the punishment—cutting out the liar's tongue, cutting off the thief's hand—was ultimately abandoned, and those countries that still employ such means are seen as barbaric.

Here in the United States, the clock has recently been turned back to a time before pure incarceration was the only means of punishment, and chain gangs and other forms of hard labor have been reintroduced in some states. Other punishments have been suggested, but returning to state-sanctioned and institutionalized torture or dismemberment would be a horrible mistake because— disregarding, for a moment, issues of decency and humanity—a state with that kind of power is dangerous to everyone. Furthermore, institutionalizing physical cruelty will only legitimize and encourage further physical cruelty and violence on the part of the felonious public.*

Perhaps not surprisingly, since the general public today believe that prison barely serves the purpose of punishment, they do not believe that treatment in a maximum-security hospital is punishment at all. But what the public do not realize is that for many violent offenders, psychiatric treatment is a harsher punishment than mere incarceration. In my experience, dangerously ill mental patients definitely view it as worse. They hate the medications; they hate the prying and unrelenting scrutiny of the professional staff; and they hate being forced to confront their lives. Clinicians call this treat-

---

* When the practice of state execution and torture began to fall off in France at the end of the seventeenth century, there was a coincidental decrease in violent crime.

ment because the focus of the psychiatric hospital system is not the nature of the criminal act so much as the mental condition of the patient, and what someone did is not as important as how someone thinks. Forensic hospital treatment is based on psychiatry, not punishment. Nevertheless, it causes suffering.

Whether we call it punishment, rehabilitation, or even treatment, incarceration of any kind causes some suffering—to a greater or lesser extent, depending on the individual. But it is important to recognize that although prison incarceration really seeks to change not a person's mind but merely his behavior, incarceration in a mental institution *always* seeks to change both mind and behavior. And unlike the prison system, from which still-dangerous people are released every day, people in forensic hospitals who are considered dangerous because of mental disease are not supposed to go free. To hold a criminal convict beyond his sentence would violate the U.S. Constitution, but there is no term limit to incarceration for mental patients. Thus, even as a form of revenge, the forensic hospital system has features that should appeal to the public at large. It is punishment with no term limit.

And it has advantages that highly publicized approaches, such as Megan's Law—the public identification and registration of child sex offenders after their release from prison—lack. Megan's Law offers merely a "scarlet letter"; it doesn't require a change in the mental condition of a sex offender. The man who killed eight-year-old Megan Kanka was released from prison after duly serving his time for an offense against another child. If he had been sent to a mental hospital instead, Megan might be alive today.

But in New York, at least, the insanity plea would not have been available for Megan's killer. It is designed only for those individuals whose mental illness is such that they are unable to appreciate the nature of their conduct or do not know that their acts are wrong. The psychopath or sadistic pedophile who lacks empathy but knows that what he is doing is wrong does not qualify for "insanity treatment" under the Mnaghten test, even if he is compelled to do wrong by some other dysfunction of brain or conscience. Because he hides his activities—and this behavior is taken as evidence that he knows they are wrong—at present he can be sent only to prison and not to a mental hospital, even when it is agreed that his behavior is "sick." According to the traditional standards of psychiatry, this knowledge of wrongfulness makes him ineligible for the insanity plea. He is classified as sane, theoretically held responsible for his conduct, and sent to prison with a definite sentence. Yet, like the serial killer who claims his actions are the result of an uncontrollable compulsion, many sexual predators do not see their behavior as involving choice.*

If the convicted sexual predator has not killed, he is virtually assured of eventual emancipation from the penal system. He will emerge the same sick fuck he was when he went in.† He may or may not have minded prison, but so long as he remains dysfunctional he is a time bomb waiting to go off. Wouldn't society be better served if the bomb were defused, or at least allowed to explode somewhere other than in our midst?

The hard evidence indicates that sexual predators cannot change their ways.‡ Many, particularly the most violent and sadistic, return to their lives of sexual sadism. And, like vampires, they make at least

---

* Westley Allan Dodd, a convicted sex murderer of children, was once asked whether sex offenders could be stopped. His actual answer: "If I do escape, I promise you I will kill and rape again, and I will enjoy every minute of it." But he will not strike again. Westley Allan Dodd was executed.

† Pedophiles rarely seek treatment, even if it is available, and often require both a court order and a personal commitment to recover before they will enter and complete a treatment program.

‡ One Canadian study showed a recidivism rate of 43 percent regardless of therapy, and that number indicates only those who got caught again. A recent Minnesota study of 767 rapists and child molesters found that treatment only made things worse.

On the other hand, another study of results of treatment programs at one sexual behavior clinic found, after a mean follow-up of 34 to 57 months, that the clinic "seems to be effective" according to the following numbers:

	Recidivism After Treatment	Untreated Counterparts
Child Molesters		
of girls	17.9%	42.9%
of boys	13.3%	42.9%
Incest Perpetrators	8.0%	21.7%
Exhibitionists	47.8%	66.7%

some of their victims carriers of their disease. Each new generation is thus infected.

In my view, we should stop sending child rapists to prison to serve five- to seven-year terms. Serial sexual predators who prey on children, more than any other group, need *indeterminate sentences*. If we were to send such people—be they strangers or, worse, parents, uncles, or cousins—to forensic psychiatric hospitals, the pedophilic sexual predator who couldn't be broken of his compulsion would theoretically be held as a patient indefinitely.

Alternatively, we could limit at least the repetition of sex crimes, or for that matter, any violent crime, by changing the nature of sentencing. Those crimes that feed the cycle of violence through childhood victimization should be subject to an indeterminate sentence—

Certainly, on a numerical basis, this shows improvement. But, particularly considering these individuals have supposedly completed a "successful" program, such numbers do not invoke much of a spirit of security. Moreover, the studies that I've seen never put a human face on the victims or even the transgressors; they just report numbers. Do these numbers take into account the enormous amount of undetected sexual crime? Do they rely on self-reports, which are notoriously unreliable? How is information verified? Are physiological methods such as penis circumference measurements used to detect arousal, and, if so, what adjustments are made for nonlaboratory conditions? (Interestingly, many "normal" males have shown significant arousal to deviant stimuli in the laboratory; what distinguishes them from sexual deviants is action in deed.) And perhaps most important, what is the treatment? (All these questions are beyond the scope of this book, but they need to be addressed.)

Although today there is no treatment for sex deviants that is universally recognized, the term *chemical castration* has recently come much into vogue. Medroxyprogesterone acetate (MPA, or Depo-Provera), a synthetic progesterone that decreases plasma testosterone and results in a decrease in sexual tensions, is the drug most frequently used in the United States to treat the sexual urges of pedophiles. Originally developed as a form of birth control for women, it has not been approved by the Food and Drug Administration for the treatment of pedophilia, but the FDA's approval of how a legally marketed drug is used by a doctor in his practice is not necessary. The loss of libido that results from treatment with MPA has been termed by the clinical community to be more effective than physical castration, which, they say, does not avert the sexual impulse as successfully. Thus actual castration would be closer to vengeance.

But "chemical castration" is not castration at all. The very term castration is being used to imply something horrible and violent, an attempt to mollify the vindictive impulses of those opposed to treatment that "coddles" violent offenders, a view championed by victims and/or their surviving families. Moreover, even if effective as a treatment, chemical castration has an inherent problem of enforcement. Whether by monthly injection or otherwise, treatment must be maintained.

a true life sentence if necessary—wherein release does not become an option without demonstrated change in the fundamental character of the perpetrator. And each indeterminate sentence can have a minimum-sentence component, regardless of the mental condition, to satisfy the public that the perpetrator is being punished.

Once such a perpetrator is in custody, let's offer him treatment—and the scrutiny of medical science. But we must recognize that a sexual predator's "debt to society" will be paid only when his impulses are fully abandoned, even if it takes his lifetime. We can do this right now by changing the law; it seems so obvious, but it hasn't been done yet. We must either lock sexual predators away for life or find a treatment that works, and the issue of whether it's the perpetrator's "fault" should be completely beside the point. Let's plug the loopholes and make society safer. Once a system of treatment is devised that has proven itself effectively to change behavior, we can consider what might be done to apply its lessons to other crimes.*

Theoretically, this system is already in place at the forensic hospital. When a patient wants to be released or the hospital wants to retain the patient, psychiatrists examine the patient and make recommendations in the form of testimony. Lawyers argue the points of view, and a judge decides. As faulty a system as it is, it still works better than standard penal release and parole. So let us eliminate the insanity defense, if we must, to get public support, but let us also be realistic and bring to the prisons a release system based on compliance with conditions that must be fulfilled by offenders in order to gain and then maintain their freedom. If we do, we may yet learn how to make irresistible sexual impulses ancient history.

If the insanity defense is something that should be done away with, however, honestly confronting mental illness is not. Some forms of

---

* Plea bargaining accounts for such a huge percentage of dispositions of criminal cases that proposing an indeterminate sentence on a broad scale becomes merely an intellectual exercise. Any accused faced with such a sentence would not plea-bargain; he would insist on taking the case to trial. So a complete overhaul is not practicable—even aside from the vested interests and political infrastructure—because it would log-jam the criminal courts. But we can institute something on a smaller scale, and we can do it now.

mental illness are readily treatable, through medication or otherwise, and successful treatment can decrease future violence. And although treatment is often unsuccessful, recidivism rates for released formerly dangerous mental patients are lower than for released convicts* because, for one reason of many, patients who are "obviously dangerous" continue to be held.† Moreover, mental hospitals have been proven to be more likely than prisons to change behavior in a positive way. Rather than do away with the methods established for rehabilitative treatment in the forensic hospital setting, we would be better served by deconstructing the current organization of prisons and remodeling it after the hospital system: smaller, decentralized facilities where inmates are not organized into gangs run by criminal bosses and where a serious attempt to decrease post-release violence is still a part of the agenda.

At the same time, we must recognize that we cannot afford to keep locked up everyone who might ever again become violent. It's just too expensive. What we urgently need instead is to improve postinstitutional supervision. Whether it is called outpatient treatment or post-prison parole, a good and regular follow-up after release will help check future violence. (This idea is not new; it just hasn't been followed seriously.) Certainly one reason that recidivism rates are lower for insanity acquittees on conditional release than for ex-convicts is the follow-up assessment, including regular blood tests for monitoring compliance with medication regimes, to which the former are subject.

Even the best postrelease mental health programs, however, still have an obvious flaw. Currently, insanity-acquittal outpatients are mixed into the general outpatient population and absorbed into the vastly larger body of the merely mentally ill, 97 percent of whom are purely civil outpatients without connection to the criminal justice

---

* See recidivism rates in first footnote on page 209.

† However, let's not pretend that there is anything accurate about psychiatric guesswork on an individual, nonstatistical basis. According to one study, 53 percent of the patients predicted to be violent indeed committed a violent act within six months; among a group of patients judged not to be a threat, 36 percent committed violent acts. At the present time there really is no accurate means to predict future violence.

system. The therapy they receive is provided by various kinds of clinicians* whose average caseload is thirty-seven clients—only one of whom is likely to be an insanity acquittee. These clinicians don't have special training to deal with insanity acquittees, and such heavy caseloads mean that they have a daunting, confusing job.

Moreover, lumping insanity acquittees into the general pool of mentally ill individuals (the vast majority of whom are nonviolent) contributes to the climate where most communities think of *all* mental patients as dangerous—if not immediately, then soon; the expression "escaped mental patient" is akin to a cry of "Fire!" in its ability to engender public panic. Whether or not we eliminate the insanity defense, we should treat outpatient insanity acquittees in a different context from ordinary mental outpatients. Historically violent people need special assessments by clinicians experienced with such a population. And assessments after release should be done where these individuals *live*, rather than at clinics or offices, because people act differently in different settings. That means house calls, even for doctors.

Another area of mental illness that must be confronted is the strictly medical side. Psychiatrists today know as much about the brain as physicians knew about the body in the nineteenth century—which is to say, not very much. But there have been amazing advances in surgery and medicine over the last hundred years. Doctors can fix hearts and reattach limbs—even penises—successfully. Today there are organ transplants, sex-change operations, and other elective procedures undreamed of even a short time ago. But we are still so ignorant of so much about the brain. Eventually, that is going to change; one hundred years from now, people may look upon psychiatrists of today the way we currently look upon witch doctors. Some day psychiatrists may be able not only to predict future dangerousness but to treat it—and not only with better drugs.

My friend Dr. Bellows insists that psychosurgery will make a

---

* In the following percentages: social workers, 39 percent; psychologists, 19 percent; nurses, 12 percent; others, 30 percent. (OMH, the source of this information, does not indicate what proportion of this last group is made up of psychiatrists.)

comeback.* "Consider this," she said while we were having coffee after court the other day. "Charles Whitman, who killed seventeen from a Texas tower, had a stimulatory tumor in the amygdala. Theoretically at least, if a neurosurgeon had known about that tumor, she could have removed it. She would have saved all those lives and never even have known it, because nobody would ever have heard of Charles Whitman if he hadn't killed all those people. Just look at the comeback ECT [electroconvulsive therapy] has had recently. If ECT can overcome all that bad press, why not psychosurgery?"

"Why not?" I answered her, taking up the argument. "Well, to begin with, there's the image of the lobotomized patient, a living vegetable, where once a person had been."

"Forget lobotomies for a moment! I admit lobotomies have given psychosurgery a bad name. But listen . . . Harvard just got a one-hundred-million-dollar grant to do studies of brain physiology. Some smart guy is going to get on to something about how the brain works that we don't know yet. Mark it: Some other form of psychosurgery will become accepted treatment in the future, and I don't mean the distant future. I'm willing to bet something will happen within the next ten years—some kind of sophisticated surgery

---

* The idea of using psychosurgery to address violence had been proposed and discredited years before. In 1970, psychiatrist Frank Ervin and neurosurgeon Vernon Mark, both associated with Harvard Medical School, published *Violence and the Brain,* in which they suggested that psychosurgery could sharply decrease criminal violence. But they had already sown the seeds to discredit themselves in a 1967 letter by advocating psychosurgery as a remedy to riots, citing "medical evidence" that violence was due not to environmental but to biological factors. This caused a stir. Dr. Alvin Poussaint, a black psychiatrist also associated with Harvard, charged whites with regarding blacks as "so animal and savage that whites have to carve on their brains to make them human beings. . . ." Eventually Mark would concede that psychosurgery for treatment of aggression was appropriate only in the presence of a specified brain disorder; but opponents of psychosurgery did not accept it as appropriate treatment for anything. They deemed it brain mutilation, harmful by definition.

In one case in Michigan, Louis Smith, a patient at an institution for the criminally insane, consented to a brain operation that was intended to change his fundamental nature. (Smith had murdered a student nurse and raped her dead body while in a mental hospital for psychiatric evaluation seventeen years earlier.) An attorney named Gabe Kaimowitz brought suit to prevent the procedure on grounds that the coercive atmosphere of the institution made it impossible to give informed consent to psychosurgery. The court agreed. When Smith was freed on the ground that the "criminal sexual psychopath" statute under which he had been incarcerated was unconstitutional, he decided he did not want the surgery after all.

technique using lasers, no doubt. And that taint on psychosurgery, left over from the early days of the ice-pick-through-the-eye-socket lobotomies, will be forgotten.

"It will be less invasive than medications, which are, by anyone's account, toxic substances," she continued in her off-the-cuff manner. "And, unlike medications, it won't go on for years and years. Just—*zap!*—a neat, clean way to remove a dangerous cluster of living mass. It will be as accepted as excising a tumor. And Johnny will be cured of his need to rape and kill.

"As a doctor, I find the death penalty repugnant—especially when we have a chance to develop a permanent cure. I save lives, I don't take them. But do we really want to wait until 'three strikes and you're in,' a life-without-parole system for offenders like Johnny? A stupid sound bite for politicians does not make for good reform," she said, her voice rising. "How many children must be ruined before we stop one person's rampage? Three or more? *That* is insane!"

"Perhaps the libido has no center and floats around the brain like a free agent, taking over those neurons that can do its bidding," I said, playing along. "What makes you think Johnny's disorder could be effectively treated with a simple surgical procedure?"

"At least we'd be trying. It would be better than killing him."

I thought of Hugh Kelly and remembered his theory on the death penalty: A killer's punishment should not be determined by his mental state—because that is impossible to know—but by the degree to which his victim was innocent.* I could imagine what he'd say about psychosurgery. I could hear his voice in my head. "Let's cut their fucking brains out!" is how he'd put it, I'm sure. He wouldn't mince words.

I believe I understand the logic behind such a position. If it's deterrence that we're after, what could be more deterring to the potential offender than the idea of a lobotomy? All the romance of execution, of

---

* I suspect, however, that Kelly's views on this have been changing since capital punishment was signed back into law in New York State. I suspect that he will abandon his blue-collar views and reject the idea of capital punishment because, given his experiences and his own potential brush with the electric chair, that is the only rational position he can take. And I believe he is rational.

dying a rebel to the end, would disappear. For those serial sexual perpetrators who can exercise free will, the idea of psychosurgery might
work as a deterrent. For those who cannot, pinpoint laser psychosurgery could be an alternative to life imprisonment or death.

But it is not a logic with which I can entirely agree.

"But Adrienne, don't you see," I said to Dr. Bellows, "there are
going to be mistakes. There always are. What about the new monsters that science will create as it gropes toward an understanding of
brain physiology? Some post-surgical patient will go off on a rampage because the wrong part of his brain has been burned away.
How will the surgeon feel about that? What responsibility will he
have for the carnage of this futuristic Frankenstein monster?

"And the choice is not simply between today's real, live Dracula
who preys on victims and makes them like himself and merely a
possible future Frankenstein made that way by medical science. It's
far more frightening than that. The real potential monster is not the
individual, but the state. Bigger than my fear of human monsters is
my fear of a state that is a monster."

"And that is why I draw the line at treatment only for those suffering from some unregenerate propensity toward violence," she responded calmly, sounding again like the professional psychiatrist.
"In my scenario, the state's power would be severely curtailed."

But I have serious concerns about Dr. Bellows's theory. Her approach to the future of psychosurgery is an assault on American civil
liberties. And I, for one, am very suspicious. Psychiatry has been
misused before. It is worth noting that in an address to the Kirby
professional staff, Tatyana Dmitrieva, M.D., the director of Serbski
National Institute for Social and Forensic Psychiatry in Moscow,
stated that 20 percent to 50 percent of the patients there were dissi-
dents diagnosed as suffering from "sluggish schizophrenia," a kind
of creeping mental illness whose primary symptom was a dissatis-
faction with a system of government. The regime's reaction to its internal critics was to find them "crazy" and lock them up in mental
hospitals for failing to recognize the greatness of the Soviet system.
If psychosurgery had been an accepted practice, many of those people would no doubt have lost pieces of their minds. A state with that
kind of power will undoubtedly abuse it.

Dr. Bellows had been present when Dr. Dmitrieva made her presentation, and I was surprised it wasn't coming to her mind.

"Yes, I thought of that," she said when I asked her about it. "It's truly scary. But this is a truly scary business. I have a lot of frightening thoughts."

Aside from my fears about the state, I also feel that to address violence in America solely in terms of the effects of incarceration or treatment is to miss the broader context. To make any change in the levels of violence, we must confront the roots of violence.

The predisposition to become violent starts early in life. Theoretically, at least, we could cut future levels of violence by restructuring children's lives. And this is the crux of the liberal–conservative debate. If we could fix families—provide parents with jobs and self-respect, provide nurturing environments for youngsters—certainly we would lower future crime rates and raise the level of public mental health. And certainly the public give lip-service to the idea that all parents should be able to raise their children in an environment that's happy and healthy, but public willingness and ability to pay for vast social projects just isn't there. The holistic-liberal approach, that we need to help people from womb to tomb, is unrealistic—and not only because it is far too expensive. The liberal–conservative debate also turns on the issue of personal responsibility. We must face the philosophical underpinnings of criminal law: the issue of free will.

The great fiction in American life is that violent crime is a matter of choice. But the roots of violence, which take hold during childhood, are something about which the children have no say.* Should

_____

* Although the quiet poor, the children, get relatively little real attention, the system cannot afford to ignore violent felons. Squeaky wheels get grease, in the form of prisons. But not all solutions to violence are expensive or complicated. There are a few soft squeaks—soft because the victims are children—that could be dealt with quite simply and (compared to their cost to society if nothing is done) relatively inexpensively. For example, lead intoxication, the number one environmental hazard for children of the urban poor, has a proven correlation to problems in behavior and self-control (number two is anemia, which causes the blood to absorb lead more quickly). Since lead intoxication is preventable yet pervasive among inner-city children, what we have is a form of social negligence that contributes to dangerous behavior. We can spend the money now for the protection of our children, or later, for jail cells and/or mental hospitals, but we will spend it. We have to choose.

childhood victimization be allowed to negate adult criminal intent? What about the disturbed mentality of a young child who was raped by a trusted member of the family? Is this person responsible years later for any ensuing mental illness and repressed rage? What about repeated rapes of the child over a period of years? Where does one draw the line of subsequent responsibility for an adult who as a two-year-old had gonorrhea of the throat? Is the resultant anger that eventually explodes their fault? Of course it is not. But neither can we afford to make a history of childhood abuse, however horrible, an excuse for violent behavior in adults.

Wouldn't we all be in trouble if those who claimed themselves unable to resist their impulses and desires, sexual or otherwise, were treated as not responsible for their acts? How hard must we struggle against the devil before giving in? Is each one of us merely a product of our genes and our environment? Do we choose the lives we live? The illusion of free will tells us that we do, but the reality of our lives makes clear that our choices are made in a context that will decide for us what "choices" we perceive. This debate over whether violence is a matter of individual responsibility is what has gotten us, as a society, to the current impasse. The question before us is not one of individual responsibility; it is a question of protecting our families, our children, our lives. Can we stop victims from becoming victimizers? Can we break the cycle of abuse?

The breakdown of families, the victimization of children, the wiring of the human brain, and the question of personal responsibility are all difficult issues. But we must engage them. If we excuse violent conduct we can only expect both excuses *and* violence to strengthen and grow. New ways will be found to assert that the perpetrator of violence was ultimately a historical victim who had no free will at the moment of his act. And the struggle of free will to triumph over impulse will be lost. Perhaps Sartre was right when he said that we are free to be anything but free, that we are condemned to freedom. But if we give up the struggle, if we allow excuses and absolutions to relieve responsibilities—or allow politics to prevent us from using the knowledge we do have—the virus of violence will continue to spread.

Acknowledgments

I am truly grateful to the many people who helped make writing this book possible. I am deeply indebted to Susan Arellano, my editor at The Free Press, who shepherded my manuscript through the rigors of the publishing process with unbridled and infectious enthusiasm. I also give heartfelt thanks to John Ekizian, whose professionalism, combined with a terrific sense of humor, made the post-production work so enjoyable. I am indebted to my agent, Faith Hamlin, who believed in this book when it was merely a vague idea and did so much to help me conceptualize it more fully, and to Dr. Rebecca Prussin, who referred me to Faith. I also want to thank Alexia Dorszynski, whose advice on language and form was so invaluable, and to acknowledge my debt to the late Erwin A. Glikes.

I am also deeply grateful to Dr. Abraham L. Halperin, formerly a psychiatrist at Kirby Forensic Psychiatric Center, whose discussions with me helped me to consider the forensic psychiatric system in the context of the greater whole. I am indebted to Dr. Dan Martell, also formerly of Kirby, for providing some details about Kirby which were important if not essential to the full flavor of this book. He too has moved on to greener pastures—in his case, working with Dr. Park Eliot Dietz in California as a forensic expert. I also want to thank Dr. John Jannes, also formerly of Kirby, whose Freudian interpretation of my first book (which was for children) led to many interesting discussions about writing in general.

In fact, there are many other psychiatrists and psychologists to whom I am indebted, but many are still employed within or close to the Kirby system and therefore shall remain nameless. I believe they know who they are.

I also want to thank Faye Bernstein, Eileen Blum, Billy Cobin, Carla Sarr, and Matt Zuckerman, all of whom were willing, through the goodness of their hearts, to read parts or all of the manuscript in its various stages and offer helpful criticism and advice.

There are also a great many people in the legal profession to whom I owe a great deal. The late Hon. Ken Shorter is one. He taught me the meaning of compassion. The Hon. Bruce McM. Wright is another. He taught me that compassion can be fun. Alan Drian, Esq., currently with the Orange County D.A.'s office in upstate New York, is a third. He taught me that you can have fun even without compassion and still get the job done. And finally, there are the unnamed attorneys, many of whom requested specifically to remain anonymous in the acknowledgments of this book. (Attorneys on the whole tend to be a conservative lot.) I honor their requests.

Thank you, all.